The Name's Familiar

The
Name's Familiar

Mr. Leotard, Barbie, and Chef Boyardee

By Laura Lee

PELICAN PUBLISHING COMPANY
Gretna 1999

The word "Pelican" and the depiction of a pelican are trademarks
of Pelican Publishing Company, Inc., and are registered in the
U.S. Patent and Trademark Office.

Library of Congress Cataloging-in-Publication Data

Lee, Laura, 1969-
    The name's familiar : Mr. Leotard, Barbie, and
Chef Boyardee / Laura Lee.
        p.   cm.
    ISBN 1-56554-394-7 (pbk. : alk. paper)
    1. English language—Eponyms—Dictionaries. 2.
English language—Etymology—Dictionaries. 3. Names,
Personal—Dictionaries. 4. Biography—Dictionaries.
    I. Title.
PE1596.L44 1999
423'.1—dc21   98-56131
                                                      CIP

Manufactured in the United States of America

Published by Pelican Publishing Company, Inc.
1000 Burmaster Street, Gretna, Louisiana 70053

Contents

Introduction

Mary Elizabeth Sawyer had a little lamb. The followers of Franciscan John Duns Scotus were the first "dunces." James Kilroy was here. Yes, Virginia, there was a Good King Wenceslas. The Reverend Thomas Lushington was the first "lush." Jules Leotard wore tight pants. And yes, there really was a Peggy Sue, a Duke of Earl, a Barbie, a Dennis the Menace, a Dr. Pepper, a Mother Goose, a Chef Boyardee, a Huey, Louie, and Dewey, a Sweet Adeline, and a Rambo.

The names are familiar, and now you can place the face. *The Name's Familiar* introduces you to the actual people who inspired, conspired, or were just plain unlucky enough to have their names immortalized. Names such as "lynch," "goblin," "hooligan," "boycott," "hooker," and "guillotin" once belonged to real people.

And then there are the scientists who have given their names to comets, electrical currents, parts of the body, and deadly diseases, and the entrepreneurs whose names are found in your pantry, bathroom, and garage.

This book began as the story of a girl named Alice, and a radio program. As the morning announcer at radio station WAGE in Leesburg, Virginia, I was always looking for interesting questions for Tuesday Trivia.

I lived in a small apartment that was sparsely furnished, with the exception of large piles of reference books. One afternoon, while browsing through my collection, I came across the story of Alice Liddell, the inspiration for Alice in Wonderland.

Although she bore little physical resemblance to her Walt Disney animated namesake, Alice was real. Not only had I found my Tuesday Trivia question for that week, I had found a new hobby—collecting the stories of the people behind familiar names.

Whenever I went to the supermarket I began to wonder: was there an Oscar Mayer? A: Yes. Was there a Mr. Pringle behind Pringle's Potato Chips? A: No. The plant was originally located on Pringle Street in Chicago. (And no, there was no Mr. Coffee or Mr. Clean, either.)

A growing number of "people questions" appeared in my show. For example:

Which were there more of, Ringling Brothers or Warner Brothers? What do the M&M on the candy bag stand for? What were the first names of Harley and Davidson? (You can find the answers in this book.)

In addition, a growing number of biographies began appearing in the "Names" file on my hard drive. Those biographies eventually became this book. Each entry in the book tells the story of a real person, and how his name managed to slip into the language. Most save the familiar word or product name for the very end so you can play along and try to guess the magic word before the final sentence.

Of course, every field has its own jargon and its own set of words derived from people's names. Some of the references in this book may seem somewhat obscure. On the other hand, you may use terms every day that do not appear in the book. For the most part, I used a completely subjective selection process. If I've heard of it, I figured other people probably have too. Since I have a degree in theatre and a career in broadcasting behind me, you'll find more entries related to things such as stage lighting that border on the obscure than doctors who gave their names to relatively uncommon diseases, for example.

Then there were the people who fall into the "way too obvious" category. For example, I didn't think I needed to waste too much ink pointing out that Washington State and Washington, D. C., were named for George Washington.

Similarly, there are some expressions that other authors

have included in collections of eponyms (words derived from people's names) that I have not. Many prominent people are familiar enough that people make references to them. If the expression outlasts the celebrity's fame, then it is included in this book. If, however, the expression is in vogue during a celebrity's heyday and fades quickly thereafter, I consider it to be a reference to a celebrity, and not an eponym.

At one time, people referred to a life jacket as a "Mae West," a reference to the actress' shape. Mae West is still a film legend, but the expression has fallen out of use. It is doubtful that anyone ever fastened on a "Mae West" and wondered how it had gotten that name.

Many people today refer to wire-rimmed glasses as "John Lennon glasses," an allusion to the member of the Beatles who helped popularize what were once known as "granny glasses." Perhaps people will still call their glasses "John Lennons" after they have forgotten the Beatles, but I doubt it.

Similarly, Sigmund Freud, though long gone, has not faded from our cultural memory. People who use the expression "Freudian" these days generally know that they are making a reference to Sigmund Freud. It is likely that the expression "a Freudian slip" will still be around after most people have forgotten its origin, but I don't believe that has happened yet, and so you will not find a Freudian entry.

While compiling this book, I discovered that I was getting an education in the origins of ordinary things. Behind the names are a lot of firsts and a lot of improvements and innovations that helped lay the foundation for the way of life we take for granted today. I hope that you will enjoy meeting the people behind the names as much as I did.

The Names

A

Adams, Samuel

Sam Adams, a man who has given his name to a popular brand of ale, achieved great success in life after he failed as a brewer. Adams was the son of a Boston maltster, and Sam began his career following in his father's footsteps. But brewing didn't work out for the younger Adams, so he did the logical thing. He went into politics. There he was much more successful. He quickly rose to prominence in the Massachusetts Assembly in opposition to the Stamp Act in 1765. He was an organizer of Boston's Sons of Liberty. During the 1760s and 1770s he recruited Josiah Quincy, Joseph Warren, and his second cousin John Adams into the Patriot cause. It was Samuel Adams who conceived of the Boston Committee of Correspondence and took a leading role in its formation and operations from 1772 through 1774. He soon found himself rebelling against another beverage—tea—as one of the men behind the famous Boston Tea Party. He later worked for the creation of the Continental Congress and became the representative for Massachusetts. Although Sam Adams left the world of brewing behind, you can order a bottle of Sam Adams in your local bar today.

Addams, Charles

Charles Addams was born January 6, 1912, in New Jersey. He studied at Colgate and the University of Pennsylvania, then went to art school in Manhattan. In 1932, he sold his first drawing to the New Yorker for $7.50, and by 1935 he was on contract. His darkly comedic visions of death and the macabre were extremely popular. It was a book of Addams cartoons that caught the eye of television producer David Levy. Levy approached Addams about adapting his cartoon to the small screen. He agreed, and "The Addams Family" was born. Interestingly, the Addams family home was based on Charles Addams' real Manhattan apartment. He also kept antique crossbows and suits of armor lying around. He resembled his creations in other ways as well. His first wife, Barbara Day, was said to bear an uncanny resemblance to Morticia. She divorced him in 1951. His second marriage ended in 1956. His third wedding, to a widow named Marilyn, was celebrated in pure Addams family style. The bride wore black, and the ceremony was held in a pet cemetery. Addams died September 28, 1988. A sports car enthusiast, he returned from a driving trip, parked in front of his Manhattan apartment building, and died while sitting behind the wheel of his car.

Albright, Jacob

Jacob Albright was the son of a German immigrant who spelled his name Johann Albrecht. Albright began his career as a brick and tile maker, but after several of his children died, he turned to religion for solace. He became a minister and in 1803 founded the Evangelical Church. Its members were then known as *Albrights*. In 1807, a dispute between Methodists and the Albrights, who spoke German, led to the formation of what was called the Newly-Formed Methodist Conference. Albright was elected the group's bishop. Once German was made the official language, the name Evangelische Gemeinschaft (Evangelical Association) was adopted. In 1895, an Evangelical institution, Albright College, was named in Jacob Albright's honor.

Alger, Horatio

Horatio Alger was born in Massachusetts in 1843, the oldest of a Unitarian minister's five children. Horatio attended Harvard Divinity School and became a minister himself in 1864. He was a minister for only six years, however, before he left for New York to become a writer. There he began writing what would become a series of novels for boys. During his lifetime he published more than 118 books. They were formula stories about the triumph of clean living and hard work. A typical book tells the story of a teenaged boy with a rural background who goes to the big city to seek his fortune. He faces difficulties and temptation but overcomes both. Just as he is about to achieve success in his career, he is betrayed or falsely accused by one of his peers. Ultimately, through honesty and perseverance, the hero is vindicated. Thus, any story of a poor boy who overcame great odds to succeed became known as a *Horatio Alger story.*

Allen, Sara Sandy

Sara Sandy Allen was an art school dropout and an air hostess when she happened to run into a struggling musician on the streets of New York. That musician, John Oates, invited her over to the apartment he shared with his song-writing partner, Daryl Hall. Allen was a lyric writer who not only wrote for the duo, but she also had lyrics written *about* her. Oates wrote the song "Las Vegas Turn Around" about her. She wrote the songs "Nothing At All" and "It Doesn't Matter Anymore." Later she would contribute to such hits as "Maneater" and "Private Eyes." Allen and Daryl Hall quickly fell in love and moved in together. Hall wrote the song "*Sarah Smile*" for her. It was Hall and Oates' first hit.

Alzheimer, Alois

Alois Alzheimer grew up in a small house in the German wine country near the River Main. He began his career as a professor of psychology in Breslau. Alzheimer published several treatises on cerebro arteriosclerosis in 1904 and on *Huntington's chorea* early in 1911. But it was an event in 1906 that made him a household name. That year a 51-year-old woman named "Auguste D." was admitted to the Hospital for the Mentally Ill and Epileptics in Frankfurt-am-Main, Germany. Alzheimer, then 42, was called in to help the woman, who had difficulty answering even the simplest of questions. When he asked her name, she said it was "Auguste." Asked what her husband's name was, she also replied "Auguste." She could not remember her address or place of birth. When reciting the alphabet she stopped at G, and she could no longer remember the order of the months. She continued to lose memory up to her death five years later. Alzheimer was fascinated by the case. At the autopsy, he paid careful attention to the atrophy in her brain. He wrote about his findings, the first study of what is now known as *Alzheimer's Disease.*

Ames, John

If you are in the hardware business, you are probably familiar with Ames shovels. What you may not know is that the company began before the Revolutionary War, and that at the time manufacturing in the Colonies was considered an act of treason. Prior to that famous war, American shovels were made of wood. That is, until Massachusetts blacksmith John Ames began making shovels out of metal like the British imports. He started by using the labor of farmers, who had little to do during the long New England winters. It took 20 people to make a shovel in those days. Nowadays each shovel receives less individual attention, and Ames has become the largest manufacturer of shovels in the world.

Amman, Jakob

Swiss farmer Jakob Amman was a Mennonite who believed in simplicity and separation from the world. His beliefs eventually caused him to separate, not only from the world, but from the Mennonite faith. He insisted that discipline within the church be maintained by excommunication. Those excommunicated would be completely shunned by the faithful. Fathers, sons, husbands, and wives were no longer to be acknowledged if they strayed from the faith. In the 1690s, a group of Amman's followers split from the Mennonites to follow this stricter lifestyle. They became known as *The Amish.* Persecuted in their native Europe, The first Amish colonists came to America on a ship called the *Adventurer,* which arrived in Philadelphia on October 2, 1727. Today there are Amish communities in 20 states, with most Amish living away from villages and towns, preferring farms and small rural communities. They have completely disappeared from Europe.

Amos, Wally

Wally Amos began his career inauspiciously as a high school dropout. He went on to graduate from a secretarial school, then entered the Air Force where he was a radio and radar repair specialist. He then became a Saks Fifth Avenue executive before moving on to the William Morris Agency in New York where he eventually became a personal manager for Hollywood celebrities. In 1975, he decided to try his hand at a new business. He took his Aunt Della's chocolate chip cookie recipe and $25,000 borrowed from friends and opened a store on Sunset Boulevard. *Famous Amos Cookies* lived up to their name, making their creator a celebrity. In 1985, Amos sold a majority interest in the company, and in 1989 he left the company altogether, losing the right to his own name, for business purposes, in the process. Today the Famous Amos brand is owned by a Taiwanese food conglomerate, and Amos has returned to the baking business. He now sells muffins under the Uncle Noname' (pronounced no-nam-eh) brand.

Ampère, Andre Marie

Andre Ampère was born in Polémieux-au Mont-d'Or, near Lyon, the son of a Lyon city official who subsequently lost his head to the *guillotine* during the French Revolution. His electro-dynamic theory and his views on the relationship of electricity and magnetism were published in 1822 and served as the basis for modern electrodynamics. He was the first to show that two parallel conductors carrying currents traveling in the same direction attract each other and, if traveling in opposite directions, repel each other. In honor of his work, a unit of electrical current is called the "*ampere*."

Anheuser, Eberhard

In 1860, Eberhard Anheuser was a successful St. Louis manufacturer of soap and candles. He heard about a struggling neighborhood business called the Bavarian Brewery. First he financed a loan to the brewery's owner, and later Anheuser and a partner, William O'Dench, bought the brewery outright.

Anheuser had a son-in-law named Adolphus Busch, the owner of a brewer's supply store in St. Louis. It seemed natural for the relatives to merge their businesses, and that is what they did in 1865. The two became equal partners. In 1876, Busch developed a "Bohemian-style" lager named for a town in what was then Bohemia. Brewers in that region would generally name the beer after their town with the suffix "er" added. Beers produced in the town of Plzen, for example, were called Plzners, or Pilsners, as English speakers came to know them. There was another nearby town known for its breweries called Budweis. Like Pilsner, "Budweiser" originally referred to a type of beer—beer like that produced in Budweis. In the late 1800s, there were several breweries producing beers called Budweiser. Miller and Schlitz both produced Budweiser. But as the name became so strongly associated with another company, they stopped selling beer under that name. In this country, the next to last Budweiser producer was DuBois Brewing, which stopped making its Budweiser in the late 1970s. Overseas it is a different story. In modern day Bohemia, or the Czech Republic, as it is now called, there is still a rival Budweiser. In 1895, almost 20 years after Busch's Budweiser was first brewed and bottled, a Bohemian company called Budejovicky Pivovar started making a beer. Within the town, it was known as Budvar, a shortened version of the name of the brewer, Budejovicky Pivovar. It was exported, however, under the name Budweiser Budvar. A legal battle between Buds has raged for years. America's Budweiser went on to become the nation's best selling beer and one of the most widely recognized brands in the world. Adolphus Busch died in 1913, and his son August took control of the company. In 1919, the company was renamed *Anheuser-Busch*, the name by which it is known today. You might be interested to know that Anheuser-Bush is now also a leading operator of theme parks, including Sea World, Sesame Place, and *Busch Gardens*.

Archimedes of Syracuse

Archimedes of Syracuse, a mathematician, lived from 287 to 212 B.C. One day as he was taking a bath, he pondered a question one of his kinsman had asked him. The kinsman had given a goldsmith a quantity of gold to make a crown. When he received the crown it was the right weight, but the kinsman believed that the goldsmith had replaced some of the gold with silver. What did Archimedes think? As he bathed and pondered the question, Archimedes noticed that the lower he sank in the tub, the more water was displaced. He imagined that the amount of water displaced must be related to the weight of the submerged object. Recognizing the answer to his kinsman's question, Archimedes leaped from his bath and ran down the street shouting, "Eureka! I have found it!" After some experiments he discovered two things. The first was that the goldsmith had cheated his friend. The second was *Archimedes's Principle*, which states: "The solid will, when weighed in the fluid, be lighter than its weight in air by the weight of the fluid displaced."

Armani, Giorgio

Giorgio Armani was born July 11, 1934, in Piacenza, Italy. After studying medicine for two years, Armani left his education behind to pursue a career in the world of fashion. He got his first job in the field in 1957 as a buyer for the La Rinascente Department Store. He held that post until 1964, when he became a fashion designer for Hitman, a men's clothing company. He was with Hitman until 1970, when he offered his design services to various companies on a freelance basis. Over the next five years, he established a strong reputation, and in 1975 he created, together with Sergio Galeotti, his own label of men's and women's ready-to-wear clothing, which he humbly named Giorgio Armani. Today, the Giorgio Armani fashion empire has sales of roughly $8.5 million. More than 2,000 stores worldwide sell Armani.

Armour, Phillip Danforth

Phil Armour grew up on a Stockbridge, New York, farm. He was expelled from school when he was 17. The year was 1849, the height of the gold rush. Armour joined the adventurous souls heading to California to seek their fortunes. When he finally got to the West Coast, he found thousands of miners who had gambled away their life's savings. Few of them found any gold. Instead of joining them, Armour decided to profit from them. He built sluiceways that allowed the miners to use water to pan their gold. Thus, he was able to put aside $8,000. He took the money and visited his brother Herman in Milwaukee. He liked Milwaukee so much that he decided to stay. In 1863, Armour formed a partnership with a meatpacker named John Plankinton. Shortly after the Civil War, the first refrigerator railroad car had been built. This allowed farmers to expand the market for their meat products, specifically, hogs. Armour believed that this, coupled with the fall of the Confederacy, would lead to lower hog prices. He sold hog futures to New York traders at $40 a barrel. As he predicted, prices fell, and he was able to fill the orders with pork he bought at only $18 a barrel. In 1867, Armour and his partner set up their own packing plant in Chicago. They called their business Armour and Company.

Armstrong, Thomas

In 1860, 24 year-old Thomas Armstrong used the money he had saved working in a glass factory to buy his own cork-cutting shop in Pittsburgh. Besides stopping wine from escaping from bottles, cork was used in insulation, gaskets, cork board, and floor coverings. By the late 1800s, cork, or, more specifically, cork flour, was being used in a new floor covering, linoleum. Linoleum, by the way, gets its name from one of its principal ingredients, linseed oil. It also contains cork flour and mineral fillers pressed onto a burlap backing. When the Armstrong Cork Company began selling linoleum in 1908, the product had been available for some time, but Armstrong was the first to sell it in bright colors for home use. Author Vince Staten wrote: "It was Armstrong who made floor covering available and desirable for the common man. He was the *Henry Ford* of flooring." Linoleum made Armstrong a household name. Unfortunately, Thomas Armstrong did not live to see it happen. He died the same year his company rolled out its first sheet of colored linoleum.

Arquette, Rosanna

Rosanna Arquette was born into a family of actors on August 10, 1959, in New York City. She is the daughter of actor-director Lewis Arquette and actress-poet Mardi, and the granddaughter of Cliff Arquette, better known as Charlie Weaver on the "Hollywood Squares." Her younger sister, fellow actress Patricia Arquette, describes their childhood years as unconventional. For seven years, beginning in 1969, the family lived in a commune in Virginia. "It wasn't like the free-love, free-drug communes," Patricia Arquette said in a 1987 interview. "It was a family place. We'd paint, garden, catch fireflies. It was a nice way to grow up." In 1977, the family relocated to Los Angeles. Rosanna began her acting career as a teenager with a role in the television Movie of the Week *Harvest Home*, which starred Bette Davis. Several television roles followed, including an Afterschool Special and a part on the series "James at 15." Her first film role was in 1980 in *Gorp*. In 1982, while working on the television movie *The Executioner's Song* and the film *Baby It's You*, she met a keyboard player named Steve Pocaro, and a romance followed. Around that time, Pocaro and his brothers, Jeff and Mike, were forming a band called Toto. Arquette spent a lot of time with the musicians, and she and Pocaro were apparently quite serious. The liner notes of Michael Jackson's album "Thriller" has Arquette in the "Thank you" list as "Rosanna Porcaro." Her presence led the band's lead singer, David Paitch, to write a song about her. "*Rosanna*" hit number 2 on the *Billboard* charts on May 8, 1982. It hit number 12 on the British charts on April 9, 1983. The relationship was less enduring than the song, however. Today, Rosanna is married to Jon Sidel.

Ash, Mary Kay

Mary Kay Ash was born in Texas in 1913. In 1920, when she was only seven, her father was stricken with tuberculosis and became unable to work. Her mother went to work while Mary cared for her father and the home. She married a young musician named Ben Rogers right out of high school. After eight years of marriage and three children, her husband was drafted to serve in World War II. He did not return from his tour of duty. Forced to earn her own income, she became a salesperson with Stanley Home Products, which used house parties to sell its products. She left Stanley in 1953 and took a job with the World Gift Company. She quickly developed business in 43 states and became national training director. Then she came face to face with the glass ceiling—a barrier that was much thicker in 1963. An efficiency expert told World Gift that Mary Kay had gained too much power in the company. Instead of accepting reassignment, she resigned and wrote a book about selling for women. While writing the book she became inspired to start a business of her own. On September 13, 1963, with her life savings of $5,000, she launched the *Mary Kay Cosmetics Company*.

Austin, Stephen Fuller

Stephen Fuller Austin was born in Wythe County, Virginia, in 1793 in a town now known as *Austinville*. Austin is often referred to as the "Father of Texas" because he convinced so many families to move to the region. In 1822, he founded a settlement of migrant Americans on a tract of land purchased by his father, Mose Austin. The land was between the Brazos and Colorado rivers in Texas, which was then part of Mexico. In 1833, a convention of Texas colonists delegated Austin to persuade Mexican authorities to grant them self-govern-ment. Under the theory that it is easier to get forgiveness than permission, Austin advised the Texans to set up their own government without waiting for official approval. This earned him free room and board in a Mexican jail until 1835, when he returned to Texas and assumed command of the settlers' army. In that same year, he headed a Texas delegation to Washington, D.C., where he obtained government financial and military support for the newly formed Republic of Texas. In 1836 he ran for the presidency of Texas but was defeated by *Sam Houston*. He thereafter served as secretary of state in Houston's cabinet until his death. Austinville, Virginia, is not the only town to bear Austin's name. There is also a little town in Texas that so honors him.

Avis, Warren

Warren Avis grew up in Detroit and started his career as a teenager selling bikes and used cars. He later moved up to his own car dealership. During World War II, Avis joined the Air Force as a combat flying officer. He traveled extensively, and found the hardest part of the trip was getting from an airport to his final destination. The experience inspired him upon his return to open his own Rent-A-Car system at Detroit's Willow Run Airport. He quickly opened a second branch in Miami, a hub for tourists. Many other branches followed. Since he was a Ford salesman, Avis was able to strike a deal with Ford for cheap new cars each year. He explained that customers would be test driving new Ford models and that the advertising would help sell cars. By the time Avis sold his Rent-A-Car system in 1954, there were 185 locations in the country.

B

Bacardi, Don Facundo

Don Facundo Bacardi emigrated from Catalonia, Spain, to Cuba when he was 14. He worked in Cuba as a wine importer. In his spare time he dabbled with another alcoholic beverage, rum. Using the island's ample sugarcane to make molasses, Bacardi experimented with different formulas and lengths of fermentation until he hit upon the idea of filtering the rum through charcoal to remove impurities. Finally he was pleased with the taste, and he was ready to sell the stuff. On February 4, 1862, Bacardi and his three sons bought a tiny distillery with a tin roof and a colony of fruit bats to keep the distillers company. Bacardi considered the bats to be a sign of good fortune, so they were allowed to live there. At the suggestion of Mrs. Bacardi, the bats were adopted as the company's trademark. *Bacardi* was soon the most popular rum in Santiago and quickly became the top seller in all of Cuba. Today, Bacardi Rum is sold in more than 170 countries. Now headquartered in Bermuda, its two primary rum-producing facilities are located in Puerto Rico and Mexico.

Baker, Frances

In 1899, Frances Baker, a 22-year-old African-American domestic worker from St. Louis, shot her 17-year-old boyfriend, Albert. She was later acquitted of the murder on the grounds of self-defense. But from that day forward Baker was haunted by a song. The song was *Frankie and Johnny*. The origins of the song are somewhat obscure. Some claimed that a man named Jim Dooley wrote the ballad after reading about

Frankie in the news. Others claim that versions of the song predate the Baker shooting. In either case, other than the fact that Frankie shot her lover, little of the story line of the song appears to match the story of Baker's life. *Frankie and Johnny* is the tale of a woman who shoots her lover after finding him with another woman. In reality, according to court accounts, Albert had come to Frankie's apartment and threatened her with a knife. She shot him once, not three times, as in the song, and he was dead. The popularity of the song drove her from St. Louis to Omaha, where she hoped to live out her days anonymously. Instead, the song followed her. She moved to Portland, but heard it there, too. The song was made into a play, then into a movie. Finally, she had had enough. She sued Republic Pictures for $200,000 for defamation of character. Her biggest objection was to the suggestion that she was a woman of loose morals. After listening to her testimony, the court ruled that there was not enough evidence that the "Frankie" of the song was actually supposed to be Frances Baker. After losing the suit, Frankie was committed to a mental institution and died two years later at the age of 75.

Ball, Frank and Edmund

In 1880, Frank and Edmund Ball, two of five brothers from Buffalo, New York, borrowed $200 from their Uncle George to launch their own business. They began by selling wood-jacketed tin containers to store paint, varnishes, and kerosene. They named their venture the Wooden Jacket Can Company. Their product was so successful that they expanded their line. Soon the brothers had refined their original product to make longer-lasting tin-jacketed glass containers. In 1884, the renamed Ball Brothers Glass Manufacturing Company began manufacturing glass canning jars for the home. The items made Ball a household name. In 1887, Edmund and Frank were joined by brothers George, Lucius, and William. They moved their business to Muncie, Indiana, to take advantage of a natural gas boom in the Midwest. By the early 1900s, the brothers were quite well off. They were able to donate $300,000 to the Muncie Normal Institute for a gymnasium.

Following the donation, the institution was renamed *Ball State Teachers College*. The fruit jar business has expanded considerably. Its subsidiary, *Ball Aerospace & Technologies Corporation*, built the corrective optics used to repair the *Hubble Space Telescope*. The packaging company no longer manufactures the famous *Ball jars*.

Barnet, Angela

Angela Barnet was an aspiring actress living in London. In 1969, a mutual friend introduced her to a then-unknown David Bowie. (Bowie's family name was Jones but he had to come up with a new last name to avoid confusion with Monkee Davy Jones). During her marriage to the musician, Barnet came in contact with many of England's top rock stars, including Mick Jagger and the Rolling Stones. She is the *Angie* of the Rolling Stones' song. She calls the tribute "very flattering." But when she asked for permission to print the lyrics to the song in her kiss-and-tell autobiography (she and Bowie are divorced), the Rolling Stones denied the request.

Bartlett, Enoch

Enoch Bartlett was an enterprising Massachusetts merchant, always looking for new products to sell. In the early 1800s, Bartlett heard of a farm owned by Captain Thomas Brewer that was growing delicious pears imported from England. The pears had been known for some time in England as William pears and were gaining popularity among the New England population. Bartlett bought the Roxbury farm from Brewer and began marketing the fruit as *Bartlett pears*. The yellow pear is the most common American variety, representing 70 percent of the annual U.S. pear crop.

Bartlett, John

John Bartlett was a high school dropout who left school in 1836 at the age of 16. He saved the money he earned working at a *Harvard University* bookstore until he had enough to buy the shop. He may not have been well educated, but Bartlett was well read. He earned a reputation for being able to quote from any famous book and for being able to name the source of any famous saying. In 1855, he began selling a collection of quotes he had assembled. The original collection of *Bartlett's Familiar Quotations* was 258 pages long.

Bausch, John Jacob

John Jacob Bausch was born in 1830 in Switzerland, one of seven children. When Bausch was only six years old, his mother died. Bausch's first job was assisting in his older brother's spectacle-making business. In 1848, the younger Bausch got word of an opening at an optical shop in Berne, so he left on foot for the city. When he arrived, he got the job at a starting salary of 36 cents a day. After only a year, however, Bausch decided to try his luck in America. He traveled to Buffalo, New York, where he worked as a cook's assistant, then moved to Rochester, where he found work as a wood-turner. There he suffered an accident. His hand got caught in the machinery, and he was forced to leave the trade. Once he had recovered from the accident he tried selling his brother's optical supplies. The business seemed promising, and he convinced a friend to join him in business making eyeglasses. That friend's name was Henry Lomb.

Bayer, Friedrich

Friedrich Bayer was born in 1825, the only son in a family of six children. His father was a weaver and a dyer, and Bayer followed in his father's footsteps. In 1840, he opened his own dying business. He was very successful. In the past, all dyes had come from organic materials, but in 1856 coal tar dyes were discovered. Bayer and a partner saw great potential in the coal tar, and they began to experiment in a small laboratory. In 1863, they formed Friedrich Bayer et Compagnie to manufacture the dyes. Bayer died on May 6, 1880, while the company was still in the fabric dye business. The company went on to employ chemists to develop innovative dyes and products. In 1897, Felix Hoffmann, a Bayer chemist, chemically synthesized a stable form of salicylic acid powder that relieved his father's rheumatism. The compound became the active ingredient in a new pharmaceutical product called aspirin. The name borrowed the letter "a" from acetyl, and "spir" from the spirea plant, the source of salicin. In 1899, the Bayer Company distributed this drug for the first time. It sold very well, indeed.

Bayley, Elizabeth Ann

Elizabeth Ann Bayley was born in 1774 to a highly religious Protestant family. She married a wealthy young merchant named William Magee Seton. Elizabeth Seton became well known for her generosity and tireless service to others, earning herself the nickname "the Protestant Sister of Charity." When her husband fell ill, they traveled to Italy, hoping the climate would help him recover. It did not, and he died. Seton turned to the Catholic Church for guidance, and eventually became a Catholic Sister of Charity. She opened a school for girls in Maryland called Sisters of Charity of St. Joseph. Her family could not accept her conversion, and she was estranged from most of them. One nephew admired Mother Seton, however. He was Bishop James Roosevelt Bayley of Newark. In 1856, he established a college in South Orange, New Jersey, and named it *Seton Hall* in her honor.

Baylor, Robert Emmett Bledsoe

Robert Baylor began his political career in his home state of Kentucky. He later became an Alabama congressman and then moved to Texas, where he rose to prominence as a lawyer and a Baptist preacher. For many years, Baylor served as the moderator of the Texas Baptist Union Association and president of the Baptist State Convention. In 1841, he wrote a report as corresponding secretary of the Baptist Union Association recommending that a special committee make proposals regarding higher education. The result was the Baptist Education Society, which, not surprisingly, elected Baylor as its first president. When the Reverend William M. Tryon suggested that a new academic institution be named for Baylor, he objected, insisting that he was not worthy of the honor. Baylor was overruled, and the institution came to be known as Baylor College, and later *Baylor University*.

Beam, James Beauregard

In 1880, when Jim Beam was only 16, he went to work in the distillery built by his great-grandfather, Jacob Bean, in 1795. By the time he was 30, Jim Beam was running the operation. He continued as president of the thriving operation until exactly midnight on January 16, 1920, when the Volstead Act made alcoholic beverages illegal in the United States. Beam tried his hand at various alternative careers, from farming to coal mining, during the dry years, but they were no substitute for his earlier career. When Prohibition was repealed in 1933, Jim Beam celebrated by building an even larger distillery in Clermont, Kentucky. He also introduced a new bourbon, which he named for himself. By 1964, the government had changed its mind about alcohol. That year Congress passed a resolution designating bourbon whiskey as "a distinctive product of the United States."

Bean, Leon Leonwood

The somewhat redundantly named Leon Leonwood Bean lived in Freeport, Maine. He was an avid outdoorsman, but he found that the heavy leather woodsman's boots of his day left his feet cold and wet. He decided to take matters into his own hands, or feet, and craft a boot that combined light-weight leather tops with waterproof rubber soles. He sold 100 pairs of the boots to fellow sportsmen through the mail. They quickly discovered a flaw in Bean's design. All but 10 of the pairs were returned because the stitching gave way. Bean tried again, and replaced the defective boots. Originally, L. L. Bean sold his products only through the mail, but so many people dropped by his Freeport workshop that Bean decided to open a showroom in 1917. The company grew and prospered, and Bean gradually added other types of clothing to his product line. L. L. Bean died in 1967 at the age of 94. His grandson, Leon A. Gorman, took over the company. Today L. L. Bean is one of the world's leading international mail-order companies, with sales over $1 billion a year.

Begon, Michael

Michael Begon began his career in the French navy. After marrying a noble woman, he was named the royal commissioner of Santo Domingo by King Louis XIV. During his stay in Santo Domingo, Begon took care of the native people's medical needs, which required him to study the variety of plant life on the Caribbean island. Among the hundreds of specimens he collected was a flowering plant that grew in the shade. When Begon returned to France, he brought the plant with him. Because of its ability to grow in the shade, the species became popular both as a garden plant and as a house plant. The *begonia*, as it came to be called, was not given that name until it was brought to England 67 years after Begon's death.

Begum, Arjunaud Banu

The wife of Mughal Emperor Shah Jahan was so beloved that she was known by the title Mumtaz Mahal, meaning "Crown of the Palace." In 1631, after she had given the emperor 13 children and was in labor with her 14th, complications set in. As she was dying, Jahan promised that he would build the most beautiful palace in the land in her honor. It was built between 1632 and 1643. The white marble palace, known as the Taj Mahal (Taj is a short form of Mumtaz), was described by poet Rabindranath Tagore as "whispers in the ear of eternity." A 19th century surveyor, Col. J. A. Hodgson, said the Taj seemed to be made from pearl or "of moonlight," and suggested that it be preserved under a glass case. The name Taj Mahal has since been given to other ornate buildings, including one of Donald Trump's hotel/casinos. Blues singer Henry Fredericks also adopted it as his stage name.

Bell, Alexander Graham

Alexander Graham Bell was born in Edinburgh, Scotland. Besides his formal education at the University of London, Bell also studied with his grandfather, a speech and elocution teacher also named Alexander Bell. After his training, Bell taught at a school for the deaf in England. In 1870, Bell and his parents immigrated to Canada. Two years later, he moved to Boston and established a school for the deaf. In 1873, he became a professor of speech and vocal physiology at Boston University. It was there that he began experimenting with devices to help the deaf learn to speak, including methods of recording sound waves graphically. At the same time he was studying methods of transmitting several telegraph messages simultaneously over a single wire. These two areas of study led him to the idea of transmitting speech telegraphically. Bell was not the first to try to build such a device. In fact, the word "telephone" was coined as early as 1849. He was, however, the first to patent a working telephone. The patent was granted March 7, 1876, and three days later Bell staged the first demonstration. He transmitted the first telephone message to his assistant in the next room. "Watson, come here. I want you," he said. Over the next few years some 600 suits were filed against Bell's patent, none of them successful. The telephone made Bell rich and famous. With the help of his father-in-law, Bell founded the first telephone company, *the Bell Telephone Company*, often referred to as "Ma Bell." Bell also contributed his name to the measure of sound intensity, the *decibel.*

Bell, Glen W.

In 1946, just after World War II, 23-year-old Glen Bell left the Marine Corps and returned to his hometown of San Bernardino, California. With $400 he had made by selling his refrigerator, Bell decided to open the only business he could afford, a hot dog stand, which he called Bell's Drive-In. In 1952, he sold the stand in favor of a larger restaurant. The first day in his new hamburger and hot dog shop Bell took in $20. Meanwhile, elsewhere in San Bernadino, two brothers named McDonald had opened their own hamburger restaurant, which was doing quite well. Instead of competing with the *McDonalds* on their own turf, Bell decided to add Mexican food to his menu. Soon Bell's tacos were outselling his hamburgers, so he decided to open a few restaurants devoted entirely to them. He called the restaurants Taco Tia. Later, he would name the taco restaurants he opened after himself—Taco Bell.

Benedict, Samuel

Word experts agree that eggs benedict was named after someone named "Benedict." Beyond that, there is little agreement. The inventor of the poached egg, English muffin, and hollandaise sauce dish could be Samuel Benedict, a customer at the Waldorf Astoria who ordered it to cure his hangover. Others say it was a banker by the name of E. C. Benedict. It's possible that Benedict was a woman, Mrs. Le Grand Benedict, who, the story goes, ordered up the egg concoction at the Delmonico Restaurant in New York City.

Bengue, Dr.

Dr. Bengue was a French pharmacist in the late 1800s. His area of expertise was muscle aches. He developed several ointments and treatments, including a balm made of wintergreen oil and menthol. The ointment relieved muscle pain by causing "counterirritation." The stinging ointment stimulates the receptors for dull pain and as the brain receives the signal it overrides the previous signal for sharp pain. Dr. Bengue called his treatment Baume Bengue. In 1898, a Canadian named Thomas Leeming, Jr., met the good doctor on a business trip to Europe. He was impressed with the preparation and bought the rights to market it in America. At first he imported the product, but later began manufacturing it in New Jersey. Leeming renamed it *Ben-Gay* to help American consumers pro-nounce it correctly.

Berlitz, Maximilian

Maximilian Berlitz grew up in the Black Forest region of Germany. In 1872, he came to the United States. With a background as a teacher and an ability to speak six European languages as well as Greek and Latin, he found work teaching foreign languages. Berlitz later joined the Warner Polytechnic College. The staff was somewhat limited— limited, in fact, to Berlitz. One of his first acts as president and dean of the school was to look for an assistant to help him teach French. One day a letter of introduction came from a young Frenchman named Nicholas Joly. His French, of course, was perfect, and Berlitz hired him right away and brought him to America. But Berlitz had failed to ask if Joly spoke English. He didn't. As luck would have it, just as Joly arrived, Berlitz took ill. He had no choice but to leave Joly in charge of the class while he recovered. Joly was forced to use a combination of mime and pointing to explain concepts to his students. When Berlitz returned to the classroom, he was surprised to find that the students had learned more quickly than students he had taught using a traditional approach. Berlitz used this discovery to develop a system of language instruction that was the basis for the *Berlitz* courses.

Bessemer, Henry

Henry Bessemer was born in 1813 in England. He was a metal worker, a creative young man responsible for many innovations in the metalworking field. Among his inventions were a ventilator and a process for pulverizing metals. During the Crimean War, Bessemer began to study ways of improving the quality of the metal used in cannons. At that time, steel was relatively new and difficult to produce. It was made by heating iron in small crucibles to remove carbon and other impurities. The process was labor intensive and inefficient. Bessemer developed a system in which air was blown through the metal, oxidizing the carbon, leaving pure steel. The procedure was known as the *Bessemer process*. It was used for years to make steel rails for the railroad industry, but by the turn of the century it had been replaced by a more efficient process.

Bich, Marcel

Marcel Bich began his career at age 18 selling flashlights door to door in Paris. After one too many doors had been slammed in his face, Bich got a job with an ink manufacturer. That employment was interrupted by World War II. After a stint in the Air Force, Bich returned to the Paris area where he and a partner, Edouard Buffard, went into business selling ink refills for the highly priced American import—the ball point pen. Bich believed that an inexpensive disposable pen of that type would sell much better than its refillable counterpart. So he went to work developing his own pen. Finally, in 1953, he perfected the design he wanted. He dropped the "H" from his name and called his pen *Bic*.

Birdseye, Clarence

Clarence Birdseye was born in Brooklyn, New York, in 1886. He began his career in a unique way for a Brooklyn youth by offering lessons in taxidermy. He later attended Amherst College, where he had a part-time job finding frogs for the Bronx Zoo and rats for a biology professor at Columbia University. He apparently did not catch enough rats, because a shortage of funds forced him to quit school. He then headed west where he worked as a field naturalist for the U.S. Biological Survey. Out west, he discovered a new career, fur trading. As a fur trader, Birdseye traveled to the Canadian peninsula of Labrador, where he stayed for five years. He lived mostly on fresh fish. When shipments of vegetables would arrive, he would preserve them in barrels of frozen water. Birdseye would later say that he learned his quick-freezing technique from the Eskimos. When he returned to the U.S., Birdseye started a frozen food company.

Birkenstock, J. A.

J. A. Birkenstock began making shoes in the 1700s. Little is known about the man, except that church records in a small German village list him as a shoemaker. Years later, Konrad Birkenstock followed in his grandfather's footsteps, only more comfortably. In the 1890s when he was making shoes, all his competitors were making flat insoles. Birkenstock believed that an insole contoured to the shape of the foot would be more comfortable. In 1902, he developed the first flexible arch support, to be inserted in shoes that were now being made in a factory, instead of by hand. Birkenstock's shoes gained popularity throughout Germany and were soon exported to Switzerland, Austria, and Czechoslovakia. It was Konrad's grandson, Karl, who in 1964 designed the first Birkenstock sandal. No one in America would have heard about this were it not for a woman named Margot Fraser, who took a trip to Germany in 1966. Her feet began to ache from too much walking, so she tried a pair of Birkenstocks. She was so impressed with the shoes that she began importing them to California. They became quite popular, especially among those with long hair.

Biro, Ladislas and Georg

Ladislas and Georg Biro were brothers from Hungary. Ladislas was a newspaper editor. Much of his time was spent filling inkwells and fountain pens, and cleaning up the smudges the pens inevitably created. He turned to his brother Georg, a chemist, to come up with a solution to the problem. The brothers began experimenting with roller ball pens. They were not the first to do so. In 1888, an American leather tanner named John Loud had patented a roller ball pen, specifically designed to mark leather. Although Loud received the first ball point pen patent, he never manufactured the pen. Hundreds of other inventors came out with their own ball points in the following years, but most of them were leaky and clogged easily. The Biros' pen was not much better, but a chance meeting helped to popularize their brand. In 1938, the brothers took a vacation. While at the beach they showed one of their pens to an old man they met. It so happened that he was the president of Argentina. He invited the Biros to his country, and when World War II broke out, they quickly took him up on his offer. In the early 1940s they improved upon their original pen design. They came up with an improved ink tube that worked on capillary action, so the pen could write even at an angle. The pen became popular with pilots in the Royal Air Force because it didn't leak at high altitudes. Because of the pen's popularity with British soldiers, the word "biro" is still synonymous with "ball point pen" in England today. Unfortunately, sales of the pens fell off after the war and the Biros went broke.

Bissell, Melville and Anna

Anna and Melville Bissell were shop owners in Grand Rapids, Michigan. When packages of goods would arrive at their store they would contain sawdust. In 1876, Melville bought his wife a carpet sweeper, a new invention at the time, to remove the sawdust from the floor. The sweeper was ineffective, so Bissell took it apart and tinkered with it. Unlike the appliances on "Home Improvement," the sweeper was much improved. Melville Bissell died of pneumonia in 1889, and Anna went on to build a company to market the sweepers. She began selling Bissell sweepers across the country and overseas and became one of the first female CEOs in America.

Black, S. Duncan

S. Duncan Black worked for the Rowland Telegraph Company. In 1910, he and a friend, Alonzo Decker, decided to form their own company. They called the company *Black and Decker*.While they were perhaps not creative at coming up with company names, they were creative when it came to business. The Black and Decker company produced industrial machines and tools. During World War II they heard reports of employees stealing portable power tools from U.S. defense plants. They correctly surmised that there would be a big market for those kinds of tools after the war. Black and Decker's line of home power tools was introduced to the market in 1946.

Blair, John

John Blair was the chief promoter and builder of the Chicago and Northwestern railroads. As his railroads cut through the West, new towns were created and Blair had to name them. He named a town in Iowa for his good friend Oakes Ames. He then named another Iowa town for his daughter Alta. He couldn't name a town for one daughter and not the other, so Aurelia also got her own town. Once he'd tired of naming towns for other people he began naming towns for himself. There is Blairsburg, Iowa, Blair, Iowa, and Blair, Nebraska. One day Blair's faithful dog Colo died. Yes, there is a Colo, Iowa.

Bloch, Henry and Richard

Brothers Henry and Richard Bloch went into business together in 1946. They offered bookkeeping and management services to businesses and called their venture the United Business Company. As time went on, the Blochs found that they were spending more and more of their time on income tax returns. They decided to focus entirely on taxes, and so they changed the name of their business. They decided to name their tax company after themselves, but found that people were always mispronouncing their last name. They changed the spelling so that Americans could pronounce it more easily— *H&R Block.* Today H&R Block prepares one out of every ten income tax returns in the United States.

Bloomer, Amelia

Amelia Jenks Bloomer lived in Seneca Falls, New York, in the 19th century. She described herself as "a simple young thing with no education in business." Be that as it may, Bloomer became the editor of the *Lily,* the publication of the Seneca Falls Ladies' Temperance Society, the first women's magazine in America. This would not have been enough to record Bloomer's name in history had her publication not taken up the cause of dress reform for women. Women of the day wore unwieldy hoop skirts, and when Bloomer appeared in public wearing a short skirt covering a kind of baggy trouser, people were shocked. Although Bloomer was not the designer of the outfit, she became famous for introducing it to the public. *Bloomers* still carry her name.

Bloomingdale, Lyman and Joseph

In the late 1800s, hoop skirts were all the rage, and the Bloomingdale family was more than happy to supply them. Lyman Bloomingdale and his father opened Bloomingdale's Hoop Skirt and Notions Shop, while Joseph took to the road as a traveling skirt salesman. In 1872, Joseph tired of the road, and the brothers decided to open a ladies' notions shop together. Their East Side building was small and far from the main shopping district. Unlike most stores at the time, the East Side Bazaar sold a variety of fashions. On their first day, they sold only $3.68 worth of merchandise, but receipts would soon increase dramatically. By 1880, *Bloomingdale's* had grown into a five-story building, and it continued to expand. Joseph Lyman retired in 1896, and died in 1904. Lyman was the sole proprietor of the business until his death in 1905.

Blurb, Belinda

In 1907, a humorist named Gelett Burgess published a book called *Are you a Bromide?* When the book made its debut at a booksellers' dinner, it featured a dust jacket with a photograph of a stunning young model named Belinda Blurb. Underneath her picture was text describing the model's fine appearance. Booksellers from the dinner soon were referring to any text on a dust jacket as a *blurb*. You may not have heard of the book *Are You a Bromide?* but you have probably heard one of Burgess' other works:

> I never saw a purple cow
> I never hope to see one
> But I can tell you anyhow
> I'd rather see than be one.

He was also the author of a lesser-known sequel poem:

> Ah yes, I wrote the "Purple Cow"
> I'm sorry now I wrote it
> But I can tell you anyhow
> I'll kill you if you quote it!

Boeing, William

William Edward Boeing was born in Detroit in 1881. He graduated from *Yale University* in 1904, one year after the Wright brothers' historic flight. He was excited by the possibilities of aviation. After moving to Seattle where he worked as a timberman, he took up flying as a hobby in 1911. He built his first airplane in his boathouse in 1915. He had found a new career, and a year later he started his own company, Pacific Aero Products. Somehow, the name wasn't quite right. So the next year he changed the name to Boeing Airplane Company. By 1928, the Boeing Company had become one of the largest U.S. aircraft manufacturers. Boeing retired in 1934 from the company he had founded, but his company continued to soar. In 1954, Boeing developed the Dash 80, the prototype for the 707, which was destined to revolutionize air travel. The Boeing 747, which made its first flight in 1970, was the first "jumbo jet." Boeing, who died in 1956, was inducted into the Aviation Hall of Fame in 1984.

Boiardi, Hector

Yes, there is a Chef Boyardee, although his name is not spelled that way. Hector Boiardi, an Italian immigrant, came to the United States in 1914 when he was only 17. Upon his arrival, he immediately got a job as a chef at New York's Plaza Hotel, where his brother worked as a waiter. After moving to Cleveland, he perfected his spaghetti and meatball recipe in 1929. His customers kept asking for bottles of his pasta sauce so they could have it at home, and he obliged. He then added cheeses and pasta to the sauce. The results were so popular that he started to sell the products in area stores, and later in stores outside the area. Boiardi remained an advisor in the canned pasta business until his death at age 87 in 1985. And yes, that is Hector's picture on the label.

Bond, James

James Bond, known to his friends as Jim, was a Philadelphia ornithologist and the author of a book called *Birds of the West Indies*. While the bird-watching book may not have been a bestseller, it did catch the attention of an Englishman named Ian Fleming. At the time, Fleming was living in Jamaica and writing a book of his own. It was the story of an as yet unnamed British secret agent who had the code name 007. One day, as Fleming was sitting at breakfast looking through his favorite non-fiction title, he found the perfect name for his hero: Bond, James Bond. Interestingly, the name Bond was not chosen because it was strong, exotic, or even memorable. As Fleming later wrote, "It struck me that this name, brief, unromantic and yet very masculine, was just what I needed." Jim Bond didn't know about his fictional namesake until the early 1960s when he read an interview in which Fleming explained the origin of his character's name. In 1961, Bond's wife, Mary, wrote to

Fleming and half jokingly threatened to sue him for defamation of character. Fleming replied, "I must confess that your husband has every reason to sue me. . . . In return I can only offer your James Bond unlimited use of the name Ian Fleming for any purpose he may think fit."

Borden, Gail

Gail Borden was born on a farm in upstate New York. He spent most of his adult life in the South, where he changed jobs frequently and turned out a variety of inventions. They included a four-wheeled wagon with sails designed to travel on land or water, giant refrigerated buildings designed to "freeze out" disease, and a flat meat biscuit. While none of these inventions ever caught on, the meat biscuit did lead to another invention that did. Since meat could be kept fresh longer by removing the moisture, Borden reasoned that the same would be true of milk. He tried boiling milk in open pans to remove the water, but the milk had a burned taste. Then on a trip to a Shaker colony, Borden had another idea. The Shakers used a vacuum process to condense maple sugar. Borden tried the process on milk and added sugar as a preservative. The process worked. By this time the Civil War had broken out. The U.S. Army heard about Borden's condensed milk and put in an order for 500 pounds for the soldiers. Thus, at age 56, Borden finally had come up with an invention that had caught on. The modern Borden Corporation owns such companies as Krazy Glue, Classico, and Elmer's Glue. Elmer's Glue, in case you were wondering, was not invented by Elmer. Elmer was created to help sell the glue. He is the "brother" of Borden's mascot, Elsie the Cow.

Borden, Lizzie

Lizzie Andrew Borden was born July 19, 1860, the younger daughter of Andrew and Sarah Borden. Sarah Borden died three years later, and Andrew remarried in 1865. On August 4, 1892, Andrew Borden and his second wife were found murdered, killed by blows to the head with a sharp instrument. On August 12, Lizzie was arrested for the murders. The trial, which ran from June 5 to June 20, 1893, was a sensation. The Bordens were rich and prominent Massachusetts citizens. The Fall River murders generated all the interest of the Menendez brothers' trial years later. But it is unlikely that the name Menendez will be remembered a century from now. That is because the Menendez story was never made into a rhyme, as was Lizzie's alleged crime:

> Lizzie Borden took an axe
> And gave her mother forty whacks.
> When the job was nicely done
> She gave her father forty-one.

In the century since the killings, Lizzie has become the subject not only of songs, but also of plays, movies, and even a ballet. In the end, Lizzie Borden was acquitted of the murders, but questions as to her guilt or innocence remain. Whatever happened on the night of August 4th, or in the courtroom, the four-line poem will always have the last word. As Dorothy Parker once wrote, "I will believe till eternity, or possibly beyond it, that Lizzie Borden did it with her little hatchet, and whoever says she didn't commits the sin of sins, the violation of an idol."

Borders, Tom and Louis

The Borders brothers lived in Ann Arbor, a Michigan college town where in 1971 they opened a bookstore. The bookstore began to amass a large inventory. To keep track of the stock, the Borders brothers developed a computer inventory system. Thanks to the system, *Borders Books* earned a reputation as a place where one could find almost any book. Soon they began to build more stores in suburban Michigan, and then across the country. In the early 1990s, Borders added music to the inventory. In 1996, *Borders Books and Music* boasted 115 stores and sales of more than $700 million.

Botolph

Botolph was born in England around A.D. 610. He grew up to be a Catholic monk. He was sent to Gaul, where he lived until

654. He then returned to England and founded the monastery of Ikanhoe in East Anglia. For his good works, Botolph was sainted. His feast day is June 17. The monastery was later renamed St. Botolph's in his honor. Although the monastery was destroyed by the Danes in 810, the town surrounding it continued to carry Botolph's name in a condensed version— *Boston*. A number of citizens of Britain's Boston eventually settled in Massachusetts, and they named a city there after their hometown.

Boysen, Rudolph

In the late 1920s, a California botanist named Rudolph Boysen crossed a blackberry, a raspberry, and a loganberry and came up with a brand new fruit. He didn't see much future in the berry and soon abandoned the project. In 1932, a man named Walter Knott heard about the fruit. Knott had come to California with his wife, Cordelia, and set up a farm. In 1932, the couple were selling their fresh produce from a roadside stand. Unlike Boysen, Knott thought the new breed of berry would be a boon to his business. So he bought six sickly plants from the botanist and named the fruit *boysenberry*. The success of the produce stand helped the couple to open Mrs. Knott's Chicken Dinner Restaurant. It was so popular that people had to wait to get a table, and the Knotts built a ghost town to entertain them while they waited. This was the first of many attractions that would be built at *Knott's Berry Farm*.

Bowie, Rezin

The Bowie brothers, John, James, and Rezin, were Louisiana slave smugglers in the 1820s. Such a dubious background does not ensure that one's name will be recorded by history. But smuggling slaves into the country could be a dangerous business. So Rezin Bowie crafted a strong, double-edged hunting knife with a long blade. He then carved the family name into the handle. Rezin gave the knife to his brother James, who was an adventurous type. He was known for fearlessly roping wild horses and alligators in Louisiana swamps. Besides slave smuggling, James made his living selling fraudulent Arkansas land grants. Perhaps his career choices played a role in his decision to move to Texas. He became a Mexican citizen in 1828, married the daughter of the province's vice-governor, and began searching for a fabled lost mine. A few years later James joined the defenders of the Alamo, where he was killed. The knife he left behind was copied by many craftsmen in the following years. Those copies were known as *Bowie knives*.

Boycott, Charles Cunningham

Boycott was born in 1832 in Norfolk, England. As a retired army captain, he became the land agent for the 3rd Earl of Erne's estates in Ireland in 1873. In 1880, the Land League demanded that Boycott lower rents by 25 percent. Boycott not only refused, but tried to evict the tenants. The tenants organized and decided to stop speaking to Boycott and to cease working on his harvest. Boycott left Ireland as the result of the actions by his tenants. His name remained as a word for organized protest.

Bowdler, Thomas

Thomas Bowdler was a medical doctor who was forced to leave the profession because he couldn't stand the sight of blood. He was extremely concerned with what we today call "family values." In 1818, Bowdler published an edition of William Shakespeare's works that had removed "those words and expressions which cannot with propriety be read aloud in the family." The volume, *The Family Shakespeare*, was actually a revised and updated edition of an 1807 collection edited by his sister Harriet. The other Bowdler did not sign her name to the work. Her brother further edited and sanitized Shakespeare's works and received the credit. While the volume did not remain part of our literary heritage, Bowdler did contribute something to the language. It was his name. Today, *to bowdlerize* means to severely edit a literary work.

Bradley, Milton

Milton Bradley was born in Haverhill, Massachusetts. The early portion of his career was marked by a long string of bad luck.

He wanted to be a scientist, and in 1854 he took his savings and enrolled in the Lawrence Scientific School at Cambridge. Unfortunately, his parents decided to move two years later, and he was forced to drop out. He commuted from his family home in Hartford, Connecticut, to Springfield, Massachusetts, where he worked as a draftsman for the Wason Locomotive Car Works. While he was working in Springfield, Bradley began to dream of another career. He wanted to be a lithographer, a dream that seemed impossible because of the lack of lithographic presses in Springfield. One day Bradley heard about a press that was for sale in Providence, Rhode Island. He traveled to Providence, learned to use the machine, bought it, and brought it back to Springfield. In 1860, Bradley got his first big project. The Republican National Convention suggested that he produce photographs of their candidate, Abraham Lincoln. Bradley pressed hundreds of thousands of the pictures, but by the time Lincoln won the election he had grown a beard and no longer resembled the photographs. No one bought them. The Civil War followed shortly after, and it seemed Bradley's business was doomed. But then an inventor brought Bradley a game called "The Checkered Game of Life." He printed 45,000 copies. The game was meant to be educational. The purpose was to finish the game with a peaceful retirement based on having made proper moral decisions. By 1868, *Milton Bradley* was the leading manufacturer of games in America. Over the years, the object of the Game of Life shifted. In the modern version, the person who retires with the greatest fortune wins.

Braille, Louis

Born in Coupvray, France, Louis Braille was blinded at age three after an accident with an awl. In 1818, he was sent to the National Institute for the Young Blind in Paris. He became a noted musician in France, playing the organ and violin. In 1828, Braille himself became a teacher. Shortly thereafter, he began experimenting with "point writing" to allow the blind to read. The system he devised is now known as *braille writing*. It is now used around the world, but was not widely used until after his death. Thomas Edison, although fully sighted, preferred braille to visual writing. Another notable person to use braille was Aldous Huxley who, although not blind, had vision problems and learned braille to give his eyes a rest. He especially liked braille because he could read in bed in the dark.

Breck, John

In 1898, John Breck, a fireman with the Chicopee, Massachusetts, Fire Department, became the youngest fire chief in America. Personally, however, Breck was troubled. He was only 21 years old and was already losing his hair. In those days, there was no Rogaine, no Hair Club for Men, not even even much shampoo. Most Americans washed their hair with the same bar of soap they used on their bodies. Breck was unwilling to accept his hair loss, so he began taking chemistry classes at Amherst College in his spare time, determined to find a cure. He earned a doctorate, and opened a scalp treatment center where he used his own liquid shampoo. Breck never did discover the cure for hereditary baldness, but he did introduce modern shampoo to the American public.

Breyer, William

William Breyer began his career in 1866 as a door to door ice cream salesman. He made his frozen dessert out of cream, fruits, and nuts, and then loaded it onto a wagon and drove through town ringing a bell. He earned enough money to open a store in 1882. The Philadelphia shop combined a soda fountain in front and a manufacturing area in back. William Breyer died later that year, but the success of his ice cream increased. His son Henry took over the business and helped Breyer's to become the largest selling ice cream in America. Interestingly, the business that began with the delivery of ice cream door to door merged with the Good Humor Company in 1993.

Brock, Alice

Alice Brock lived in the former Trinity Episcopal Church in Housatonic, Massachusetts, with her husband, Ray, and their dog Facha. In 1965, they had Thanksgiving dinner for some friends at their church home. In attendance were 18-year-old Arlo Guthrie and 19-year-old Richard Robbins. The youths offered to take out the Brock's garbage. Finding the dump closed on Thanksgiving, they dumped the rubbish over a hillside. Police Chief William "Obie" Obanhein arrested the youths for illegally dumping garbage, to which they pled guilty. Obanhein was quoted as saying that he hoped the case would be an example to others who were careless about the disposal of rubbish. Whether it was an example or not, it proved to be a boon to Arlo Guthrie, whose arrest record not only prevented him from being drafted, but also proved to be the basis for a song. The resulting recording, *Alice's Restaurant,* launched the folksinger's career.

Brooks, Henry Sands

Henry Sands Brooks was born in 1773, the son of a Connecticut doctor. He grew up and moved to New York, where he had a successful career as a grocer. Groceries were not his favorite goods, however. Brooks liked stylish clothes, and whenever he could, he would travel to Europe to do some shopping. In 1818, when he was 45, he opened his own clothing store in Manhattan. He devoted his store primarily to the latest fashions from London. The business did well enough that he was able to bring in his brother, John, and his sons, Henry and Daniel. Brooks died in 1833, but his relatives kept the business going. In 1845, in an era when most clothing was hand tailored, they introduced the first ready-made suit. In the 1850s, the Brookses were joined by four more brothers, and they adopted the name *Brooks Brothers.*

Brown, Charlie

Charlie Brown, a round-faced Minneapolis native, once took an art class at the Bureau of Engraving in that city. One of his more talented classmates was named Charles Schulz. Brown and Schulz quickly became fast friends. They often talked about Schulz' plan to create a comic strip with a central character who struggled with life and tried to do well. Schulz named the central character after Brown. The "Peanuts" character bears a striking resemblance to his namesake. Brown eventually served as program director at the Hennepin County Juvenile Detention Center, where he went out of his way to help troubled youths. Brown died of cancer on December 5, 1983. He had never married or had children. Nevertheless, a child bearing his name will live on.

Brown, John

Abolitionist John Brown worked for the Underground Railroad across the Midwest from Ohio to Kansas. It was in Kansas that he and seven others murdered five pro-slavery settlers. In 1859, Brown and a team of followers captured the National Armory at *Harper's Ferry, Virginia*. He planned to use the armory as a refuge for fugitive slaves. The following day, the arsenal was recaptured by a citizen army led by Robert E. Lee. Brown was captured and hanged for treason, becoming a martyr for the cause. *John Brown's Body* became one of the most popular Union songs during the Civil War.

Brown, Nicholas

For 20 years, John Brown, a wealthy New England merchant, served as treasurer of Rhode Island College. The Baptist institution of higher learning was founded in 1764 in Warren and later moved to Providence. It closed briefly during the Revolutionary War, but reopened and prospered largely due to Brown's contributions. In 1804, his nephew, Nicholas Brown, donated $5,000 to the school. The Browns had already donated more than $160,000 at that point. This was the type of support that Rhode Island College wished to encourage, so the name of the school was changed to *Brown*.

Browne, Sam

Samuel James Browne was a 19th century British general who served with distinction in India. At that time, soldiers carried swords on their belts. The heavy swords had a habit of pulling the belt out of line, and even pulling a soldier's trousers down. Browne came up with a solution to this uncomfortable and awkward problem. He ran a second strap over his right shoulder and connected it to the belt. This held the belt and the sword in place and made it neater and easier to maneuver. The military belt and shoulder strap combination is known today as the *Sam Browne belt.*

Brummel, George Bryan

George Bryan Brummel was born in England in 1778. As a student at Eton and Oxford, he became known for his fine dress. After graduation, he decided not to work so he could focus on his wardrobe full time. An inheritance allowed him to continue to purchase fine clothing, despite his lack of a job. His impeccable sense of style endeared him to the British aristocracy. He even advised the Prince of Wales on matters of style. He later fell out of favor with the former prince, now King George IV, when he made fun of his highness' weight. No longer the golden boy of the royals, Brummel left for France in 1816. The French gave him the nickname "Beau," meaning "beautiful." His beauty was not enough to pay his bills in France, however, and the one-time dandy died poor and disheveled. His name and reputation as a fine dresser were destined to live on. *Beau Brummel* is now an epithet for a dedicated follower of fashion.

Buick, David Dunbar

David Dunbar Buick was born in Arbroth, Scotland, in 1854. Two years later his family moved to America. Buick went into the plumbing supply business. Then in 1899 he sold the business to form the Buick Manufacturing Company. At first, the company built only engines. But in 1903 it became the Buick Motor Company and produced its first car. Buick was not a good businessman, and in 1908 the company was failing. He sold the company to William Durant, who transformed it into one of the most successful automobile manufacturers in the country. Buick himself died penniless. He was buried in the Woodmere Cemetery in Detroit.

Bullwinkle, Clarence

Jay Ward, along with partner Alex Anderson, created the first made-for-television cartoon in 1948. "Crusader Rabbit" ran until the late 1950s. When that show ended, Ward turned his attention to another idea, a cartoon that would appeal to adults as well as children. The cartoon would feature a clever squirrel and a not-so-clever moose. Ward named the squirrel Rocky because it sounded like a fitting name for a kid's cartoon hero. The moose was named Bullwinkle after a local Berkeley, California, used car dealer, Clarence Bullwinkle.

Bunsen, Robert Willhelm

Robert Bunsen was born in Göttingen on March 31, 1811, and was educated at the University of Göttingen. He was a noted scientist and invented many things. Interestingly enough, the *Bunsen burner*, which was named for him, was not among them. In 1834, Bunsen discovered the antidote that is still used today for arsenic poisoning: hydrated iron oxide. He invented the ice calorimeter, a filter pump, and the zinc-carbon electric cell. He used the cell to produce an electric arc light and invented a photometer to measure its brightness. The cell was used also in his development of a method of producing metallic magnesium. Although Bunsen popularized the burner that bears his name, it was British chemist and physicist Michael Faraday who invented it. Bunsen died in Heidelberg on August 16, 1899.

Burbank, David

Luther Burbank was a noted botanist, the originator of many varieties of fruits and vegetables, including the *Burbank potato*. His work stimulated worldwide interest in horticulture. At the time of his death he had more than 3000 experiments under way and was growing more than 5,000 different plants. That is why the city of Burbank, California . . . has absolutely nothing to do with him. In 1867, a Los Angeles dentist bought a 4,000-acre plot of land that had originally been part of two separate Spanish land grants. The dentist's name was Dr. David Burbank. For several years he ran a successful sheep ranch on his property, but a drought in 1886 forced him to subdivide the land and sell it in 1887. On May 1, 1887, the town that was created there was named *Burbank*.

C

Cadbury, John

A young Quaker named John Cadbury opened a grocery in Birmingham, England, in 1824. In 1831, he began selling bitter drinking chocolate and cocoa. In those days, sweet chocolate confections were unknown. In 1847, Cadbury was joined by his brother Benjamin to form a business called Cadbury Brothers of Birmingham. About this time the pair started making some of the first "eating chocolate" in England. Sweet chocolate quickly became a luxury of the rich. In 1853, the Cadburys received a royal warrant to make chocolates for Queen Victoria. Benjamin left the company in 1860 and a year later John Cadbury retired, leaving his sons Richard and George in charge of the business. Over the years chocolate went from being the treat of the rich to a common snack. In 1993, the United Kingdom ranked fifth in the world in chocolate consumption. The British eat an average of 16.09 pounds of chocolate per person each year, and Cadbury dominates that market. The company introduced its famous Cadbury Creme Egg in 1971 and entered the U.S. market in 1978.

Cadillac, Antoine

In 1701, Antoine de la Mothe Cadillac, a 43-year-old French army officer, established a French settlement at the waterway between lakes St. Claire and Erie. Cadillac had convinced King Louis XIV's chief minister, Count Pontchartrain, that a permanent community at this strategic location would strengthen French control over the upper Great Lakes and repel British advances. So Cadillac built Fort Pontchartrain. It was not enough to keep the British away. The French lost the fort in the French and Indian War. The British, who now occupied the region, kept the French names, even though they didn't understand them. That is why the city is called Detroit, meaning "the straits," and the waterway (which is, in fact, a strait) is curiously named the Detroit River. Had the French been victorious, perhaps the future Motor City would have been named for Cadillac. Instead, Cadillac is a small town in Northern Michigan known primarily as an exporter of Christmas trees. Cadillac's association with Detroit did not end there, however. When Henry Martyn Leland founded an automobile company in 1904, he named it the *Cadillac Motor Car Company* in honor of the city's founder.

Caesar, Augustus

O.K., see if you can follow this: He was born September 23, 63 B.C. as Gaius Octavius, named after his father, who died in 59 B.C. Octavius' mother, Atia, was Julius Caesar's niece. Octavius had two sisters, both named Octavia—Octavia the Elder, who was a half sister, and Octavia the Younger, a full sister. Both the younger and the elder Octavias were older than Octavius. In 44 B.C., Octavius changed his name to Gaius Julius Caesar Octavianus and during the following decade and a half was known as Octavian. He later dropped the Gaius Julius and adopted the title Imperator Caesar Octavianus. Finally, on January 16, 27 B.C. he received the title "Augustus," which translates roughly to "Imperial Majesty." Thereafter, he was known as Imperator Caesar Augustus. The name Augustus was used by many subsequent Roman leaders, but this Augustus was the first. When Octavius was still a boy, Julius Caesar made him an heir without the boy's knowledge. When he learned he was an heir, the younger Caesar managed to gain power following Julius' assassination. He defeated his enemies, including Antony and Cleopatra, in a series of military campaigns, and became the leader of the Roman Empire by 29 B.C. He reigned over the empire's golden age. One of his duties was to oversee the revision of the calendar, a task that Julius Caesar had begun in 46 B.C. Before that time there were 10 months in a calendar year, all named for their positions in the year. September, October, November, and December still carry their original Latin names, which mean seventh, eighth, ninth, and tenth month. You will notice, of course, that September isn't the seventh month, nor do any of those months correspond to their positions in the calendar. That is because a 10-month calendar did not match the seasons of the year. Julius Caesar first addressed this problem (see next entry). Augustus made further improvements to the calendar and in the process renamed Sextilus (sixth month) for himself. If you've ever wondered why February is 28 days long while all the others are 30 or 31, the answer is ego. Julius' month on the new calendar was 31 days long, and Augustus' month couldn't be shorter than that named for Julius. So Augustus stole a day from February.

Caesar, Julius

Gaius Julius was born around the year 100 B.C. Although historians are skeptical, legend has it that he was cut from his mother's womb. His method of birth earned him the name Caesar, meaning "to be cut." This is also the source of the term *caesarean section*. Julius Caesar made some revisions to the calendar in 46 B.C. On the advice of an astronomer who was either Egyptian or Greek, Caesar reengineered the calendar so that the year would be in step with the seasons. In addition, he ordered the New Year moved from March to the first day of Januarius, named after the Roman God Janus, whose two faces look both backward and forward in time. That year was called "the Year of Confusion" because 80 days were added to the year. It was not Julius who decided to name a month after himself. It was the Roman Senate who renamed the fifth month after him. Quintilus became Julius, or July, as we call it now. One famous Caesar that was not named for Julius was the *Caesar salad*.

Calvert, George

George Calvert was born around 1580 in Yorkshire, England. He embarked on a highly successful political career in 1606 when he became private secretary to the secretary of state. In 1609, he became a member of Parliament. He was knighted in 1617 by

James I of England and became the secretary of state himself in 1619. In 1625, Calvert became a Roman Catholic. This must have been a difficult decision, because no Catholics were then permitted to hold public office in England. His conversion forced him to resign. James rewarded him for his public service, however, by granting him large estates in Ireland and giving him the title Baron Baltimore. At this point, Calvert turned his attention toward the New World. In 1623, he received a charter for the peninsula of Avalon in Newfoundland. Despite a hefty financial investment in the colony, it did not prosper. So Calvert petitioned for a grant farther south. In 1632, King Charles I granted him a tract of land to the northeast of the colony of Virginia, an area we now call Maryland and Delaware. Baltimore prepared the charter of his proposed colony but died before it could be accepted. The grant passed to Calvert's son Cecilius and continued to be passed to subsequent Lords Baltimore. The Maryland city was named for the family. The *Baltimore oriole*, by the way, was so named because it matched the colors of the Baltimore coat of arms.

Campbell, Joseph

This was not the noted expert on mythology; this Joseph Campbell owned a canning company. In 1894, Campbell retired, leaving the company in the hands of Arthur Dorrance and John Thompson Dorrance. The industrious pair came up with a method of condensing soup. The condensed soup was easier to package and ship. Even though Campbell was gone, the new proprietors named their product *Campbell's Soup* after the founder of the company. The Campbell's Soup kids, by the way, were based on Grace Wiederseim, the wife of a Campbell's advertising executive. As a child she had drawn a picture of herself by standing in front of her parents mirror and sketching what she saw. Years later she used that portrait as the basis for the drawings of the soup kids.

Canary, Martha Jane

Martha Jane Canary was born in Princeton, New Jersey, in a very unstable home. Her parents moved to Virginia, where they eventually split, leaving young Mary Jane to fend for herself. She took care of herself just fine, thank you very much. Dressed as a man and toting a gun, she roamed the West until she landed in the Black Hills of South Dakota, where she finally settled. She was an excellent marksman, and it was said that anyone who crossed her was in for a calamity. She may have been successful at shooting, but the original *Calamity Jane* was a calamity at marriage (she went to the altar 12 times) and at finances as well. She died penniless.

Cardini, Caesar

Italian-born Caesar Cardini was the proprietor of a Tijuana restaurant called Caesar's Place. During the Prohibition era, Caesar's Place was popular with Californians who would cross the border to have legal alcohol with their meals. Hollywood stars such as Clark Gable, Jean Harlow, and W. C. Fields were among them. For the Fourth of July celebrations at Caesar's Palace in 1924, Cardini came up with a special salad comprised of romaine lettuce, Parmesan cheese, garlic-infused olive oil, eggs, croutons, lemon, and anchovy-flavored Worcestershire sauce. The guests loved it. Word quickly spread, and Caesar's salad became the rage in Hollywood. Soon they were serving Caesar's salad at other upscale restaurants in the area. When Prohibition ended, so did the popularity of Tijuana as a nightspot, so Cardini emigrated to the U.S., bringing his salad with him.

Carnegie, Andrew

Andrew Carnegie was born in 1835 in Dunfermline, Scotland, the son of a weaver. The family came to America when Carnegie was a child. In America he worked as a telegraph boy and later joined the Pennsylvania Railroad. He became a successful investor, earning millions of dollars (and this was back when a million dollars was a lot of money) in Pittsburgh steel. In 1889, Carnegie wrote, "Surplus wealth is a sacred trust which its possessor is bound to administer in his lifetime for the good of the community. The man who dies rich, dies disgraced." Today Carnegie's name is found on more than 2,500 libraries, as well as *Carnegie Hall,* the *Carnegie Foundation,* and the *Carnegie Endowment for International Peace,* which were among his gifts.

Celsius, Anders

In 1742, Swedish-born astronomer Anders Celsius pondered the thermometer that was in use at the time, one named for *Daniel Gabriel Fahrenheit.* Celsius believed that there must be a simpler system. He eventually constructed a thermometer that designated 0 degrees as the boiling point of water and 100 degrees as the freezing point. That's right, 100 degrees was freezing. During his lifetime Celsius stuck to his belief that 100 degrees should represent the point of freezing, but after his death those who felt higher numbers should correspond to warmer temperatures won out and the scale was transposed. Until 1948, the scale Celsius devised was known as the Centigrade Scale. But that year scientists decided to honor the inventor by renaming the scale *Celsius.*

Cessna, Clyde

In the early 1900s, Kansas farm boy Clyde Cessna was one of the many young men whose imagination was captured by the Wright brothers' first flight and the brand new field of aviation. So, in 1911, he taught himself to fly. In the next seven years, Cessna earned a reputation as an accomplished and daring exhibition pilot. In 1925, he teamed up with Walter Beech and Lloyd Stearman to form the Travel Air Manufacturing Company, which built biplanes. He stayed with the company only two years before leaving to concentrate his manufacturing efforts on monoplanes. His airplane business was hit hard by the Great Depression, and for a time Cessna stopped production. But, in 1933, Cessna and his nephews Dwane and Dwight Wallace reopened the factory. The business got off the ground quickly, in time to furnish military planes during the war. Today, *Cessna* sells more light and mid-size business jets than all other companies combined.

Chanel, Gabrielle

Gabrielle Bonheur Chanel, better known by her nickname Coco, was born in Saumur, Maine-et-Loire, France. In 1914, Chanel opened a millinery shop in Paris. By the mid-1920s she had launched the classic Chanel look, consisting of a wool jersey suit with a straight, collarless cardigan jacket and a short, full-cut skirt, worn with costume jewelry and a sailor hat over short hair. In 1969, Alan Jay Lerner and André Previn wrote a play called *Coco* based on her life. Today the name Chanel is probably most closely associated with the perfume *Chanel Number 5*. What happened to Chanel Number 4? Well, there wasn't one. Five was simply Chanel's favorite number. She released the fragrance on the fifth day of the fifth month of 1925.

Chateaubriand, Francois Rene de

Born in 1768 the younger son of an ancient and noble Breton family, Francois Rene de Chateaubriand traveled extensively as a young man during the tumultuous period following the French Revolution. He wrote about his travels in *Voyage en Amerique* and *Atala*. Returning home to France, he became involved in pro-Royalist political causes, served as ambassador to England, and continued to write, particularly on topics relating to American Indians. He is often called the "Father of Romanticism" in French literature. But even the non-literary know his name today, thanks to a Parisian chef who served up a tenderloin cut served with mushrooms and bearnaise sauce in honor of the author and his dinner guest, the celebrated gastronome Anthelme Batillat-Savarin.

Chauvin, Nicholas

A native of Rochefort, France, Nicholas Chauvin was a soldier fiercely loyal to Napoleon and fond of telling inflated tales of his military glory. In the early 19th century a French vaudeville production used Chauvin as a character. During his lifetime he was admired for his devotion to his leader. After his death, however, *thespians* Charles and Jean Cogniard penned a comedy called *La Cocarde Tricolore*, which portrayed Chauvin as a comic character. His blind military zeal was parodied and exaggerated. The play became very popular and made Chauvin's patriotism famous. Today his name is remembered in the word *chauvinism.*

Chevrolet, Louis

Louis Chevrolet was a French race car driver who designed his own vehicles. One day in the early 1900s, Chevrolet met a fellow race car driver, Buick executive William C. Durant. Durant was impressed with Chevrolet's cars, although they were large and costly. So Durant had Chevrolet's designs modified into less expensive models. Although his friend Chevrolet was no longer involved in the process, Durant retained the name Chevrolet for his cars because he felt it had "a musical sound." The trademarked design on the hood of the Chevrolet came from the wallpaper in a French hotel. Durant was so impressed by the pattern that he ripped a swatch from the hotel's wall to bring back to his plant in Flint, Michigan.

Chippendale, Thomas

Thomas Chippendale was born in Otley, England, the son of a wood carver and cabinetmaker. In 1749, Thomas set up his own workshop. His furniture was so well regarded that today the term *Chippendale* is often applied to any furniture of the era. Chippendale died in London and was buried on November 13, 1779. One of his 11 children, Thomas II, took over the business and managed it for more than 40 years. The Walt Disney chipmunks, Chip 'n' Dale, were given their names as a play on the word Chippendale.

Chrysler, Walter

Walter Chrysler was a railroad mechanic until 1912 when he became works manager of the Buick Motor Company. By 1916, he was president of the company. In 1919, Buick was incorporated into General Motors. Chrysler helped in the reorganization and operation of both the Willys-Overland and Maxwell Motor companies. Then in 1925 the Chrysler Company was organized with Chrysler as president. He served as chairman of the board from 1935 until his death.

Claiborne, Liz

Liz Claiborne was born in Brussels, Belgium. Her father was a banker, and the family was always on the move. By the time she was a teenager, they were living in the United States. Claiborne did not finish high school. She wanted to become a fashion designer, but her father vetoed the idea, sending her instead to Paris to study art. She won a design contest for *Harper's Bazaar* in 1949 and shortly thereafter returned to the United States, where she married. She worked as a model and sketch artist before finally getting a job as a fashion designer with Arthur Ortenberg, who later became her second husband. She then became chief designer at Jonathan Logan. In 1976, Clairborne and Ortenberg decided to start their own firm. In only two years, Clairborne was earning $23 million on her designs. The Liz Claiborne Company went public in 1981. By then, the company's annual sales had reached $2 billion.

Clark, David Lytle

David Clark was born in Ireland and came to America when he was only eight years old. His family was poor, and after only one year of grade school the boy left to find work. His first job was selling newspapers and carrying market baskets. Then, at the ripe old age of 12, he attended business college, taking courses at night after working during the day. His first job as an adult was in a frame factory where he earned $1.50 a week. After that, he moved from one job to another, working at everything from paint manufacturing to selling fish. Finally he found steady work with a small New York candy manufacturer. He drove the delivery wagon, peddling chocolates door to door. After three years in the job he had enough money to buy the wagon, horses, and merchandise, and in 1886 he went into business for himself. He manufactured his candy in a small house in Allegheny, Pennsylvania, and sold it from the wagon. The success of his chocolate business surprised even Clark. During his life, the D. L. Clark Company became a leading manufacturer of confections, and the *Clark Bar*, introduced during World War I, made Clark a household word.

Cleaveland, Moses

You may have thought the Baby Ruth candy bar was named for Babe Ruth, but it wasn't. It was named for another Cleveland (see next entry). Maybe you thought that the Ohio city of Cleveland was named for President Cleveland. It wasn't, either. It was named for General Moses Cleaveland, who surveyed the area in 1796. You probably thought Cleveland, Ohio, was spelled with only one "a." This time you are right. To save space on a newspaper masthead, a printer singlehandedly decided to shorten the city's name by one letter, from Cleaveland to Cleveland. Ohio is not the only state to boast a city named Cleveland. Twenty-six states and Nova Scotia have cities by that name.

Cleveland, Ruth

Baby Ruth was the daughter of Grover Cleveland, the first child to be born in the White House. In the 1920s, a marginally successful confection called Kandy Kake changed its name to Baby Ruth, in honor of the White House kid. It soon became the best-selling candy in America. Many people erroneously believe that the candy bar was named for baseball great Babe Ruth. It was not. In fact, Ruth once tried to market his own brand of candy, and the Curtiss Candy Company took him to court. Babe Ruth was forbidden to use his own name on the candy to avoid confusion with Baby Ruth.

Cobb, Robert S.

In 1934, Robert S. Cobb became the owner of Hollywood's famous Brown Derby Restaurant. The restaurant got its start after actress Gloria Swanson quipped that in Hollywood, "You could open a restaurant in an alley and call it anything. . . . It could even be called something as ridiculous as the Brown Derby." Her ex-husband, Herbert Somborn, decided to test her theory. He opened a hat-shaped restaurant in 1926. It was a smashing success. One evening Cobb went to the icebox and found an avocado, which he chopped with lettuce, celery, tomatoes, and strips of bacon. Later he embellished it with breast of chicken, chives, hard-boiled eggs, watercress, and a wedge of Roquefort cheese for dressing. The *Cobb Salad* became one of the most popular items on the Brown Derby's menu.

Cohen, Bennett

Bennett Cohen was born in Brooklyn, New York, in 1951 and grew up in Merrick, Long Island. He eventually enrolled at *Colgate University*, but dropped out after a year and a half. He then attended *Skidmore College*, where he studied pottery and jewelry making. He then enrolled at the University Without Walls, but again was a dropout. Finally, Cohen settled down, working as a crafts teacher at a residential school for emotionally disturbed teenagers. Cohen often treated the students to new flavors of homemade ice cream that he would experiment with in the kitchen. In 1977, Ben left the school and decided to go into business with an old high school friend, Jerry Greenfeld. They planned to make and sell bagels, but when they learned how expensive the machinery would be, *Ben and Jerry* decided to try selling ice cream instead.

Colgate, William

William Colgate grew up on a farm where his father, Robert Colgate, made soap and candles. William decided to try his own hand at the soap business. He opened a soap shop in Baltimore in 1802, but in those days most people made their own soap and saw no reason to buy Colgate's. His business folded after only a year. Undaunted, Colgate moved to New York, and in 1806 he tried again. This time he had a plan. Instead of trying to compete with the same soaps his customers made at home, he would add fragrance. Homemade soaps were made out of cooking fats and did not smell particularly pleasing. The scented soap sold surprisingly well. In 1819, now a prosperous businessman, William Colgate helped to found an educational institution then known as Madison University. He became a great benefactor of the institution and left a large bequest in his will. After his death, his son James took up the cause, contributing more than $1,000,000. In 1890, the institution was renamed *Colgate University*. William Colgate died before his company produced the product that most people associate with his name. In 1908, when the business was in the hands of five of his eleven children, they introduced a dental product sold in jars. It was called *Colgate Tooth Paste.*

Collins, John

John Collins was a bartender around the time of the Civil War. He mixed gin, citrus juice, soda water, and sugar to create a popular drink that people asked for by his name. "Give me a Collins," customers often said. At the turn of the century, people developed a taste for a sweeter gin, so they began mixing Old Tom brand gin into the beverage. (No, I don't know who "Old Tom" was.) The new drink was called a *Tom Collins.* Bartenders will also be familiar with a *Rickey*, which is a Tom Collins without sugar. Apparently, a Kentucky colonel named Joe Rickey preferred his Tom Collins that way.

Colt, Samuel

Samuel Colt was born in Hartford, Connecticut, in 1814. He attended the Amherst Academy in Massachusetts until he was 15, when he was expelled. It seems he had built an underwater mine, and when he demonstrated it to a Fourth of July crowd it misfired and covered the crowd in mud. So Colt found himself a job on a ship bound for India. When he returned a year later, he brought with him a wooden model of a repeating pistol that he had designed. He gave this model to a gunsmith and paid him to craft a real pistol from his design. The prototype exploded. The gunsmith then changed the design to the point that it would not fire at all. Colt fiddled with the design, and by the time he was 22 he had perfected it. He opened the Patent Arms Manufacturing Company in Paterson, New Jersey, but it went bankrupt. He returned to working with underwater mines but never missed an opportunity to demonstrate his repeating pistol. Gen. Zachary Taylor was sufficiently impressed with the weapon that he ordered a thousand for his 1846 war with Mexico. With no factory of his own, Colt had to subcontract the work to Eli Whitney, the son of the famous inventor. By 1851, Colt had supplied the United States Army with 6,000 revolvers. Four years later he incorporated Colt's Patent Arms Manufacturing Company. During the Civil War, the Colt Company furnished hundreds of thousands of weapons to the Union Army. Samuel Colt died of a stroke on January 10, 1862. He was 48.

Sir Condom

Most experts believe there was a Dr. Condom—or perhaps a Dr. Conton, who was fond of a method of birth control that is evident in the name. The experts do not agree, however, on who he was. One theory is that he was in some way associated with the court of King Charles II. He may have been court physician to the king, and thus supplied His Majesty with the royal birth control devices. One version says that the king was so delighted with the invention that he made Condom a knight. Another source traces the word to a mid-17th century Colonel Condum of Britain's Royal Guards. Some word watchers doubt there was a Dr. Condom at all. They claim condom is simply derived from the Latin "condus," which means receptacle. In any case, condom use predates the court of King Charles II. The first known published description and clinical trials of condoms were recorded by *Gabrielle Fallopius*. His sheath was made of linen. There is a town in France called Condom, by the way. It's the center for the production of Armagnac, a type of brandy. Town officials say that they have to replace the sign bearing the name of their town five or six times a year. They are frequently stolen by British tourists. The French word for "condom" is "preservatif."

Constantine

Constantine was born in Thessalonika and later moved to Constantinople, the capital of the Byzantine Empire. There he became the protégée of imperial minister Theoctistos. After his teacher's assassination in 855, Constantine, by now an ordained priest, joined his brother, Methodius, in a monastery in Asia Minor. Because of their speaking skills, the brothers were selected to be missionaries. In 862, Prince Ratislave of Moravia, now Czechoslovakia, asked the Byzantine emperor to send priests to instruct his people in Christian liturgy in his country's native tongue. Since Constantine and Methodius had spoken the language in their youth, they were the perfect choice. Arriving in Moravia, they found that there was no alphabet into which they could translate the Bible, so Constantine created one. Once he had completed this task, Constantine returned to the monastery and adopted the name Cyril. He died two years later. Cyril and Methodius were the patron saints of Czechoslovakia and the Slavs. The alphabet Cyril created is still used in that part of the world. It is known as *Cyrillic* in his honor.

Coors, Adolph

Adolph Coors was born in 1847 in Barmen, Prussia. At age 14, he began an apprenticeship at the Henry Wenker Brewery. Then his parents died, and the Prussian War tore his homeland apart. Unwilling to serve King William I, he stowed away on a ship bound for America. He was discovered in the cargo area and agreed to work off the price of passage once the ship arrived in the United States. In 1868, with no money in his pocket, Coors arrived in America. He worked as a bricklayer for a year before traveling west to Naperville, Illinois, where he was able to put his brewer's training to work as a foreman for the Stenger Brewery. He continued to work his way across the country. In 1872, he arrived in Denver, Colorado, ready to pursue his dream of owning a brewery. To earn the money to finance this dream, he labored as a gardener. Within a month, he had enough to purchase a partnership in a Denver bottling company. By year's end he was the sole owner. Still, he wanted to own a brewery. Then on a Sunday afternoon, his only day off, Coors discovered an abandoned tannery on the banks of a Golden, Colorado, river. He thought this would be the ideal place for his brewery, and he convinced one of his customers, Jacob Schueler, to invest in his dream. In less than a year the brewery was turning a profit, and by 1880 Coors had earned enough to buy out his partner. The brewery continued to grow. It survived the Great Depression only to be shut down in 1914 by Prohibition. The company was forced to dump 17,000 gallons of beer into the river, leaving the fish with quite a hangover. Coors died before Prohibition ended, but the company survived to brew again. Of the 1,568 breweries operating before Prohibition, Coors was one of only 750 to survive and reopen in 1933.

Coriolis, Gustave-Gaspard de

Gustave-Gaspard de Coriolis was born May 21, 1792, in Paris. From 1816 to 1838 he was assistant professor of mathematics at the École Polytechnique, where he studied mechanics and engineering mathematics. He introduced the terms "work" and "kinetic energy" with their present scientific meaning. You can impress your friends by quoting the title of his 1835 mathematical paper, *Théorie mathématique des effets du jeu de billiard,* which translates to "Mathematical theory of the effects of billiards." But it is not for this title that he is best remembered. In the early 1800s, army officers noticed that their new long-range artillery pieces were consistently missing their targets. Even though they were carefully aimed, the shells always landed too far to the right. Coriolis studied the problem and came up with an explanation: $f = -2vV \sin f$ where v is the angular velocity of the earth's spin, f is the latitude, and V is the velocity of the moving object. Or, to put it in plain English, the earth is spinning, producing the *Coriolis effect,* which makes winds traveling north from the equator appear to bend to the right while those traveling toward the equator bend to the left. A common misconception about this phenomenon is that it causes the water in a sink to drain in the opposite direction in the Southern Hemisphere. While the Coriolis effect does exist, it only affects large bodies of air or water. Minuscule imperfections in the surface of a sink's bowl and the angle of the spigots would have more of an impact than the Coriolis effect. The myth probably persists because most people spend so little time watching the water drain in their sinks.

Cornell, Ezra

Ezra Cornell was born on January 11, 1807, in Westchester, New York, the eldest son of Elijah and Eunice Cornell. During his childhood, Cornell and his 10 younger siblings moved frequently. Opportunities for formal education were limited. As a teenager, Cornell could only attend school three months each winter. His lack of formal education did not prove to be a great hindrance. He made his fortune improving upon the work of *Samuel B. Morse*. Cornell devised a method of stringing insulated wires along telephone poles. This made the telegraph practical, providing telegraph service to the northeastern United States. His work on the telegraph made Ezra Cornell a wealthy man, with an annual income of $140,000. When he reached this milestone he wrote: "My greatest care now is how to spend this large income to do the greatest good to those who are properly dependent on me, to the poor and to posterity." What he decided to do was to donate $500,000 to help establish an institution of higher learning. Today the institution is known as *Cornell University*.

Cornell, William Wesley

W. W. Cornell was a distant cousin of *Ezra Cornell* (see above). He and his brothers were doing quite well in the iron business in New York. In 1856, Iowa Conference Seminary's Board of Trustees voted to make the school a four-year college. They also thought a change of names was in order. The first suggestion for a new name was Mount Vernon College, but the name *Cornell College* was adopted in the hopes that W. W. Cornell would be generous with donations. He donated enough to start a library for the school, but that seems to be the extent of his generosity. In 1868, representatives of *Cornell University* suggested that, to avoid confusion, the college should change its name. Since the college had been called Cornell for 10 years before Cornell University chose the name, it remained unchanged.

Corrigan, Douglas

For two years Douglas Corrigan had been trying to get permission from the U.S. Department of Commerce to fly across the Atlantic to Ireland. The Bureau of Air Commerce refused his request, saying that his craft was not airworthy. It had no radio and no fuel gauges for the auxiliary tanks. A leak in one of the tanks was simply coated with shellac. According to Corrigan, an official told him to "get lost," and so he did. He departed from New York ostensibly en route to Los Angeles. He later explained that his compass failed and that he accidentally set the backup compass exactly in reverse. When he landed in Dublin his feet were soaked in gasoline from the leak that the shellac had failed to keep sealed. He jumped out of the plane and asked airport officials, "Is this Los Angeles?" Corrigan became an instant celebrity, earning the nickname "Wrong Way Corrigan." He would not admit until years later that he had, in fact, meant to fly to Ireland all along.

Cowen, Joshua Lionel

Joshua Lionel Cowen was born in New York in 1880. He loved tinkering with mechanical things. At age seven he carved a train out of wood and attached a tiny steam engine. The engine exploded. Next he produced a battery-illuminated flower pot. The market for glowing flower pots did not prove to be great, but the combination of a battery and illumination led to the development of Eveready flashlights. Cowen later produced the first electric door bell and then turned his attention to his first love, toy trains. In 1903, he issued his first catalog of trains. By 1921, a million Lionel trains were entertaining children (and fathers) in America.

Crapaud, Johnny

This story may not be true, but I'm not going to let that keep me from telling it. According to Robert Hendrickson, Johnny Crapaud ("Johnny Toad") was the nickname of French gambler Bernard Marigny. As the story goes, Crapaud introduced dice to New Orleans around 1800. With the dice, people began playing a game they called craps, a shortened form of the gambler's nickname. When making bets on the origin of words, however, the final authority rests with the *Oxford English Dictionary*, which contends that the game of craps already had that name well before 1800. It suggests that the name evolved from the word "crabs."

Crocker, William

William G. Crocker was an early director of the Gold Medal Flour Company and, after a fashion, the father of Betty Crocker. In 1921, the flour company held a contest. Those who completed a Gold Medal puzzle could send it in and receive a pin cushion. Along with the pin cushion the company sent a letter of congratulations, which they thought should be signed by a woman, the kind of woman who could work magic with Gold Medal Flour and an oven. They liked the idea of "Crocker" for a last name, with all its connotations of cooking. Finally "Betty" was chosen, because it had a homey feel. The famous "signature" that appears on boxes of Betty Crocker products today was the winner of a contest among office employees. By 1945, a survey showed that Betty Crocker was the second-best-known woman in America after First Lady Eleanor Roosevelt—not bad for someone who never existed!

Crow, Jim

In Charleston, South Carolina, in the early part of the 19th century there was a hotel keeper who owned two slaves—both named James. To keep them both from answering each time he called one of them, he dubbed one "Jim." Because of his darker skin, the last name of "Crow" was added. Jim Crow was born in Richmond, Virginia, around 1800 and was sold to the hotel keeper in Charleston. The hotel keeper sold him again to someone in New Orleans, where he was later emancipated. It is said that Crow went on to London, where he acquired a fortune. The name Jim Crow came to be associated with any man of color, so the segregated railway coaches at the time of the Civil War were dubbed *Jim Crow cars*. Laws requiring segregation of whites and blacks became known as *Jim Crow laws*.

Cuervo, Jose Antonio

In 1758, Jose Antonio Cuervo obtained land from the King of Spain. The land was in Mexico, which was not yet an independent republic. The town was known as Tequila. There Cuervo concocted a mezcal from a desert lily called the blue agave, or scientifically speaking, the *agave azul tequilana Weber* (Weber was a Mexican botanist). The drink he created was named for the town of its origin. In 1795, Cuervo's relative, Jose Maria Guadeloupe Cuervo, received the first official permit from the King of Spain to produce tequila commercially. *Jose Cuervo* is now the world's largest-selling brand of tequila. Mexico is not the largest consumer of tequila. It comes in second to the United States.

Culligan, Emmett

Emmett J. Culligan was born in Yankton, South Dakota, on March 5, 1893, the son of an Irish farmer. He was the second of four children. In 1913, after two years in college, he dropped out and began to buy prairie land that he planned to farm, then later sell at a profit. When World War I began, Culligan was not required to serve because his farming was deemed useful to the war effort. But he enlisted anyway, and began his training only a few days before the war ended. Although he qualified for veterans' benefits, Culligan would not accept them. After the war, he returned to his previous career, farming, and buying and selling farms. At first, he was highly successful, but farming is not a stable career, and when a depression hit the farm economy Culligan lost everything. He and his wife moved in with his mother, who then lived in St. Paul. A friend helped Culligan find a job with a water-softening firm in Fort Wayne, Indiana. He quickly rose to district manager for the state of Iowa. In 1924, he became dissatisfied with the position and decided to set up his own business, the Twin City Water Softener Company. During the Great Depression that business failed, but Culligan bounced back again. His new plan was to provide soft water service instead of selling water softeners to the homeowners. This plan was the ticket. The Culligan Zeolite Company, founded with only $50, prospered and expanded, eventually becoming simply *Culligan Inc.*

Currier, Nathaniel

Nathaniel Currier was born in 1813 in Roxbury, Massachusetts. Around 1834, he set up shop as a lithographer in New York City.

His first successful print depicted destruction from an 1835 fire that leveled a large part of lower Manhattan. The firm's prints were devoted to contemporary subjects such as scenes of social and domestic life, public disasters, and Indian raids. There was a bookkeeper in Currier's shop named James Merritt Ives. Impressed with his work, Currier promoted him to full partner. Thereafter all prints published by the firm were trademarked as *Currier & Ives* prints. After the deaths of the partners, the firm continued until 1907. Today original Currier & Ives prints, some hand-colored, are valuable collectors' items. The most famous of the prints are wintery images of sleighs and family life that often appear on Christmas cards, earning the printers a mention in the well-known carol "Sleigh Ride."

D

Daguerre, Louis Jacques Mande

Louis Daguerre first made a name for himself as a painter, staging exhibitions in Paris and London. But he made an even greater impact as a photographer. Together with a collaborator, Daguerre developed a photographic process whereby a metal plate was treated with iodide of silver and exposed to light in a camera. It was then developed using mercury vapor. The process marked a milestone in the history of photography and became known as the *Daguerreotype*. Daguerre's partner, by the way, was named Joseph Niepce.

Daniel, Jasper Newton

One of 13 children, Jasper Newton Daniel, known to his friends as Jack, was born in 1850. Raised by a family friend, he was hired out to work with the Dan Call family at the age of seven. A Lutheran minister, the Reverend Call owned a whiskey still. He taught young Jack the art of whiskey brewing. In 1860, Call's congregation objected to having a whiskey-making pastor, so Call sold his still to the 13-year-old Jack Daniel. Decades later, Daniel entered his Old No. 7 Tennessee sipping whiskey in an exhibition at the 1904 World's Fair in St. Louis, Missouri. It won the World's Fair Gold Medal and a fair amount of renown. Jack Daniel died in 1911 as a result of blood poisoning from a toe that he broke kicking his office safe in anger. Beside his tombstone are two white chairs. It is said they were put there for the many young ladies who came to mourn the bachelor's passing. Jack Daniel's name lives on.

Davies, Meta

While Meta Davies was working as a meter maid in London, she came across an illegally parked vehicle and wrote out a ticket that carried a fine of 10 shillings. The car's owner returned while she was still there. The owner, Paul McCartney, was not especially upset by the ten-shilling fine. He looked at the name on the ticket—Meta—and asked her about it. Before he pulled away he remarked, "That would be a good name for a song. Do you mind if I use it?" With a slight syllable change the result was McCartney's "Lovely Rita."

Davy, Humphrey

In the early days of mining, explosions caused by the deadly contact of flammable gas with lamp flames were common. Most of these explosions were small and killed only a miner or two. In 1812, however, a calamitous explosion brought the problem to the attention of the public at large, including a chemist who had never been near a mine. Humphrey Davy began working on the problem of how to illuminate a mine without blowing up the miners. He discovered that flame would not pass through minute tubes. He concocted a lamp that featured a series of small tubes that would encircle the lamp's flame. Gaseous air could get to the flame, but could not emerge again to ignite the surrounding air. The Reverend John Hodgson tested the first Davy lamp in a mine near Newcastle. According to one account, "Mr. Hodgson descended Hebburn pit, walked about in a terrible atmosphere of fire-damp, held his lamp high and low, and saw it become full of blazing gas without producing any explosion." Humphrey Davy would not accept royalties for his life-saving invention. A "davy" became a miner's term until technological improvements made the lamp obsolete.

De Bergerac, Cyrano

Cyrano de Bergerac lived from 1619 to 1655. He was an eloquent writer and was said to have inspired the French dramatist Moliere. He also had a reputation as a great lover, but he was sensitive about the size of his nose. An expert swordsman, he would run anyone through who dared to make fun of it. He didn't die in a sword fight, however. He was hit on the head by a falling beam at a friend's house and died of the injury. This real historical figure caught the imagination of Edmond Rostand, who wrote a play called *Cyrano de Bergerac* in 1897.

De Pauw, Washington C.

Washington C. De Pauw was a wealthy banker and plate glass manufacturer. As he was preparing his will, De Pauw thought he would leave a large portion of his fortune to found a new institution of higher learning. The founders of a Methodist institution, Indiana Asbury University, had other ideas. Indiana Asbury University was founded in 1837 "to be conducted on the most liberal principles, accessible to all religious denominations, and designated for the benefit of our citizens in general." It was named for Bishop Asbury, the first Methodist bishop in America. Asbury's founders convinced De Pauw that, instead of starting his own university, his money could be put to better use in theirs. De Pauw donated $300,000 to the institution while he was alive and included a large bequest in his will. Bishop Asbury's name was dropped. The school is now known as *De Pauw University*.

De Sade, Donatien Alphonse Francois

Count de Sade was an 18th century French novelist whose books were filled with lurid tales of sexual fantasies, mostly involving torture. De Sade was arrested and sentenced to death in 1772 for "an unnatural offence." He managed to escape to Italy, where he was arrested several times on similar charges. He died in 1814 in the Charenton Lunatic Asylum. In his will de Sade wrote, "The ground over my grave should be sprinkled with acorns so that all traces of my grave shall disappear so that, as I hope, this reminder of my existence may be wiped from the memory of mankind." That was not to happen, however. More than 50 years later, a sexologist by the name of Richard von Krafft-Ebing immortalized him by adopting the term *sadism* for those who derive sexual satisfaction from the pain of others.

De Sade, Laura

On April 6, 1327, the Roman poet Petrach saw Laura for the first time. He later cited that date as the day he began writing poems. Laura was the wife of Hughes de Sade, a descendant of the French nobleman *Donatiene de Sade*. Petrach loved Laura and wrote some of the most famous love sonnets in history in her name. The collection is called "*Rime in Vita e Morte di Madonna Laura.*" While Petrach wrote her love poems, Laura bore de Sade 11 children. She died in 1348 at the age of 40. Petrach lived to write about Laura until 1374.

De Seingalt, Giacomo Casanova

Giacomo Casanova de Seingalt was nobly born in Venice in 1725. At the age of 16 he was expelled from the seminary because of immoral conduct. He further alienated his distinguished parents by becoming a *thespian*. As an actor, he visited many of Europe's capitals. He worked at various times as a journalist, a preacher, a diplomat, and a businessman. He gained notoriety in 1755 when he was jailed as a secret agent in Venice. But he escaped to France. His exaggerated accounts of the events made him sought after among the well-to-do of Europe. A popular figure in France, he was made the head of the national lotteries and earned a fortune, which he spent on travel and romancing women. When he died in 1798, he left behind a racy 1,500,000-page memoir that made the name *Casanova* forever synonymous with a great lover.

Deere, John

John Deere began his career as a blacksmith's apprentice in 1821. He earned $30 a year, and a valuable education. By 1825, Deere had earned a reputation for his smithing, especially his quality pitchforks. Things seemed to be going well in 1831 when an investor, Jay Wright, helped him open his own blacksmith shop. Unfortunately, the shop burned to the ground. He opened the shop again—and again it burned. As Deere planned to try a third time, Wright decided he had had enough, and he sued Deere to get his money back. Deere left his business and his family behind and headed for Illinois, where in 1837 he finally opened an inflammable blacksmith business. One day in his shop Deere began to experiment with a broken steel saw blade. He reasoned that the steel would be a much better material for plows than the iron and wood that were then being used. He built a prototype, and within 20 years Deere's factory was producing 10,000 steel plows a year. John Deere's company still makes farm equipment.

Derrick, Godfrey

Derrick was an executioner at London's Tyburn prison in the 17th century. During his illustrious career, he was responsible for more than 3,000 executions. He served in the Earl of Essex's expedition against Cadiz. During the conflict, Derrick was found guilty of rape, and the executioner was, himself, sentenced to death. The Earl of Essex thought Derrick's services were too valuable to let him die, however. He pardoned Derrick, only to find *himself* brought before the executioner at a later date. The name *derrick* came to be associated with the gallows, and later with any hanging apparatus.

Dewey, Melvil

Melvil Dewey was born in Adams Center, New York, on December 10, 1851. While he was a student employed in the Amherst College library, he became frustrated with the way the books were organized . . . or disorganized. At the time, books in libraries were numbered according to their locations on the shelves, not according to their relationships to each other. If a shelf were moved, every book had to be renumbered, and the numerical system was different from library to library. So Dewey set to work on a system that would classify all books by subject matter. Called "the Edison of the library field" by his admirers, the father of the *Dewey Decimal System* went on to found the New York Library Association, the American Library Association, the *Library Journal*, and the first library school. He died the day after Christmas in 1931 in Lake Placid, New York.

Diesel, Rudolph

Rudolph Diesel was a young German living in Paris in 1870 when the Franco-Prussian War broke out, and the Diesels were forced to escape to England. His parents later put young Rudolph on a train back to Germany where he would stay with his uncle. The journey took eight tension-filled days. When he got older, Rudolph made it his mission to improve upon the steam engines that made his journey take so long. The first engine that Diesel constructed exploded, nearly killing him. After years of work and improvements, the engine was adopted for use in trains, ships, and automobiles. Diesel became rich and famous before his mysterious death in 1913. In September of that year, Diesel traveled to England on a steamer called *Dresden*. One morning he did not show up at breakfast. Ten days later his body was fished from the water by another boat. Whether his death was an accident, suicide, or murder was never determined.

Disney, Walter Elias

Walt Disney was born in Chicago in 1901. He studied at the Academy of Fine Arts in Chicago and began his career as a cartoonist in 1920. On October 16, 1923, Walt and his brother Roy Disney founded the Disney Brothers Studio. Before long, his career took off, and he owed it all to a mouse. On March 16, 1928, the cartoonist was on a train from New York to Hollywood when he began sketching a cartoon version of a real pet mouse. The mouse's name was Mortimer, and Disney had trapped him in a wastebasket and kept him as a pet in his early days as an artist. When Disney told his wife about the character, she suggested the mouse be named Mickey instead. Mickey Mouse made his first appearance in the film *Steam Boat Willie* in 1928. It was Disney's first attempt to use sound film, and he provided the voice for Mickey himself. Mickey Mouse was an immediate hit. At the height of his fame, *Film Daily* estimated that more than 100,000 people a day saw the mouse on screen. He was known as Michael Souris in France, Miki Kuchi in Japan, Miguel Ratoncito in Spain, Mikki Maus in

Russia, and Muse Pigg in Sweden. Of course, a character of his renown had his detractors. In the 1930s, he was banned in Nazi Germany, the Soviet Union, Fascist Italy, and Yugoslavia. In the 1950s he was banned in East Germany. As for Walt Disney, he went on to produce some of the most beloved animated films of all time, including *Lady and the Tramp, Cinderella,* and *Fantasia.* He opened *Disneyland* in Anaheim, California, in 1955. Walt Disney died in 1966, but the *Walt Disney Company* continued to grow. An even bigger amusement park, *Walt Disney World,* opened near Orlando, Florida, in 1971. In the 1980s, Disney Studios began making films for adults. Today there are Disneylands in Japan and France. The Disney Company had revenue of approximately $1.4 billion in 1996.

Dodge, John and Horace

Where John Dodge went, his brother Horace, the younger by four years, was sure to go. They grew up in Niles, Michigan, where their father owned a machine shop. After graduating from high school, they worked as machinists in various locations in Michigan before settling in Detroit in 1886. There they got a job at Murphy Boiler Works. After John suffered a bout with tuberculosis, the brothers decided to take a less strenuous job at the Dominion Typograph Shop that sold the unique product combination of typesetting machines and bicycles. In 1897, the pair left to start their own business with another partner. They named it Evans & Dodge Bicycle Company. The company was purchased by the National Cycle and Automobile Company two years later. The company put Horace to work in Windsor, Ontario, and they sent John to Hamilton, Ontario. It was the first, and last, time the brothers would be separated. It was only a year before another company bought National Cycle, and the brothers returned to Detroit where they went into business together again. This time they opened a machine shop. Their big break came when a man named *Ransom Olds* came into the shop for engines for his new automobiles. *Oldsmobiles* became quite popular indeed, and the Dodges supplied the transmissions for all of them. In 1903, the brothers signed an agreement with the brand new *Ford Motor Company* to supply gears and components in exchange for part ownership in the company. In 1906, *Henry Ford* announced that he would make his own engines. The Dodges resigned from Ford in 1913, and on November 14, 1914, they rolled out the "Old Betsey," the first Dodge car. They cashed out of Ford with $25 million in 1919. In 1920, when Horace Dodge became ill, his brother John never left his side. Then John fell ill and died at age 56. Horace also died within 11 months. Both were buried in the Woodlawn Cemetery in Detroit, which is also the final resting place of *Edsel Ford*. In 1928, Chrysler bought the company from the Dodge heirs.

Dolby, Ray

You might call Ray Dolby an over-achiever. He began his career with Ampex Corporation in 1949, working on audio and instrumentation projects. There he played a major role in the invention of the world's first practical videotape recorder. What makes this all the more impressive is that Dolby didn't receive his bachelor of science degree from *Stanford University* until years later. Shortly thereafter, he was awarded a Marshall Scholarship and a National Science Foundation graduate fellowship, which he used to study at Cambridge University in England. In 1961, he earned his Ph.D. in physics while at Cambridge serving as a consultant to the United Kingdom Atomic Energy Authority. He then took a two-year appointment as a United Nations advisor in India. Upon his return in 1965, Dolby founded his own company dedicated to the development of new audio noise reduction techniques. Since then, consumers have purchased more than 630 million audio products licensed to use Dolby technologies. More than 7,000 feature films have been released with Dolby soundtracks. They have been shown at the more than 43,000 movie theaters worldwide that have Dolby equipment to play them. There are more than 50 weekly television shows currently running in the United States that are encoded in Dolby Surround Sound.

Dole, James Drummond

A New Englander named James Drummond Dole graduated from Harvard in 1899 with degrees in agriculture and business and decided to seek his fortune in Hawaii, where his cousin Sanford was governor. His unlikely scheme was to harvest pineapples. Pineapples are not native to Hawaii. They were imported from South America in 1813 and they thrived. In the days before commercial aviation and refrigeration, however, perishable pineapples would, well, perish, before they reached the contiguous United States. Dole's plan was to can the fruit in Hawaii and ship it back home. In 1900, he bought 61 acres of farmland at auction for $4,000. A year later he incorporated the Hawaiian Pineapple Company, built a cannery in 1903, and produced 1,893 cases of canned pineapple in the first year. In 1907, he built a larger cannery in Honolulu, which was closer to the port and the can factory. Unfortunately, economic hard times in the states reduced the demand for what was then considered a luxury food. So Dole and eight other pineapple packers pooled their pennies. As the Hawaiian Pineapple Growers Association, they launched a $50,000 campaign advertising not one brand but Hawaiian pineapples in general, something that was not common practice at the time. Pineapple demand skyrocketed. A major breakthrough occurred in 1913 when Dole engineer Henry Ginaca invented a machine that could peel and core 35 pineapples per minute. Until then, each pineapple had to be cored by hand. Dole developed the pineapple business into Hawaii's second largest industry. The first product to bear the *Dole* trademark was not the canned pineapple but canned pineapple juice, which was sold during the Great Depression. Dole retired in 1948 and died in 1958, the year that Hawaii became the 50th state.

Douglas, David

David Douglas, a gardener at Glasgow's botanical gardens, traveled to America in 1923 to study the native plant life and collect specimens for the Royal Horticultural Society. During his travels across the great land, Douglas wrote about more than 200 plants that were unknown in Europe. Among the plants he described was a massive pine tree he first observed in 1825. The *Douglas fir* is the second tallest tree in America (after the sequoia). It can grow to 300 feet tall and 12 feet around.

Douglas could have used a plank of its hard wood in 1834. During a visit to Hawaii that year, he was killed by a wild bull.

Dow, Charles Henry

Charles Henry Dow was born on November 6, 1851, in Sterling, Connecticut, the son of a farmer. He grew up to become a journalist, working on the *Springfield Republican*, the *Providence Star*, the *Providence Evening Press*, and the *Providence Journal*. He moved to New York City in 1880 and became a reporter for a financial news service called the Kiernan News Agency. Dow remembered a friend and fellow writer from his days at the *Evening Press* named Edward D. Jones. He brought Jones into the company. By 1882, they had developed their own ideas about how to report financial news. They formed their own company in a basement on Wall Street, next to the stock exchange. The firm, known as *Dow Jones and Company*, delivered news by messenger to the financial wizards of Wall Street. By 1889, the handwritten bulletins had evolved into *The Wall Street Journal*, a four-page afternoon paper. On May 26, 1896, Dow and Jones launched the *Dow Jones Industrial Average*, then a daily composite of 12 "smokestack" companies that produced coal, leather, cotton, and sugar. A year later, they came out with a ticker to provide instant stock market updates. The first publication of an average comparable to today's 30 industrial stocks was on October 1, 1928. The Dow closed that day at 240.01.

Dow, Herbert Henry

Herbert Henry Dow was born February 26, 1866, in Ontario, Canada. He attended the Case School of Applied Science and graduated with a B.S. degree. He moved to Midland, Michigan, where he earned himself the title "Crazy Dow" because of his plan to extract bromides from the prehistoric saltwater sea buried beneath Michigan's soil. His first of many patents was issued in 1889. His patents attracted the attention of the Midland Chemical Company, which agreed to invest in Dow's scheme. The process of removing chlorine and bromides from the brine produced bleach, which Dow thought Midland

Chemical could mass produce. They turned him down, and his backing ran out. Dow then left for Ohio, where he created his own company—the *Dow Chemical Company*—on May 18, 1897. Dow perfected his bleach and bromide production technique, and in 1900 he returned to Michigan and bought out the Midland Chemical Company. When he died in 1930, Dow owned more than 90 patents.

Draco

Before Draco became chief magistrate of Athens in 621, Greece's legal system was in utter chaos. Crimes were usually punished by revenge killings, and prominent people could literally get away with murder. Draco stepped in to straighten out the mess. He composed Athens' first written constitution and set forth clear laws. The punishments for various crimes were spelled out clearly as well. To simplify matters, death was the punishment of choice for most crimes. Because of Draco's strict and uncompromising enforcement of the law, the expression *draconian justice* has survived through the ages to mean legal repression.

Dubuque, Julien

The first white settler in Iowa was a fur trader named Julien Dubuque. In his travels, he heard that lead was being mined in the area, so he approached Indian leader Kettle Chief for permission to dig. Assuming the chief would refuse him, Dubuque decided to take matters into his own hands. While he was talking with the chief about mining, he had a friend go upstream on Catfish Creek and pour oil on the water. Dubuque warned the chief that he would set the creek on fire if he did not get permission to mine. Kettle Chief refused, so Dubuque threw a burning branch into the patch of oil and the water burst into flames. Kettle Chief changed his position on the mining issue. Dubuque used women from the tribe to do the mining, and he and his crew melted the ore into bars and sold them. A white settlement sprang up around Dubuque's mine. A statue made of the ore from the mine stands today in the town that bears Dubuque's name.

Duke, Washington

Tobacco made Washington Duke a wealthy man. Having done well for himself, Duke wanted to give something back, so he bought a large plot of land that had once been a race track and offered it and a large sum of money to a group of Baptists who wanted to start a girls' school. The Baptists didn't want to found their school on a former race track or with tobacco money, so they turned him down. Duke offered his generosity to another educational institution, Trinity College, which had been founded in 1838 by Quakers and Methodists. Duke's gifts of $400,000 persuaded Trinity to move to Durham. When he died, his two sons, James and Benjamin Duke, continued to support the institution. In 1924, Trinity College decided to change its name to *Duke University*. One factor may have been James Duke's endowment of $6 million.

Duncan, Donald

In the 16th century, Philippine hunters devised a weapon so fierce, so cunning that it could be called only one thing—the *yo-yo*. The weapon was hurled, capturing its prey in its twine. As time passed, the yo-yo proved to be particularly ineffective against the machine gun, and its use as a weapon declined. The outdated weapons began stacking up, like so many eight-track tapes, until one day someone discovered that it was fun to make the yo-yo go up and down. When Filipinos started to move to the U.S. in the 1920s, they brought these exotic toys with them. It was then that they came to the attention of Donald Duncan. He believed that American children would enjoy the former weapon as well, and he made a version of the toy in 1929. His patent application was rejected, however, because a Filipino named Pedro Flores had already patented a yo-yo. So Duncan simply bought the rights from Flores. Duncan's first yo-yo went on sale in 1932. By 1965, he was selling nine out of ten yo-yos in the country. Until that year, Duncan was the only company allowed to sell a toy called a "yo-yo." The courts then ruled, however, that yo-yo was merely the name of the toy, and not a trademark.

Duns Scotus, John

Franciscan theologian John Duns Scotus wrote treatises on metaphysics, theology, logic, and grammar. He was educated at Cambridge and Oxford and received a master's degree from the University of Paris. In 1303, when King Philip IV funded his war effort against England by taxing the Church, Pope Boniface VIII threatened to excommunicate him. Duns Scotus was banished from France for supporting the Pope and attacking the Dominicans, especially Thomas Aquinas. The Dominicans fought back against the Franciscan's followers, branding them as unintelligent. John Duns Scotus' followers were known as Dunses. And so it was that a noted scholar's name gave us the word *dunce.*

DuPont, Eleuthere Irenee

Eleuthere Irenee DuPont and his father and brother emigrated from France to New Jersey in 1800. DuPont had studied with chemist Antoinne Lavoisier and listed his career as "botanist" on his passport. In those days, most Americans relied on their rifles for hunting, yet they could not always rely on their gunpowder. Dampness in the powder was known to cause rifles to misfire with surprising regularity. Using his background in chemistry, DuPont set to work to solve the problem. A year later he created E. I. DuPont de Nemours and Company to manufacture and sell a better grade of gunpowder. Among the fans of the new product was Thomas Jefferson, who used DuPont's gunpowder to clear the land at his estate, Monticello. In 1902, three of DuPont's great-grandsons, Thomas Coleman DuPont, Alfred I. DuPont, and Pierre Samuel DuPont, bought the firm, set up a new research department, and issued stock in the company. By the 1920s, DuPont had changed its focus to synthetic materials. The company's research yielded such materials as Teflon, Lycra, Mylar, and nylon. The company that began as a gunpowder manufacturer is today a $43.8 billion company with 97,000 employees in 70 countries.

E

Eastman, George

George Eastman was a bookkeeper who invented the snapshot camera and roll film. He went on to form the Eastman Kodak Company. He chose the name "Kodak" in 1888 because it was "short, vigorous, could not be misspelt, and to satisfy trademark laws, meant nothing." Besides roll film, the company also manufactured flexible, transparent film, which proved to be vital to the subsequent development of the motion picture industry. Eastman was also a great philanthropist, donating more than $75 million to various projects, including an endowment for the establishment of the *Eastman School of Music* in 1918 and a school of medicine and dentistry in 1921 at the University of Rochester.

Edgerly, Dr. Albert Webster

Dr. Albert Edgerly wrote a popular health book in the late 1800s called *Life Building* under the pen name Dr. Ralston. In 1898, Ralston was approached by an animal feed seller named William Danforth. Danforth had learned that when grain was milled, the germ was separated from the wheat and then was discarded. He decided to use the by-product as a breakfast cereal. He called his product "Purina" in reference to its purity. Dr. Ralston was pleased to give his endorsement. Thus, the Ralston-Purina Company was born.

Edwards, Earl

The Duke of Earl was not a historical figure; but there was, in fact, an Earl. Earl Edwards was the founder of the doo-wop group known as the Dukays. The Dukays recorded a handful of songs for Nat Records, including "Duke of Earl." Due to contractual problems, when VeeJay Records released the record in 1962, it could not be credited to the Dukays. One member of the band left the group and put it out under a pseudonym, Gene Chandler. So when "Duke of Earl" hit number one on the Billboard charts, Earl of the Dukays was no longer part of the band.

Eiffel, Alexandre-Gustave

In 1886, 53-year-old Alexandre-Gustave Eiffel was considered France's master of metal. He would later be dubbed "le Magicien du Fer," or "the Iron Magician." So when the French government began looking for an architect to design a tower for an exposition to celebrate the 100th anniversary of the French Revolution, Eiffel was the obvious choice. Officially, the government held a design contest, but weeks earlier French minister Edouard Lockroy had met with Eiffel to discuss plans for a tower. Lockroy was so impressed by Eiffel's ideas that he rigged the contest in the architect's favor. In January 1887, Eiffel signed a contract with the government. Eiffel and Company agreed to contribute $1.3 million of the tower's estimated $1.6 million cost. In exchange, Eiffel would receive all revenues generated by the tower during the exposition and for the next 20 years. Then, ownership would revert to the city of Paris. The *Eiffel Tower* was completed in record time, and under budget. Although many critics thought it was an ugly blight on the Parisian skyline, it soon became the most recognizable symbol of that city. Few people know that Eiffel built a love nest at the top of the tower so he could carry on his personal affairs. The room is now open to the public. For a time, the tower became a huge billboard. From July 4, 1925, until 1936 the tower sported an electric Citroen sign that could be seen for more than 20 miles. Trivia fans will be pleased to know that the Eiffel Tower contains 2,500,000 rivets.

Elmo

Elmo was a Syrian bishop. According to legend, Saint Elmo was preaching when lightning struck just inches away. He continued his sermon without missing a beat. Another legend has it that Elmo was captured and set fire by pagans, before escaping in a boat piloted by an angel. Sailors call the static electricity that discharges on ships St. Elmo's Fire. Besides being the patron saint of sailors, Elmo is also the patron of women in labor (though few women remember that at the time).

Epicurus

Epicurus, who lived from 341 to 270 B.C., began his career as a soldier before becoming a popular teacher and philosopher. He traveled to Athens in 306 B.C. and opened a school. He taught that the purpose of life was pleasure, but his view of pleasure, derived from proper living, was different from the hedonism his detractors imagined it to be. He defined pleasure as "freedom from pain in the body and from trouble to the mind. Not continuous drinkings, nor the satisfaction of lusts." His pleasure-seeking followers were atheists who dropped out of the mainstream of society, shunned marriage, and had no children. But their focus on the pleasures of the senses gave us the word *epicure*, meaning one who cultivates fine appetites for food and wine.

Etherelda

Etherelda was an English princess in the year 640. She was better known as Audrey, and later, Saint Audrey. Audrey died of a neck tumor she claimed was divine retribution for the ornate jewelry she had worn in her youth. Throughout the Middle Ages the English held a fair on Saint Audrey's day. Women wore necklaces called "Saint Audrey's Lace." The necklaces were often of very poor quality. Soon 'Taudrey's Lace (corrupted later to *tawdry*) became synonymous with cheapness.

Eustachius, Bartolomeo

Eustachius was born in San Severino around 1520. For a time, he served as the personal physician of the Duke of Urbino and of a Roman cardinal. In those days, doctors learned about the human body by dissecting animals and guessing that human beings were pretty much the same inside. The practice of dissecting human corpses was controversial, but maverick doctors such as Andreas Vesalius and *Gabriel Fallopius* had started to do just that. Eustachius was against the practice. To show the medical establishment just how useless it was to dissect real humans, Eustachius took his knife to a corpse. Instead of converting the others, however, he converted himself. He wrote essays on what he found, including a canal that connects the middle ear to the back of the throat to equalize pressure on the eardrum. The canal was named the *eustachian tube* in his honor.

Everest, Sir George

In the mid-1800s, India was ruled by Great Britain. At that time the imposing mountain peaks in nearby Nepal had not been named. (At least, they had not been named by the British. The natives had a name for the highest peak—Chomolungama.) In 1856, the surveyor general of India, Sir Andrew Waugh, suggested the world's highest mountain be named for George Everest, who had served earlier as surveyor general. Everest himself was not taken with the idea of being immortalized in stone. He pointed out that "Everest" could not be written in Persian or Hindi. Nevertheless, the name was adopted. Everest may be hard to pronounce for some, but Chomolungama proved far too difficult for the English to pronounce.

F

Factor, Max

Max Factor was born in Lodz, Russia, in 1877. At the age of 14 he became an apprentice to a wig maker. At 20, he was running his own makeup shop. In 1904, Factor brought his family to America for the St. Louis World's Fair, and they never left. First, Factor opened a cosmetics shop in St. Louis, but the motion picture industry, then beginning in Hollywood, beckoned. Factor moved to California and got a job with the Pantages Theatre. By 1914, he was perfecting makeup for the movies. He found that the grease paint used in the theatre looked dreadful on screen, so he improvised. He created false eyelashes, the eyebrow pencil, lip gloss, and pancake makeup. Of course, once they had been made to look so stylish on screen, actresses wanted to maintain that allure off camera, so they wore the makeup in personal appearances. It was not long before non-actresses were asking for the makeup so that they too could look glamorous. It was in 1927 that Max Factor introduced his first cosmetics to be sold to non-theatrical consumers. Before Max Factor, few women used cosmetics. Factor popularized both the word "makeup" and the wearing of the stuff.

Fahrenheit, Gabriel Daniel

Gabriel Daniel Fahrenheit was born in 1686 in Danzig, Poland, and was raised in Holland and England. After failing as a merchant, he developed an interest in meteorology. Among his contributions were a pumping device for draining the Dutch polders; a hygrometer, for measuring atmospheric humidity; and a thermometer that used mercury instead of alcohol. Of course, a thermometer really does no good unless there are numbers on it, so he developed a temperature scale, too. On his scale, 32 degrees is the freezing point of water, and 212 degrees is the boiling point. This scale is called Fahrenheit. Later a Swede from Stockholm would suggest a more logical scale, with a temperature range of 0-100. His name was *Anders Celsius.*

Fallopius, Gabriel

Gabriel Fallopius, born in 1523, studied to be a priest, but soon found a different calling. He became a professor of anatomy, and focused his attention on the previously uncharted female reproductive system. He was the first to scientifically observe that virgins have hymens. Some accounts actually credit Fallopius with the discovery of the vagina, but one suspects that a few people may have been aware of the organ before 1523. What is undisputed is that Fallopius gave the organ its anatomical name, derived from the Latin word for "sheath." The word vanilla, by the way, comes from the Spanish word *vanilla,* a diminutive form of *vaina,* the Spanish form of the Latin *vagina.* The scientist coined other words relating to his studies: "placenta" and "clitoris." Thanks to his studies, the scientist will remain forever a part of every woman, in name at least. One of his discoveries was the tubes that carry the egg from the ovaries to the uterus. They were named *Fallopian tubes* in his honor.

Farmer, Fannie

At age 17, Fannie Farmer suffered a paralytic stroke. Her college hopes were dashed. But hidden in this terrible setback was a new career. As she was recovering, Farmer took up cooking as a hobby, and eventually she was able to enter the Boston Cooking School. After she graduated, she earned a teaching post at the school and years later became its director. In 1896, she wrote *The Boston Cooking School Cookbook.* Unlike most cook-books of the day, Farmer's book contained exact measurements of the ingredients instead of the common "pinch of this" and "large amount" of that. She took the manuscript to Little, Brown and Company, but the only way the company would agree to publish it was if she paid for the printing. She agreed, and 3,000 copies were printed. Company officials had no idea they would still be selling the book 4 million copies later. Following the success of her cookbook, Farmer opened her own cooking school, Miss Farmer's School of Cookery. She later suffered another stroke but kept teaching, even though she was confined to a wheel chair. She died in 1915 at age 58. Four years later, a man named Frank O'Connor asked for permission to name his new Rochester, New York, candy shop after Farmer. The estate agreed, provided he spelled the name "Fanny" instead of "Fannie."

Farrow, Prudence

In 1967, Mia Farrow's younger sister, Prudence, attended a meditation course with the Maharishi Mahesh Yogi in India. Also in attendance at the course were the Beatles. Farrow took meditation seriously, so seriously that she seemed to be in a constant trance-like state. One of the people concerned about her was John Lennon, who wrote the song "Dear Prudence" to urge her to come out and play. These days dear Prudence is a meditation instructor in Florida.

Fawkes, Guy

As an American in England, I was walking down the street one November 5th, when a young girl came up to me, saying, "Penny for the Guy?" She pointed to a stuffed scarecrow-type man lying on the ground. "Penny for what guy?" this American asked. "That guy," she said, pointing again to the scarecrow. "You want me to give you a penny for THAT guy?" I asked, confused. "Well, not necessarily a penny, some people give me 10 pence," she explained. Figuring that I was not understanding something, I gave the girl 10 pence and went on with my business. Later I asked a British friend what that was about. As it turns out, November 5th is a national holiday in England. It is Guy Fawkes Night. Fawkes was caught on this date in 1605 in an aborted attempt to blow up the House of Parliament. To commemorate the absence of a revolution and the continuation of the status quo, the British burn Guy Fawkes in effigy. Fawkes was so hated in his day that his name was synonymous with "bum." When the term migrated to America, *guy* became the term for any man.

Fechit, Stepin

Stepin Fechit was a racehorse. On at least one occasion he won a race, and an African-American vaudeville performer by the name of Lincoln Theodore Monroe Andrew Perry won a tidy sum. Perry, realizing that his name had perhaps a few more syllables than the average theatre goer could remember, decided to adopt the name of his winning horse for professional purposes. As Stepin Fechit, he moved from vaudeville to the silver screen. In the 1930s and 1940s he appeared in such films as *The Galloping Ghost, Wild Horse, Miracle in Harlem,* and *Stand Up and Cheer.* Unfortunately, in those days there were few plum roles for black actors, and Fechit was often relegated to bit parts with stereotypical dialogue. During the Black Power movement of the 1950s, the actor became a symbol of a black man who demonstrates servility before whites; the term retains a negative connotation today.

Fender, Leo

Before World War II, Leo Fender worked as an accountant and radio repairman. As the war came to an end, Fender saw opportunity in post-war prosperity and the growing popularity of western swing, country music, and rhythm and blues. Those musical styles were soon to come together and produce an offspring—rock and roll. In 1953, Fender began designing a new guitar to appeal to these musicians. Fender's business partner, Don Randall, suggested that the company's newest guitar be called a "Stratocaster." Fender shipped the first few by May 15, 1954. The Stratocaster sold well in the 1950s, but did not dominate the market until the 1960s. Dick Dale helped popularize the *Fender Stratocaster* with his surf music in the early 1960s. Beatles George Harrison and John Lennon had matching Stratocasters, and Jimi Hendrix's guitar gymnastics made the Stratocaster impossible for aspiring rock stars to ignore, assuring Fender's place in rock and roll lexicon.

Fermat, Pierre

Pierre de Fermat was educated in law and spent many years as a counselor of parliament at Toulouse. Fermat also had a hobby, mathematics, and he was quite gifted. He would make notes on the margins of the treatises he was reading. When there wasn't enough space, he would write down his results without writing down the proof. One day in 1637, for fun, Fermat was reading *Arithmetica*, written by Diophantus of Alexandria. In the margin Fermat wrote: "On the contrary, it is impossible to separate a cube into two cubes, a fourth power into two fourth powers, or, generally, any power above the second into two powers of the same degree: I have discovered a truly marvelous demonstration which this margin is too narrow to contain." And so *Fermat's Theorem* became the challenge of mathematicians for generations. It wasn't until 1993 that Princeton professor Andrew Wiles was able to recreate the proof for this truly marvelous demonstration. Too bad the margins weren't a little wider.

Ferrari, Enzo

Enzo Ferrari was born in Modena, Italy, on February 18, 1898. While Enzo was still a youth, his father died, forcing the young man to abandon his education. He found work as an instructor in the Modena Fire Brigade's workshop. He enlisted in the army during World War I and found himself shoeing mules for the military. Upon his return in 1918, he became a test driver in Turin before moving to Costruzioni Meccaniche Nazionali in Milan to work as a test driver and a race car driver. He made his racing debut in 1919. After retiring from a celebrated racing career in 1929 at the age of 31, he returned to Modena and oversaw mechanical work and started a racing club. During World War II, Ferrari moved his workshop from Modena to Maranello and began making powered grinding machines for ball bearings. The workshop was bombed in 1944. Ferrari rebuilt it in 1946 and went back to work designing and building the first *Ferrari* automobile.

Ferris, George Washington, Jr.

George Washington and Martha Ferris had a son in 1859 and named him after his father. Young George studied at *Rensselaer Polytechnic Institute* and became an engineer. In the 1880s he built railroads, tunnels, and bridges, including a series of bridges across the Ohio River. By the early 1890s, he had earned a reputation as an engineer, and so he was called upon to design something special for the World Columbian Exhibition in Chicago. What Ferris came up with was a wheel 250 feet in diameter that could carry more than 2,000 passengers into the air and back down again. The ride was the highlight of the exhibition, attracting 1.5 million passengers. It spawned many imitators, and soon no fair was complete without its own *ferris wheel.*

Field, Marshall

Marshall Field began working as a store clerk at age 16. He advanced to the position of junior partner four years later and to senior partner in 1865. In 1881, Field bought out the remaining partner's interest and organized the new firm under the name Marshall Field and Company. He came up with new marketing ideas that made his store a great success. He was the first to allow customer returns, to place a price tag directly on the merchandise, and to open a bargain basement. In 25 years, he expanded his business to the largest wholesale and retail dry goods enterprise in the world, with annual sales of more than $60 million and branches in New York City, Great Britain, Germany, Switzerland, France, and Japan. As his fortune grew, Field became a noted philanthropist. His gifts included a donation of $1 million in 1893 for the founding of *Field Museum of Natural History.*

Fields, Debbi

Debbi Fields says that she started her career because she was embarrassed at a party. The Fieldses were invited to the home of a client of Debbi's economist husband, Randall. They were eager to make a good impression on the client. The host showed Debbi Fields his large library, which she found a bit intimidating. Then he asked her what she was doing with her life. Not wanting to admit to being a housewife, she said, "Well, I'm trying to get orientated." As she would later tell *Redbook* magazine: "He went to the shelf, practically threw a dictionary at me, and said, 'The word is *oriented*, not *orientated*. If you can't speak the English language, don't speak at all.'" Fields said that she was inspired then and there to launch her own business and make something of herself, if for no other reason than to show this man up. So in 1977, as a young mother with no business experience, *Mrs. Fields* opened her first cookie store in Palo Alto, California.

Firestone, Harvey

Harvey Firestone was born on an Ohio farm. In 1890, he joined his uncle's buggy company as a salesman. He moved up quickly, and by 1892 he was in charge of the entire Michigan district. In 1896, however, the company went bankrupt. A friend helped Firestone buy a tire company in Chicago. With money he earned from that enterprise, Firestone left for Akron, Ohio, which thanks in part to B. F. Goodrich was known as the rubber capital of the world. There he opened the *Firestone Tire and Rubber Company* with a staff of 12. His big career break came in 1906 when *Henry Ford* decided to put Firestone tires on the first mass-produced cars, placing the largest single order for tires at the time.

Fisher, Herman

Herman Fisher worked his way through Penn State as a *Fuller Brush man*. After graduating, he got a job as a salesman for a toy company, but after only a few years decided to start his own business. He traveled to East Aurora, New York. There he met a school board member, Irving Price. Price had moved to town after retiring as eastern district manager for Woolworth at age 36. Now he was active in the community and looking for a new business. The pair met a woman named Helen Schelle, the owner of a Penny Walker Toy Shop in Binghamton. The three decided to go into business together. They raised

$71,600 and converted an old house into a toy factory. All of their original toys would be made of pine, they agreed. Perhaps they thought Fisher-Price-Schelle sounded too much like a law firm. When they opened in 1930, they called their company *Fisher-Price*.

Fitzgerald, Edmund

Edmund Fitzgerald was the president of the Northwest Mutual Life Insurance Company. In 1958, the company launched a new ship. Mrs. Fitzgerald had the honor of christening the ship, which was named after her husband. The vessel was 729 feet long and 75 feet wide, the flagship of the line. It was the largest ship to sail the St. Lawrence Seaway. At the time she was christened, no one could have predicted that she would also be the largest ship to end up at the bottom of Lake Superior, that the entire crew would go down with her, or that Canadian folksinger Gordon Lightfoot would write a popular ballad about the event.

Fleischmann, Charles and Maximillian

The Fleischmann brothers, Charles and Maximillian, arrived in the United States from Austria-Hungary in the 1860s. They formed a partnership with a businessman named James Gaff to build a yeast plant in Cincinnati. They patented a compressed yeast cake that, because of its leavening power, revolutionized home and commercial baking in the United States. They introduced their new product at Philadelphia's Centennial Exposition of 1876. Almost 10 million visitors had the opportunity to sample bread made with the yeast. The experience helped to make *Fleischmann's Yeast* a household name. One of the biggest steps forward for the company, however, came during World War II. So that soldiers could have fresh bread in the field, Fleischmann Laboratories developed and manufactured the first active dry yeast. Previously, yeast was sold only in compressed cakes, which required refrigeration. In 1945, *Fleischmann's Active Dry Yeast* became available to America's home bakers for the first time.

Fokker, Anthony Herman Gerard

Anthony Fokker was born April 6, 1890, at Kediri, Java. In 1895, his father, a coffee planter, retired and moved the family to the Netherlands. Early on, Fokker showed an interest in mechanical things. He quickly moved from building models of airplanes to constructing a full-sized functional airplane. He completed his craft and taught himself to pilot a plane in 1911, the same year that both *William Boeing* and *Clyde Cessna* learned to fly. As Germany headed into World War I, it needed a squadron of fighter planes and called on Fokker to supply them. During the war, 8,000 Fokker pursuit planes did battle against the British *Sopwith Camel*, designed by *Thomas Sopwith*. Manfred von Richthofen, the Red Baron, piloted a Fokker. It wasn't until 1919 that Fokker was formally founded as a company. Over the next 75 years, Fokker designed and built 125 different types of aircraft.

Foley, Jack

If you're one of those people who reads film credits, you've probably seen a listing for a "Foley editor." Jack Foley was a technician at Universal Studios in the 1950s. He was the first to develop a process of "looping" sound effects using a special studio, now called a *Foley studio*, designed for watching the picture and creating the sounds at the same time. In this way, the *Foley editors* can add the sounds of footsteps, rustling clothing, and background noises. You may be wondering why they didn't record the real sound of the actor's footsteps in the first place. The answer is that in real life, background noises can be as loud as foreground noises, but we are able to focus our attention on certain sounds. That's why the friend you're talking to on a New York street is not drowned out by the traffic and crowd noises. On film, the sound effects editors and re-recording mixers have to do the focusing. First they record the dialogue and later add other sounds at just the right levels. Perhaps you were wondering about some of those other mysterious job titles you've read in the credits? What is a boom operator or a gaffer, and what does the best boy do best?

The answers: the "boom" is a microphone that is suspended on a large pole over actors in a scene, just above camera range. The boom operator moves the boom as necessary. In Old English, "gaffer" meant "old man." Now it refers to the head of the electrical department. Gaffers work closely with grips, who are the folks responsible for the production equipment. The key grip is, of course, the person who holds the keys. Actually, the key grip is the chief grip. The best boy is the chief assistant to the gaffer, or the second in command of another group. Traditionally, women as well as men are called the "best boy," but I recently spotted a listing for a "best person" in a film's credits.

Ford, Edsel

Edsel Bryant Ford was the son of *Henry Ford*, founder of the *Ford Motor Company*. Naturally, Edsel went into the family business. In September of 1957, the company rolled out a new car. If the Ford family had had its way, the car would have been called the Ventura, the stylists' name for it. That original choice was overridden by the Ford board of directors, who wanted to honor Edsel. Edsel Ford's grandson, Edsel Ford II, was eight years old at the time. "My grandmother, my dad, and both my uncles were against naming the car Edsel," he says. "But Board Chairman Ernie Breech waited until all the family members were out of town, then put the *Edsel* name to the board. They passed it." The Edsel automobile line was an unprecedented market disaster. The name "Edsel" quickly became synonymous with failure. These events occurred when Edsel Ford II was at a vulnerable adolescent age. About the period, he simply says, "Kids can be cruel."

Ford, Henry

When New York Central Railroad president Chauncey Depew's nephew asked him for advice on whether to invest in a new company started by Henry Ford, Depew advised him, "Nothing has come along that can beat the horse and buggy." Henry Ford was born on July 30, 1863, on the family farm in Wayne County, Michigan. His first job was with Detroit's Edison Company. In 1903, he formed his own company to try to beat the horse and buggy. The company's innovations in mass production reduced the time it took to build each car and enabled Ford to sell cars for only $500. This made automobile ownership a possibility for a greater number of people than ever before. In 1908, Ford introduced the car that would put the *Ford Motor Company* on the map—the Model-T. During the years of its production, the Model-T accounted for half the world's output of cars. Today we see very few horses and buggies on the New York State Thruway.

Ford, John Thompson

John T. Ford owned several theatres. One was located on 10th Street NW in Washington, D. C. One Friday night, April 14, 1865, the play *Our American Cousin* was being staged starring an English-born actress named Laura Keene. One of Keene's fellow actors was about to earn himself a place in history. His name was John Wilkes Booth. The Civil War had ended only the week before, and President Abraham Lincoln and his family had decided to attend the performance for an evening of relaxation. Box 7, where the President was seated, was to be the site of his assassination by Booth. Following the tragedy, the government confiscated the theatre. Ford tried to reclaim the theatre in July of that year but public outcry prevented it. In 1968, *Ford's Theatre* was finally restored and dedicated "to the arts . . . and to the American people."

Foster, Samuel

Samuel Foster's family moved from Austria to New England in 1897 when he was 14. His first job was as a fireworks salesman, but he abandoned the work after an explosion. He held various jobs after that, including working as a waiter and as a jewelry maker, before he got a job with a plastic comb company in 1907. After 12 years, Foster left the company to launch his own business, Foster Manufacturing Company. Shortly thereafter, he was joined by a partner named William Grant. Grant did not stay with the company long, but Foster couldn't afford to change the name of the venture again, so the name *Foster Grant* stayed. The company's first big order was for rhinestone-encrusted plastic dice. Believe it or not, the *Kresge* company needed lots of them. Soon Kresge's supplier was buying all his plastic goods from Foster's company. The first Foster Grant sunglasses appeared in the mid-1920s. They were children's sunglasses, and sold for 10 cents.

Francis of Assisi

In 1811, a child was born to a wealthy cloth merchant and a French immigrant. The child was christened John, but his French mother gave him the nickname of Francis, meaning "the little Frenchman." As a youth, Francis was a knight and a troubadour. On a pilgrimage to Rome, something changed Francis. When he returned to Assisi, he donned beggar's garb and began praying in a ruined chapel. In the chapel, he had a vision of Christ asking him to "repair my falling house." The 26-year-old took cloth from his rich father's warehouse and sold it to raise funds to repair the church. His father was not amused by the changes in his son and disinherited him. Francis threw off the clothes he was wearing, as they had come from his father. The church bishop gave the naked Francis a brown gardener's tunic to wear. He left for the countryside, where he begged and preached, eventually gathering a sizeable group of followers who adopted his gardener's attire and vows of poverty and discipline. From then on Francis' followers were referred to as *Franciscan Friars*.

Fresnel, Augustin

French scientist Augustin Fresnel was fascinated by light. He developed the mathematical theory of refraction and polarization, and the *Fresnel Reflection Coefficients*, which I would gladly explain if I understood them. In 1818, Fresnel submitted a paper on the theory of diffraction to a competition sponsored by the French Academy. He believed that light was a wave, not a bombardment of particles. A member of the judging committee, Siméon Poisson, was critical of the wave theory of light. He argued that if the theory were true, a bright spot should appear behind a circular obstruction. This effect was subsequently observed by Dominique Arago, another member of the committee, thus verifying Fresnel's theory. Fresnel won the competition, and the spot has become known, not as "Arago's bright spot," but as "Poisson's bright spot." Fresnel's name has been attached to the compound lens he designed to concentrate a beam of light in a horizontal direction so that it can be seen for long distances. *Fresnel lamps* are used in lighthouses and in theatres. According to *New Theatre Words* by Theatre Crafts International, Fresnel's name is associated with the spotlight in every language except German. The Germans call it a "Stufenlinsenscheinwerfer."

Frisbee, William Russell

In 1871, William Russell Frisbee founded the Frisbee Pie Company in Bridgeport, Connecticut. Back in 1920, Frisbee pies became popular with students at *Yale University*. They discovered that not only could you eat the pie, but you could also play with the tin afterward. It was another 30 years before the Wham-O Toy Company, fresh from its success with the hula hoop, would try to market a flying saucer toy. Wham-O called its toy the Pluto Platter. In 1959, a company executive heard about the game they played at Yale and decided to change the product's name. Frisbee is remembered today, not for his pies, but for the aerodynamic properties of his pie tins.

Fuchs, Leonhart

Leonhart Fuchs was born in Wemding, Germany, in 1501. His father, Hans Fuchs, was Burgermeister of Wemding. He died when Leonhart was four years old, and the boy was raised by his grandfather. Fuchs had an interest in living things, so he studied botany and pharmacology before earning a medical degree in 1524. He worked as a teacher and a doctor before being appointed court physician to Georg von Brandenburg, Margrave of Ansbach, at a salary of 50 gulden in 1528. He gained widespread acclaim for his treatment in a 1529 epidemic. But Fuchs wanted to teach. He had only become court physician in the first place because of Von Brandenburg's plans to found a university. When these plans fell through, Fuchs moved on. In 1535, in addition to his medical practice, he became professor of medicine at Tuebingen University. There he wrote a book called *De Historia Stirpium*, which discussed medicinal plants. It was his interest in plants, in fact, that earned Fuchs a place in our lexicon. Fuchs introduced a colorful flowering shrub to Europe. It was not until 1703, many years after the scientist's death, that the flower and its bright pink color were named *fuschia* in his honor.

Fuller, Alfred Carl

Alfred Carl Fuller was reared on a farm, which he left in 1903, bound for Boston. With only $75 in his pocket, the unemployed 18-year-old moved in with his sister and her husband. He got a job as a trolley conductor, but his employer was somewhat displeased when Fuller took a trolley for a joy ride. He was fired from a host of other jobs, including gardening and grooming horses. His own brother-in-law dismissed him from a job as a delivery boy because he kept delivering packages to the wrong addresses. Finally, just before his 20th birthday, Fuller went to a former business partner of his late brother. They had sold brushes door to door, and Fuller thought he could take over the trade. As he went door to door, he discovered that many potential customers wanted custom-made brushes. In 1906, he built a workshop in his sister's basement to make such brushes. He earned enough with these brushes to move out of his sister's house to his own place in Hartford, Connecticut. There he opened the Capital Brush Company, which he later renamed *Fuller Brush*. Within a few years, Fuller's salesmen were all over the country. In 1922, *The Saturday Evening Post* labeled them *Fuller Brush men*.

Funk, Isaac Kaufman

Isaac Kaufman Funk was born in Clifton, Ohio, on September 10, 1839, and educated at Wittenberg College. He became a Lutheran minister, but he always had a passion for language. He founded and edited the *Literary Digest* in 1889, and from 1901 to 1906 he was chairman of the editorial board of *The Jewish Encyclopedia*. It was a publishing firm he started in 1878 with a partner, Adam Willis Wagnalls, that made his name familiar. *Funk & Wagnalls* Publishing Company, established in 1876, has become the third-largest publisher of general reference encyclopedias in North America and the leading seller of encyclopedias through supermarkets. Surprisingly enough, it gained some hip pop cultural credentials in the 1960s when "Look that up in your Funk & Wagnalls" became a catch phrase on the television comedy show "Laugh-In." The "Laugh-In" references raised Funk & Wagnall's dictionary sales by 20 percent.

G

Gallo, Ernest, Julio, and Joseph

It was under unhappy circumstances that the Gallo brothers inherited the family vineyard. In 1933, their father murdered their mother and then killed himself. Ernest and Julio, in their early twenties, took on the responsibility of raising their teenaged brother, Joseph. With the money their father had left, they invested in a winery. At the time, the young men had no idea how to make wine. Julio checked out some books on winemaking from the public library, and they were on their way. In the 1950s, Ernest discovered that poor blacks were buying large quantities of 40-proof port and mixing it with lemon juice. He decided to develop a wine suited to those tastes. The result was Thunderbird. The wine earned the company a great deal of money (2.5 million cases were sold in the first year), but it also earned Gallo an unwanted reputation as a producer of cheap wine. The Gallos survived, however, to produce more Gallo wine and the popular wine cooler Bartles and Jaymes. Today *Ernest and Julio Gallo* is the largest producer of wine in the United States. The youngest Gallo grew up and bought himself a ranch where he raised cattle and sold Gallo cheese. In 1986, a family feud erupted. The older Gallos sued the younger for the use of the Gallo name. Ernest and Julio won, so today you will find no Gallo cheese to go with your Gallo wine.

Gallo, Joey

Joey Gallo did not own a vineyard. His field was organized crime. He was known in his neighborhood as "Crazy Joe." He had some unusual habits for a mobster. He was fond of literature and philosophy, as well as the more typical criminal pursuits of murder, wife beating, and child abuse. He was killed for revenge at Umberto's Clam House while eating dinner with his family. After the hit, the tale of Joey Gallo made its way to a young song-writer who liked to pen topical songs. Bob Dylan apparently did not know about Gallo's predilection for beating his family when he wrote the song *"Joey."* It was later recorded by Johnny Thunder, and Gallo's story was told in the 1974 film *Crazy Joe.*

Gallup, George

George Gallup was born in Iowa and received his doctorate in journalism from the state university in 1928. In the early 1930s, he became a journalism professor. He also conducted reader surveys for midwestern newspapers. One of the surveys he conducted for the *Des Moines Register and Tribune* showed that readers were interested in photography. In response, the publishers decided to put out a photo-heavy magazine called *Look.* In 1936, Gallup spent $250,000 on a new polling technique that he was sure would be an improvement upon the then-reigning pollster, *Literary Digest.* Instead of polling a large number of people, Gallup polled a only small representative sampling and forecast the results from that sampling. The big test of Gallup's system came during the 1936 presidential campaign. The *Literary Digest* polls had shown that Alf Landon would be the next president. Gallup's results showed that Franklin Roosevelt would win. Gallup's prediction proved to be correct, which is why the name Gallup, and not *Literary Digest,* is now synonymous with polling.

Galvani, Luigi

Luigi Galvani was born in Bologna, Italy. He studied at Bologna and became professor of anatomy in 1762. Investigating the muscle fibre of frogs, he discovered he could make the muscle twitch by touching the nerve with various metals without a source of electrostatic charge. Furthermore, a greater reaction was obtained when two dissimilar metals were used. He attributed the effect to "animal electricity." His work inspired his friend *Alessandro Volta,* leading to the production of the electrical battery and initiating research into electro-physiology. Volta later proved Galvani's theories of animal electricity wrong, but the scientific process Galvani had developed, *galvanization*, was named after him.

Gary, Elbert

Elbert Henry Gary was born in 1846 in Wheaton, Illinois, and educated at the Union College of Law, which is now part of the University of Chicago. After graduating, he practiced law for many years. In 1882, he became a judge for DuPage County, Illinois. In 1898, he became president of the Federal Steel Company, which he helped to found. Gary was one of the organizers of the United States Steel Corporation and served as chairman of the board of directors beginning in 1903. The company built a factory in northeastern Indiana on Lake Michigan. The port was perfectly located between great iron ore reserves to the north and coal deposits to the south and east. Steel production began there in 1909, and the company town that sprang up was named in honor of the U.S. Steel chairman. Although Gary was responsible for a number of reforms in the working conditions of employees in his plants, he was against shortening the 12-hour workday. In 1919, steelworkers went on strike over the issue. The dispute was so heated that on October 7, 1919, the city that bore Gary's name was occupied by federal troops, who remained there until the strike ended on January 7, 1920. Although he won on that occasion, Gary was forced to institute the 8-hour day in 1923. In April 1927, *Forbes* magazine quoted the 80-year-old executive as saying: "I am not particularly interested in longevity. I am much more interested in life." The article went on to say, "He is as interested in (his business) as he was 25 years ago. So Judge Gary remains young." Four months later, Gary put his feet up on the table at a board meeting, leaned his chair back, and fell over. He died of complications from his injuries on August 15, 1927. The play "The Music Man" contains a song called "*Gary, Indiana.*" Despite the homey rural flavor of the song, Gary has always been a factory town. Today it is a polluted, high-crime area with a population that is shifting to the suburbs.

Gatling, Richard J.

Dr. Richard J. Gatling was born in Maney's Neck, North Carolina. He was a physician who loved to tinker with new machines as a hobby. Finding no market for his creations in North Carolina, Gatling moved to Indiana, where his agricultural inventions made him wealthy. He invented a grain-sowing machine, a steam plow, a wheat drill, a steamboat propellor, and a hemp-breaking machine. But he is best known for a later invention, the revolving six-barrel machine gun, with an effective firing range of 2,000 yards. He patented the weapon on November 4, 1862. Gatling demonstrated the gun to the federal government during the Civil War, but President Lincoln at first refused to allow the Union Army to use it because of rumors that Gatling was a Confederate sympathizer. It was not adopted until 1865, when an order for 100 was filled by the *Colt Patent Fire Arms Manufacturing Company*. By then, the Confederates were on the brink of defeat. The *Gatling gun* was widely used following the war, however, and it spawned a slang term, *gat*, meaning gun.

Gauss, Karl Friedrich

Karl Gauss was a mathematical prodigy. He was born in 1777, and by the age of three he was already annoying his father by finding errors in his bookkeeping. When he was a nine-year-old schoolboy, Gauss was presented with a complicated mathematical problem. The youngster solved it, even though he had not yet been taught how to do so. As a 21-year-old student at Gottingen, he established proof of the fundamental theorem of algebra, which had troubled mathematicians since the time of Euclid. He also developed the theory of elliptical functions. In 1801, he became more widely known to the mathematics community by publishing a book on the theory of numbers called *Disquisitiones Artihmeticae*. Around the same time, an astronomer named Giuseppe Piazzi discovered the asteroid Ceres. Gauss was able to compute the orbit of the asteroid. His method of computing orbits, still used today, is called the *Gauss method*. He also gave his name to some technical terms used in mathe-matics and statistics, including the *Gauss curve* and *Gaussian dis-*

tribution. But most people outside the scientific community know Gauss' name primarily because of his theories about electricity. A magnetic unit in electricity is called a *gauss.*

Geiger, Johannes Hans Wilhelm

Johannes Geiger was born in Rheinland in 1882. His father was a prominent rabbi and one of the leaders of Reformed Judaism. He hoped that his son would follow in his footsteps, but Johannes had a different calling. He received his doctorate from Erlangen and in 1912 became director of a radium research laboratory in Berlin. In the early 1920s, he became a physics professor and researcher at Tubingen University. It was there that he began working on a device to measure levels of radioactivity. With a partner, Wilhelm Muller, he developed in 1928 the first successful counter. Although the device is officially called the *Geiger-Muller counter,* Muller has been relegated to the Roebuck bin of forgotten partners. To most of us, the instrument is simply the *Geiger counter.*

Gerber, Frank

Frank Gerber's father, Joseph, owned a canning business in northern Michigan known as the Fremont Canning Company. In 1901, Gerber joined the company, which he eventually took over. In 1928, Frank and his wife had a daughter named Sally. Sally Gerber was not a healthy baby, and her doctor told the Gerbers to serve the child a diet of fruits and vegetables. So Gerber and his son, Dan, applied a process used to make tomato puree to produce strained fruit. Word of the baby food spread throughout Freemont, where it became very popular with mothers. What made the baby food so successful, though, was the marketing. While most commercially available baby foods at the time sold for 35 cents, Gerber's baby food sold for only 15 cents. He then advertised the product with an offer of free samples, which mothers snapped up. The move convinced grocers to carry the product, and soon the cannery was devoted entirely to Gerber baby food. The company name was then changed to *Gerber Products Company.* Gerber's hometown, Freemont, Michigan, is home to an annual baby food festival.

Gerrow, Peggy Sue

The girl in Buddy Holly's song "Peggy Sue" and the sequel "Peggy Sue Got Married" was a real person. And she did get married. When Holly brought a new song he had written called "Cindy Lou" into the studio, his good friend and drummer, Jerry Allison, asked him if he would change the name to Peggy Sue. Allison had a girlfriend named Peggy Sue, and he said he was going to marry her. The title was changed and the song shot to number 3 on the charts. Jerry and Peggy got married. Buddy Holly's dad suggested a sequel, and "Peggy Sue Got Married" was recorded. The name apparently struck a chord with other musicians, and Peggy Sues began to pop up in other songs, including Bobby Darrin's "Splish Splash" and the Beach Boys' "Barbara Ann."

Gerry, Elbridge

Elbridge Gerry was born in 1744. He served in the Massachusetts provincial congress and the Continental Congress before being elected in 1789 to the U.S. House of Representatives. He served there until 1793, and four years later he became a negotiator for President John Adams. In 1810, the Democratic-Republican became governor of Massachusetts. As governor, Gerry was in charge of determining the layout of voting districts. He sensed an opportunity and created several new districts. One of them included Gerry's hometown, Marblehead. It wound, snake-like, up to Salisbury, near the New Hampshire border. It was lost on no one that this oddly shaped district was created solely to create favorable voter concentrations for the Democratic-Republicans. In response, a popular Federalist paper printed an editorial cartoon in which the district's outline sported a head, wings, and claws. The cartoon labeled the beast a *gerrymander*. The public quickly applied the term to Gerry's redistricting technique.

Gibson, Orville

Orville Gibson was born in Chateaugay, New York, in 1856. In 1881, he moved to Kalamazoo, Michigan, where he got a job in a shoe store. In his spare time, Gibson liked to craft musical instruments from wood and started selling his mandolins and guitars. They were popular enough to allow Gibson to quit his day job. On October 11, 1902, he incorporated the Gibson Mandolin and Guitar Company. Initially, the mandolins were more popular than the guitars, but as hillbilly music and rhythm and blues became more popular, Gibson's guitars became the top seller. Orville died in 1918, two years before a Gibson employee invented a microphone that fit inside the guitar, creating a prototype of the electric guitar.

Gillette, King C.

King C. Gillette was a traveling cork salesman from Boston. He was a friend of William Painter, who invented the bottle cap. Painter suggested that in order to thrive in business, Gillette should invent something that could be used a few times and then thrown away. One morning while shaving, Gillette had his inspiration. After trying 700 different blades and 51 razors, he finally found the right combination. In 1903, he began selling *Gillette disposable razors.*

Gipp, George

George Gipp was born February 18, 1895, in Calumet, a small town on Michigan's upper peninsula. He was an avid sportsman in high school, participating in track, hockey, and baseball, but he never played organized football. That all changed when he went to college. Gipp played football at Notre Dame for four years, scoring 83 touchdowns to help Notre Dame rack up 27 wins against only 2 losses. During his years with the team, not a single pass was completed in his defensive zone. On November 20, 1920, during a game against Illinois, Gipp contracted a serious strep infection that later led to pneumonia. Legend has it that Notre Dame coach Knute Rockne visited the ailing Gipp in the hospital. Gipp, sensing that death was near, told Rockne that "when the breaks are beating the boys, tell them to win one for the Gipper." George Gipp died on

December 14, 1920, and was buried in the Calumet Cemetery. Eight years later, with Notre Dame trailing Army at half-time, Rockne told his players the story of Gipp's death-bed statement. He concluded by asking his players to "go out there and win one for the Gipper." The team did just that. Years later, a young actor named Ronald Reagan heard the tale. He thought it would make a great movie, so he started telling people in Hollywood about it and working on a script. In his mind, he pictured Pat O'Brien as Knute Rockne and himself as the Gipper. Meanwhile, Warner Brothers announced that it was going to do a movie about Rockne. They also thought Pat O'Brien would be great as Rockne, but they did not see Reagan as an actor in the film at all. Reagan auditioned anyway, but was turned down because he didn't look like a football player. Reagan rushed home and returned with his old college football picture. He won the role. It was only a small part, but it turned out to be a turning point in Reagan's career. Years later, Reagan used the catchphrase "win one for the Gipper" in his presidential campaign.

Goodrich, Benjamin Franklin

Benjamin Franklin Goodrich was born in 1841 in Ripley, New York, believe it or not. At the age of eight, Goodrich became an orphan. He was reared by relatives and at age 17 began studying medicine with his cousin. He graduated from Cleveland Medical College at age 20 and enlisted in the Union Army as a surgeon. After his experience in the bloody Civil War, Goodrich had had enough of medicine. He decided to try his hand at real estate. In 1869, his partnership traded $10,000 worth of real estate for stock in the Hudson River Rubber Company, located in Hastings-on-Hudson, New York. Goodrich eventually bought the entire company and became president. He moved the business first to Melrose, New York, where rent was cheaper, and then to Akron, Ohio, where it was cheaper still. There the company produced its first rubber product, a fire hose. In 1880, the business officially became *B. F. Goodrich Company*. Goodrich died eight years later. He was 47.

Goodyear, Charles

We know the name Goodyear today because of a fortuitous accident. In 1839, Charles Goodyear was working in his father's shop when he accidently dropped rubber and sulfur onto a hot stove. He discovered that the mixture he had created did not react to changes in temperature the way other rubber did. Goodyear imagined that a kind of rubber that did not get soft in hot weather or crack in cold weather would be the perfect material for tires. He patented vulcanized rubber in 1843, and it quickly became the standard for the rubber industry. Goodyear spent the rest of his life in court trying to protect his patent. Goodyear did not found the *Goodyear Tire and Rubber Company*. It was established in Akron, Ohio, in 1898, 38 years after Goodyear's death. It was named in his honor.

Goyathlay

Goyathlay is an Apache name meaning "He Who Yawns." The young man of that name was born in 1829. He grew up to be a brave warrior and leader. Mexican settlers had so much respect for the Apache leader that they dubbed him Geronimo, after St. Jerome, the desert dweller. In 1850, Geronimo's family was killed by the Spanish, and he declared his own personal war against the white man. He was hunted relentlessly by American and Mexican forces, but his knowledge of the deserts and mountains kept him one step ahead of his pursuers. He was able to elude capture until 1886, when Gen. George Crook and Gen. Nelson Miles finally arrested him and took him to Florida. Then an old man, Geronimo was through fighting. He settled in Oklahoma, and sold Geronimo souvenirs. He died there in 1909 of natural causes. No one is sure how the warrior's name became the battle cry of World War II paratroopers.

Grafenberg, Ernst

In 1944, German obstetrician and gynecologist Ernst Grafenberg described a "zone of erogenous feeling" that was "located along the suburethral surface of the anterior vaginal wall. . . . In the course of sexual stimulation, the female urethra begins to enlarge and can be easily felt. It swells out greatly at the end of orgasm. The most stimulating part is located at the posterior urethra, where it arises from the neck of the bladder." American researchers Beverley Whipple and John D. Perry followed up on Grafenberg's research in the early 1980s and named the area the Grafenberg spot, or *G-spot*, in the scientist's honor.

Graham, Florence Nightengale

Florence Nightengale Graham was born in Ontario, Canada, and worked at a variety of jobs until 1908, when she went to work in a New York salon. She learned about cosmetology and massage and took those skills with her when she opened her own salon a few years later. She felt that the opening of her own business marked the perfect occasion to recreate herself. The first step was to choose an exotic new name. She chose "Elizabeth Arden." As the manager of a salon, and later, a chain of salons, Arden developed her own cosmetics. Her signature product was a face cream with the consistency of whipped cream. Cream Amoretta was released in 1914. A year later, Arden decided to market the cosmetics directly to the public instead of selling them only in her salons. It was a good decision. Elizabeth Arden cosmetics were a great success. Arden once said: "Death not merely ends life, it also bestows upon it a silent completeness, snatched from the hazardous flux to which all things human are subject." Her life was silently completed in 1966 when Arden was 81, or maybe 82. Or maybe 88.

Graham, Sylvester

Sylvester Graham was born in 1794 and grew up to become a Presbyterian minister. He was obsessed with healthy living, both morally and physically. He was against alcohol and giving in to sexual urges. He believed in simple foods free of spices and seasonings. He also disapproved of eating meat and fatty foods. Ralph Waldo Emerson called the noted health food advocate "the poet of bran meal and pumpkins." He was best known, however, for recommending the use of coarsely ground whole wheat in the kitchen. The flour became known as *graham flour*, and it made good crackers.

Grauman, Sid

In 1927, Sid Grauman was a wealthy man. He had made his money in Hollywood, not as an actor or filmmaker but as the owner of several movie theaters. They were not simple movie houses, but show palaces with exotic themes. He drew patrons to the Million Dollar Theatre, The Egyptian, and the huge Metropolitan with publicity stunts worthy of Hollywood. He was, for example, the first to place huge searchlights in front of his theaters to attract attention. On January 5, 1926, Grauman ran an advertisement for his newest theater. It read: "Sid Grauman cordially invites you to attend the ground breaking ceremony for the new *Grauman Chinese Theatre Hollywood*, Hollywood Boulevard at Orchid Ave. Miss Norma Talmadge, star of all stars, will dig the first shovelful of dirt for the foundation of what will be the world's most unusual playhouse." The Chinese Theatre, with its cement impressions of film stars' hands and feet, became one of Hollywood's most famous landmarks. Sid Grauman owned the theater until 1929. After Grauman died, it was corporate owned until Ted Mann bought it in 1973. He dubbed the property "Mann's Chinese Theatre," although Grauman's name is still often associated with it.

Gregory I

Gregory was born into a wealthy family in the year 544. His mother became a nun shortly after his birth, and he followed her example, using his fortune to build monasteries. In 590 he became pope. He attempted to win converts to Catholicism, first by sending missionaries to England and then by reducing by one-third the rent of any Jew who converted. He had more success converting the English abroad than with the Jews at home, however. He held very strict views. He believed, for example, that sex is always evil, even when it produces children. Gregory forbade a man who had had intercourse with his wife to enter the church until he had purged himself by ceremonial washing. But it was his musical tastes, not his theology, that earned Gregory a place in our language. Gregory was a great promoter of "plain song" in his Church. He compiled a large collection of these limited scale musical offerings, which we know as the *Gregorian Chant*. He is not, however, the same Gregory we remember for the *Gregorian calendar*. That was pope Gregory XIII, who made adjustments to the *Julian calendar* in 1582.

Grimm, Jakob and Wilhelm

Jakob and Wilhelm Grimm were born one year apart in the mid-1780s. They were two of the six children of Philipp Grimm, a magistrate in the village of Steinau, Germany. The brothers' personalities were perfect compliments to each other, and they rarely spent time apart. Jakob, the older brother, was a serious young man. His brother, on the other hand, was gregarious and fun loving. Sadly, father Grimm died when Jakob was only 11. Without its bread winner, the family fell into poverty. A wealthy aunt came to the rescue and arranged for the children to attend a prestigious secondary school in Kassel. After graduating in 1802, the Grimm brothers went to the University of Marburg. They began by studying law, but soon found that they had a greater interest in German literature. Jakob had abandoned his study of law in 1806. Wilhelm completed his law degree a year later. Around this time, a friend named Clemens Brentano approached the Grimms and asked them help compile a collection of folk tales. From 1807 to 1810, the brothers collected stories. When they were through, they had 50. When they presented their finished project to Brentano, however, he was no longer interested. So in 1812 they published the tales themselves under the title *Kinder—und Hausmärchen*. The collection was not an instant hit. Then in 1823 a British publisher added illustrations to an English translation of the text. With pictures, *Grimm's Fairy Tales* became very popular, indeed.

Groening, Homer

Matt Groening was the successful cartoonist behind "Life In Hell," an alternative comic strip that appeared in 200 news-papers across the country. In the mid-1980s, the producers of "The Tracey Ullman Show" approached him about doing a cartoon version of his strip for the program. Rather than give

Fox television the licencing rights for "Life in Hell," Groening came up with a new cartoon about another family. He named the characters after his father, Homer, his mother, Marge, and his sisters, Lisa and Maggie. He named his own character Bart, which was an anagram for brat. "The Simpsons" became so popular that they outlasted "The Tracey Ullman Show." Their own show began on January 13, 1990.

Grosholtz, Marie

Little Marie Grosholtz was born in Berne, Switzerland. In 1762, Grosholtz' uncle, Christopher Curtius, was invited to Paris, and he took his sister and her two-year-old daughter with him. A trained doctor, Curtius had begun sculpting body parts in wax for medical study and soon found he enjoyed making wax portraits. He eventually gave up his medical practice and turned his attention fully to his wax portraits and statues. Curtius gained substantial acclaim for his skill, and such luminaries of the time as Voltaire and Benjamin Franklin sat for portraits with the artist. All the while, young Marie worked as an assistant. In 1780, she became friends with King Louis XVI's sister, Madame Elizabeth, who came to Marie to learn about modeling. In 1789, the Bastille fell. It was a bad time to be friends with royalty, and Marie was arrested. She was finally released after she agreed to sculpt the likenesses of the victims of the Revolution for posterity. In 1795, Marie married Francois Tussaud. Several years later, she moved to England, taking her late uncle's Paris wax exposition, her two children, and Tussaud's name along with her. Francois she left behind.

Guillotin, Joseph

French physician Joseph Guillotin favored capital punishment. Specifically, he favored the use of a beheading machine as a more humane method of execution. Guillotin did not invent the device that removes one's head from his or her shoulders. Such devices were known to have been used as early as 1307 in Ireland. But he was instrumental in convincing the powers that be to use such a device during the French Revolution, and it came to be known as the *guillotine*. There is a persistent story that Guillotin met his demise under the blade of his own invention. Although that is a much better story than the truth, Guillotin died of natural causes. After Guillotin's death, his children petitioned the French government to change the name of the device. Their petition was not granted, and so they changed their own name instead.

Guggenheim, Meyer

Meyer Guggenheim was born in Switzerland and emigrated to America in 1847. He became a rich man by importing embroidery from the country of his birth. He was also richly endowed with sons whose generous philanthropy would make Guggenheim a familiar name. There were seven Guggenheim boys: Isaac, Daniel, Murry, Solomon, Benjamin, Simon, and William. Daniel, born in 1856, grew up to be president of the American Smelting and Refining Company and to found the *Daniel and Florence Guggenheim Foundation*, devoted to aeronautical research and development. Solomon, born in 1861, founded the *Solomon R. Guggenheim Museum* for modern art. Simon, born in 1867, became a Colorado senator and in 1925 founded the *John Simon Guggenheim Memorial Foundation*, which grants fellowships to scholars, writers, and artists in memory of his son.

Guinness, Arthur

Arthur Guinness ran St. James Gate Brewery in Dublin. In 1759, some English friends introduced him to a new brew made from roasted barley. It was such a hit that by 1799 all his production was the roasted barley beer, which he named Guinness. By 1820, Guinness was being drunk around the world. By the end of the century, St. James Gate Brewery was the largest in the world, with distribution even at the South Pole. Today the brewery annually produces 2.5 million pints of Guinness with the same strain of yeast created by Arthur Guinness so many years ago. Arthur is also the Guinness behind the *Guinness Book of World Records*. In 1954, the managing director of the Guinness company hired two researchers to put the book together in four months. It shot to number 1 on the bestseller list and has been revised and updated regularly ever since.

Guppy, R. J. Lechmere

As president of the Scientific Association of Trinidad, R. J. Guppy discovered a small fish that is native to Trinidad, Venezuela, and the surrounding regions. In 1868, Guppy presented his catch to the British Museum, which put the fish on display. Initially, the fish were given the scientific name *Geradinus guppy*, after their discoverer. That name did not stick. Scientifically, the tropical fish are now known as *Poecilis reticulate*, but unofficially they are still known by their discoverer's name.

Guzman, Dominic

Dominic Guzman traveled to southern France in 1203 and found shameless heresy all about. He traveled throughout the land preaching a return to orthodox values. Dominic was the inventor of rosary beads. He founded an order of ultra-orthodox priest/soldiers, who came to be known as *Dominicans.* In 1963, a song called "Dominique" topped the American pop charts. The song was sung in honor of St. Dominic. The unlikely pop star behind the song was Sister Luc-Gabrielle of Belgium's Fichermont Monastery. She was dubbed "the Singing Nun." In an ironic twist following her chart success, Gabrielle forsook her vow of poverty and left the convent. The followup to her ode to the preacher of orthodox Catholicism was an ode to birth control. It was called "Glory Be to the Golden Pill."

H

Hall, Joyce

Joyce C. Hall was raised in Nebraska by his mother. His father left home when Hall was nine. In 1910, Hall headed to Kansas City to seek his fortune. He was armed with two shoeboxes full of picture postcards he hoped to sell to dealers throughout the Midwest. After only a few years, the postcard business had expanded enough to allow his bothers Rollie and William to join him and open a specialty store for postcards and stationery. Then Hall decided that selling Christmas cards with envelopes might be more profitable. He decided to call his company *Hallmark*, a play on his name and the word for quality. The word hallmark dates back to the year 1300, when gold and silver were marked for quality at Goldsmith's Hall in London. Coins of quality received a "Hall mark." The first Hallmark card appeared in 1916. It featured the greeting "I'd like to be the kind of friend you are to me." One of the innovations that made Hallmark so successful, however, had nothing to do with the sentiments contained in the cards. In 1936, Hall introduced display cases that featured rows of cards that the customer could browse. Previously, cards were purchased by asking a clerk to choose an appropriate card. When Hall died in 1982, the company he had founded was worth $1.5 billion. These days, more than 10 million Hallmark cards are sold each year. "All I was trying to do was make a living," Hall once said. "In those days, if you didn't work, you didn't eat. And I like to eat."

Halley, Edmund

Edmund Halley was born in London and educated at the University of Oxford. He was a mathematical prodigy, publishing his first paper on the orbit of planets at age 20. The astronomer was intrigued by the theories of the British physicist Sir Isaac Newton and encouraged him to write *Principia*, which Halley then published in 1687 at his own expense. Halley's most important scientific treatise was *Astronomiae Cometicae Synopsis* (Synopsis on Cometary Astronomy). In this work, Halley applied his friend Newton's laws of motion to all available data on comets. He theorized that comets are part of the solar system. In 1758, he accurately predicted the return of a comet, proving that he was right. *Halley's Comet* has continued to show up every 75 1/2 years ever since. In fact, author Mark Twain was quoted as saying, "I came in with Halley's Comet in 1835, it is coming again next year, and I expect to go out with it." Twain's prediction was accurate. He died on April 21, 1910, just one day after Halley's Comet's perihelion, the point of its path nearest the sun.

Hanes, Pleasant Henderson and John Wesley

Pleasant Henderson and John Wesley Hanes were the sons of a German immigrant. Pleasant, the older son, was born in 1845, and John Wesley was born five years later. They grew up in North Carolina. Pleasant served in the North Carolina Cavalry during the Civil War. He was a special courier for Robert E. Lee, with whom he served until Appomattox. When Pleasant returned from the war, the Hanes brothers went into business together, selling tobacco from a wagon. By 1872, they had saved enough money to start their own company, the P. H. Hanes Tobacco Company. It grew to be the third largest tobacco business in the country. In 1900, the brothers sold the company to North Carolina's tobacco giant, *R. J. Reynolds*. Each brother then launched his own business. Pleasant Hanes made men's knit underwear under the name P. H. Hanes Knitting Company. John Wesley opened a hosiery he called Shamrock Mills. John Wesley died in 1903, and his company was later renamed Hanes Hosiery Mills. Pleasant died in 1925. The two companies continued to operate separately until 1962 when they merged.

Handler, Barbie

The *Mattel Toy Company* was named for its founders, Harold *Mat*son and *Eli*ot Handler. Barbie Handler was the daughter of Eliot Handler and his wife, Ruth. When Ruth Handler saw that Barbie preferred playing with fashion-plate paper dolls to baby dolls, she guessed that she would love a three-dimensional fashion doll. Mattel created a doll to look like a combination of Brigette Bardot and Grace Kelly. The *Barbie doll* was introduced at the New York Toy Fair in 1959. The first dolls sold for $3 each. Today they are worth over $1,000. Today there is a Barbie Fan Club, with over 600,000 members worldwide. And the doll has been given her own full name—Barbara Millicent Roberts. The Handlers had a son, too, by the way. His name was Ken.

Hardee, Wilber

In 1960, Wilber Hardee of North Carolina decided to open his own version of the new quick-service restaurants that were gaining popularity around the country. Quick-service restaurants with no dining room or wait staff and a limited menu consisting only of hamburgers, french fries, and soft drinks were a new concept in those days. Hardee's Restaurant was instantly popular. During the first three months of business, its net profit averaged about $1,000 a week. "That was big, big money back then," Hardee recalled. It was not until two businessmen, Leonard Rawls, Jr., and Jim Gardner, became involved that Hardee's became the nationally recognized franchise that it is today.

Harley, William

In 1901, 21-year-old William Harley got together with some friends and his brothers William, Walter, and Arthur Davidson and began building a small engine in the brothers' backyard. They attached the engine to a bicycle and began to cause a stir riding it around town. In the next couple of years they made two more of the motorized bicycles. People began to ask the team to make such a bike for them. In 1907, they sold their motorized bicycles to the post office. Then they formed the *Harley-Davidson Motorcycle Company*. In July of 1947, *Life* magazine ran a story about an outlaw group of motorcyclists who had disrupted a California town. Their motorcycles of choice were Harleys. The group and the article about them earned Harley-Davidson a reputation as the vehicle of rebels and outlaws. Today Harley-Davidson is the only American motorcycle manufacturer and sells more than 50,000 of the two-wheelers each year.

Harper, Robert

Robert Harper was born in Oxford, England, and emigrated to Philadelphia when he was 20. He worked as an architect and builder. In 1747, while building a church in Virginia, he met a friend in a Frederick, Maryland, tavern. The friend told him about a piece of land where the Shenandoah River flows into the Potomac. Harper fell in love with the land and bought a portion from its owner, Lord Fairfax. Harper settled on the land, married, and built a ferry. The surrounding area became a town, which was subsequently named *Harper's Ferry*. Harper's Ferry went down in history as the scene of the raid on the government arsenal by abolitionist *John Brown*. It became a strategic area during the Civil War and was finally captured by the North at the Battle of Gettysburg.

Harvard, John

John Harvard was born in 1607 in Southwark, England, the son of a butcher. In 1634, he graduated from Emmanuel College, Cambridge University, and in 1637 moved to America, settling in New England with his wife. He became a teaching elder in a church in Charlestown, Massachusetts. Two years later, the General Court of the Massachusetts Bay Colony voted to found a "schoale or colledge" for the education of "English and Indian youth in knowledge and Godliness." They named the college-to-be Cambridge, after the famous British school. Only one week after Cambridge was opened, John Harvard died of consumption. But his will left 780 pounds and his library of 370 books to the new school. As Thomas Shepard reported in 1648, "The Lord put it into the hart of Mr.

Haruard who dyed worth 1600 pounds to give halfe his estate to the erecting of a Schoole. The man was a scholler and pious in his life and enlarged toward the country and the good of it in life and death." Six months later the General Court decided to rename the institution in honor of its first benefactor. Harvard College has since become *Harvard University*.

Harvey, John

John Harvey was born into a family of sailors in Bristol, England, but unfortunately he was not much of a sailor himself. He got seasick. He decided to pursue a career that would allow him to stay on dry land. So he contacted his uncle, Thomas Urch. Urch had gone into business in the late 18th century with a winemaker named William Perry. By the 1820s, the winery was a thriving business, and Urch invited his nephew to join the shop as an apprentice. The years passed, and Harvey eventually became head of the winery. In the 1860s, his sons John and Edward joined him. As the story goes, the team began experimenting in search of the perfect blend of a sherry drink that was popular at the time. It was called Bristol Milk. They invited a customer to try their new blend, and she exclaimed, "If that is the Milk, then this must be the Cream." And so, Harvey's Bristol Cream it was.

Haydon-Down, John Langdon

John Langdon Haydon-Down was born in 1828 at Torpoint in Cornwall, England. He left school at age 13 to work for his father, who was an apothecary. In 1847, he moved to London and enrolled in the Pharmaceutical Society. After a three-year hiatus to recuperate from illness, Down lectured in chemistry until 1853. He then enrolled as a medical student at the London Medical College, where he graduated second in his class. In 1859, he was appointed medical superintendent and resident physician at the Eastwood Asylum for Idiots in Surrey. He was the first to describe a medical condition he called "Mongolism." A contemporary of Darwin, Down believed that the syndrome was an example of de-evolution, a step backward to an earlier, less advanced stage in human development. He used the term Mongolism to describe the patients because children with what is now called Down's Syndrome often have features that resemble those of Asians. "A very large number of congenital idiots are typical Mongols," wrote Dr. Down. "So marked is this, that when placed side by side, it is difficult to believe that the specimens compared are not children of the same parents. . . . Here, however, we have examples of retrogression, or at all events, of departure from one type and the assumption of the characteristics of another." Despite the sound of these views today, Down was considered a liberal in his time. He advocated such things as education for women and training for children with learning disabilities. *Down's Syndrome* was named in his honor. It was geneticist Dr. Jerome Lejeune who in 1959 determined the cause of Down's Syndrome to be an extra copy of chromosome 21.

Heimlich, Henry Jay

Physician Henry Heimlich received his medical degree from Cornell Medical School and did his initial work in New York City. In 1977, he transferred to Xavier University in Cincinnati, where he became professor of advanced clinical sciences. Heimlich's main field of study is disorders of the alimentary tract. He published books on thoracic and stomach surgery. But it was his procedure for saving a choking victim developed in the mid-1970s that made his name a household word. By applying sudden pressure to the abdomen by various means, a rescuer can force air upward through the windpipe, thereby dislodging the obstruction and reopening the airway. Although it is widely used on choking victims, Heimlich has battled with the medical establishment over whether the *Heimlich maneuver* should be used on drowning victims instead of mouth to mouth resusitation. In 1994, he traveled to China to work on a controversial experimental treatment for AIDS. But Heimlich has even loftier objectives. "My ultimate goal," he wrote in *Who's Who in America*, "is to avoid needless death and promote well-being for the largest number of people by establishing a philosophy that will eliminate war."

Heineken, Gerard Adriaan

Gerard Heineken wanted to start a brewery, but his mother was adamantly opposed to public drunkenness. Unfortunately, it was Gerard's mother who had the money. Somehow, Heineken convinced her that if he could get the people in Amsterdam to drink beer instead of hard liquor, there would be less drunkenness. She relented and loaned him the money. Heineken bought Amsterdam's largest brewery, known as "the Haystack." The beer that Heineken named after himself became popular the world over. It was, in fact, the first beer to be legally imported following the end of Prohibition in the U.S. The *New York Times* in April of 1933 announced: "The first legal shipment of imported beer in thirteen years arrived Tuesday in Hoboken, N. J. It was about 100 gallons from Heineken's Brewery in Rotterdam."

Heinz, Henry

Henry Heinz began his career at the ripe old age of eight selling the surplus from his mother's garden. By the time he was 12 he had started his own garden. When he was an adult, he made his career choice official, and launched a company called Anchor Brands in 1869 to sell bottled horseradish, sauerkraut, pickles, and vinegar. The business was a failure, and Heinz went bankrupt. He even lost his home. But that was not the end of the story. By 1879, Heinz had paid off his debt, and he was more determined than ever to make his business a success. He traveled to England with samples of his sauces and quickly sold them to a London grocer. Upon his return, Heinz turned his focus to advertising. In 1892, he spotted a sign that advertised "21 styles" of shoes. He liked the strategy. At the time, his company was churning out more than 60 products, but he liked the sound of the number 57. So "57 varieties" became a fixture in his advertising. He also erected New York's first electric sign. Commonplace today, the sign captivated New Yorkers at that time. His business grew, and soon Heinz was packing more than a few pecks of pickles and peppers. By 1969, the company's "57 varieties" numbered more than 1,100.

Hellmann, Richard

Richard Hellmann was born in Vetschau, Germany, in 1876. As a boy, he was apprenticed in the wholesale food business. In 1903, Hellmann moved to America, where he opened his own grocery. Two years later, he added a delicatessen to his business. To accompany the sandwiches Hellman and his wife sold, they offered customers several sauces for 10 cents a portion. The sauces were different varieties of mayonnaise, which was popular in Europe but not yet well known in America. The mayonnaise was so popular with the customers that Hellman decided to market it more widely. He bottled the most popular variety, the blue ribbon formula. Customers snapped it up, and he simply couldn't make enough to keep up with the demand. In 1915, he built a factory to produce *Hellmann's Mayonnaise* on a grand scale.

Henry, John

John Henry was a muscular African-American who worked for the C&O Railroad in the mid-1800s. In those days, drilling was done by hand. One worker would hold and turn the drill while another struck it with a sledge hammer. The second was called a steel driver. Steel driving was a perfect job for Henry, with his great strength and endurance, but it was not to last. The newly invented steam drill threatened to replace manual laborers. In 1873, the C&O Railroad was cutting the Big Bend Tunnel near Talcott, West Virginia. John Henry refused to be replaced by a machine, and he drove steel night and day to prove he could outpace the drill. As the folk song that commemorates the event explains:

> John Henry said to the captain,
> A man ain't nothing but a man.
> But before I let that steam drill beat me down,
> I'll die with my hammer in my hand, Lord, Lord,
> I'll die with my hammer in my hand.

Henry won a partial victory. He outpaced the drill, but in the process burst a blood vessel. He died with his hammer in his hand, Lord, Lord; he died with his hammer in his hand.

Hershey, Milton

Milton Hershey was born into a family of Mennonite farmers on September 13, 1857, in Derry Church, Pennsylvania. He left school in the fourth grade to work as a printer's apprentice in Gap, Pennsylvania. He left the printing field after only a short time and became an apprentice to a Lancaster candymaker. In 1876, at the age of 18, he opened his first candy shop in Philadelphia. The business failed after six years. He then moved from city to city before finally returning to Lancaster in 1886 to open the Lancaster Caramel Company. Although he began his career making caramel, he soon realized that the candy would not retain an imprint of his name in hot weather. So he switched his focus to chocolate. His chocolate-flavored caramel had always been a big seller. In 1900, he sold the caramel company to concentrate exclusively on the flourishing chocolate business. Today the company's main plant in *Hershey, Pennsylvania,* uses about 700,000 quarts of milk each day, the storage silos at the plant hold 90 million pounds of cocoa beans, and Hershey Chocolate is the largest single user of almonds in the country. Hershey never abandoned the Mennonite values of his youth. He was never comfortable with material possessions and showy wealth. So when his chocolate bars became successful, Hershey used the profits to open the *Milton Hershey School.*

Hertz, Heinrich

Heinrich Hertz, a German professor and scientist in the late 1800s, was the first person to broadcast radio waves and measure them. Like many scientists, however, Hertz did not recognize the value of his own research. When asked what his experiments would be good for, he replied, "They are of no use whatsoever." Hertz measured the frequency of oscillations in radio waves, and today such a measurement is known as *hertz.* FM radio, by the way, stands for "frequency modulation." It operates by adjusting the frequency of the waves. Amplitude modulation, or AM, modulates the amplitude, or "height," of a wave. Hertz died at age 37 of blood poisoning, long before the computer revolution put the term *megahertz* on everyone's lips.

Hertz, John

John Hertz, a native of Austria, moved to Chicago with his family when he was five. He ran away from home in 1890 when he was only 11 years old. His first job was with the *Chicago Morning News*, where he ran copy and sold papers, earning himself $3 a week. After a year, his father found him and brought him home. He didn't stay long. After only six months he left home for good and returned to the newspaper. At 15 he fell ill and his doctor advised him to get a job with regular hours. His next job was driving a delivery wagon. He also took up a hobby, boxing. His hobby led him to a job as a sports reporter for the *Chicago Record*. He was only there a short time when the paper merged with another, and the entire editorial staff was laid off. Hertz returned to boxing, this time as a manager. His management skills earned him $10,000, and he retired, at the insistence of his girlfriend. He got a job then as a horseless carriage salesman. Sales were sluggish until Hertz came up with the idea to sell service along with the vehicle. If your Model-T broke down, Hertz would be there to help you. He then decided to go into the taxi business. To make his cabs easily visible, Hertz painted them yellow. The Yellow Cab Company opened August 2, 1915. It was a smashing success. In the early 1920s, Hertz added a rental car business to Yellow Cab. He called it Drive-Ur-Self. In 1925, General Motors acquired Yellow Cab and Drive-Ur-Self. It was General Motors that named the rental car business *Hertz Rent-A-Car*.

Hill, Joe

He was born Joel Hagglund in Gavle, Sweden. As a writer of union songs in America years later, he was known by his Americanized name, Joe Hill. He was arrested for murder and after a trial based entirely on circumstantial evidence, sentenced to death. The most famous of the folk songs and poems about Hill was "*I Dreamed I Saw Joe Hill Last Night*," with lyrics by Alfred Hayes set to music by Paul Robeson. The song has become a staple of folksingers. Joan Baez sang it at Woodstock. It is interesting to note that the murder Hill was

arrested for was not, as could be surmised from the song, part
of a labor uprising. Hill was, in fact, arrested for the shooting
of a shop owner. On the night of the shooting, witnesses
described a tall man and a shorter man fleeing the store. The
tall man was shot in the chest during the fray. Later that
evening, Hill came to a doctor's office with a gunshot wound
to the chest. He asked the doctor not to report it. He claimed
that he was shot in a fight over a woman. As the doctor was
treating him, he noticed that Hill had a gun. When the doctor
drove him back to his boarding house, Hill threw the gun from
the window. It was never recovered. Hill refused to testify on
his behalf at the trial or offer any explanation for his wound.
No woman ever came forward to corroborate Hill's story.

Hilton, Conrad

Conrad Hilton was born in 1888 in San Antonio, New
Mexico, the son of a store owner. In 1907, when receipts from
the business were slow, the Hiltons took in lodgers. Young
Hilton worked in the store by day and went to the train station
in the evening to bring potential guests to the house. When he
grew up, Hilton pursed a career in politics. He won a position
in the New Mexico state legislature, but became disillusioned
with politics two years later and returned to San Antonio.
There he organized a syndicate to establish the first bank in
the town, only to see the shareholders elect another man
president. He began working at the new bank as a cashier.
Eventually, he worked his way up to the board of directors, but
his banking career was cut short by World War I. He served in
France, returning home in 1919. Hilton went to Cisco, Texas,
with plans to buy a bank. A twist of fate forever changed his
fortunes. When he arrived, all of the town's hotels were
booked. Obviously, Cisco needed hotel rooms more than it
needed a bank. He bought the 40-room Mobley Hotel and
added new rooms in every available space. Next he bought a
hotel in Fort Worth, and another in Dallas. By 1925, his
hotels had brought in enough to allow him to build a brand
new million-dollar hotel in Dallas. This one he called *Hilton*.

Hippocrates

Hippocrates, the most celebrated physician of antiquity, was born on the island of Cos, Greece, and lived from 460 to 357 B.C. He traveled widely and became known as the "Father of Medicine." A collection of Greek medical wisdom was named the *Hippocratic Collection* in his honor, although it was not all written by Hippocrates. It probably formed a library at a medical school of the time. One part of the collection is a physicians' pledge. While physicians recite a version of the *Hippocratic Oath* to this day, the modern pledge was updated by the General Assembly of the World Medical Association in 1948 and amended by the 22nd World Medical Assembly in 1968. The revised oath is more contemporary and relevant to modern day physicians.

Hires, Charles

Pennsylvania pharmacist Charles Hires began selling packets of beverage mix through the mail in 1870. He called his drink "root tea" until a friend suggested a stronger name might help it sell better. He decided on "root beer," a name that would come back to haunt him. In the late 1800s, the Woman's Christian Temperance Union put a dent in the company's sales. Assuming that the root beer was alcoholic like ordinary beer, the group staged a boycott of the product. It wasn't until 1898 that an independent laboratory was called in to test the brew, and the Temperance Union's zeal was tempered. By the late 1800s, Hires realized that bottled beverages were selling better than powdered ones, and the mixture was replaced with a bottled version.

Hobson, Tobias

Tobias Hobson was born in Cambridge near the middle of the 16th century. A coach driver and stable owner, he made his living carrying passengers and packages, and renting horses to the students of Cambridge University. Whoever came to rent a horse could not choose which of the 40 horses he wanted. He had to take whichever horse was nearest the door, or he would get no horse at all. In this manner, Hobson could keep his horses on a strict rotation. His business practices became well known among Cambridge students. They coined the phrase *Hobson's choice* to refer to any situation where one must accept whatever is offered, or go without.

Hodgkin, Thomas

Thomas Hodgkin was an English physician, educated at the University of Edinburgh. He was an associate of the eminent physicians Richard Bright and Thomas Addison at Guy's Hospital, London. In 1832, Hodgkin wrote a paper "On the morbid appearances of The Absorbent Glands and Spleen." Although it never made the bestseller list, the paper did describe several cases of a disease that affected the lymph system. The disease subsequently came to bear his name. In more recent years it has been found that not all the cases Thomas Hodgkin described were actually *Hodgkin's Disease*. They still carry his name, however. They are called *Non-Hodgkin's Lymphoma*.

Honda, Soichiro

Imagine a young Japanese rebel with a love of engines and speed. That was Soichiro Honda. He was born in 1906, the son of a blacksmith. As a youth, he dropped out of school to race cars. Shortly after 1930, Honda built a small piston-ring company. He wanted to expand the plant, but because the Japanese government was preparing for war, cement was unavailable. Undaunted, Honda learned how to make his own cement and built his larger plant. The plant managed to survive World War II bombings, only to be leveled by an earthquake. Honda did not give up. He started again, this time building motorcycles. The motorcycle business was very successful. Honda's plan was to market the motorcycles to the middle class. By 1965, one of every two motorcycles sold in the United States was a Honda. Three years later, Honda started making cars again. In the early 1970s, Honda introduced the Civic and the Accord. "By the time we got into the business all the good names like Cougar and Wildcat were taken," Honda once said.

Hooker, Joseph

Joseph Hooker was born in Hadley, Massachusetts, and educated at the U.S. Military Academy. With the outbreak of the Civil War, he was appointed brigadier general of volunteers, and in 1862 he became brigadier general in the Union Army. His skillful leadership and personal bravery won for him the nickname "Fighting Joe." In January 1863, Hooker was assigned by Abraham Lincoln to the command of the Army of the Potomac. His command on the battlefield failed to show the qualities that had distinguished him as a corps and division commander. Besides his poor track record on the battle field, he earned a reputation for the liquor and "professional" women in his camp. Such women came to be laughingly referred to as "Hooker's division," and later, simply *"hookers."*

Hoover, William Henry

William Henry Hoover was a harness maker in Ohio at the turn of the 20th century. In 1908, as the automobile industry threatened to make saddlery obsolete, Hoover had his eye out for a new product to sell. His inspiration came from his wife. She had bought an invention built by her cousin, a janitor who loved to tinker with machines. He had attached the motor from an electric fan to a soap box to create suction, and attached a pillow case to the back to catch the dust. It was not the first vacuum cleaner, but was certainly one of the first portables. It was the product Hoover had been looking for, and in one corner of his harness shop he launched the Electric Suction Sweeper Company, later to be renamed the *Hoover Vacuum Company*. Hoover's machines so dominated the field that in Britain the term "hoover" is used instead of the word vacuum. And when one uses a hoover to clean, he or she "hoovers."

Hope, Henry Phillip

In 1830, a wealthy banker named Henry Phillip Hope had the opportunity to buy a celebrated, cut blue diamond. The 112.5-carat diamond was originally brought from India to France by a merchant named Jean-Baptiste Tavernier. Rumor had it that the diamond had been stolen from a sacred Indian idol and that it was cursed. King Louis XIV did not believe in the curse. He bought the diamond and made it a part of his crown jewels. The king had it recut into the shape of a heart, which reduced its weight to 67.5 carats. The diamond was handed down to Louis XVI, who gave it to his wife, Marie Antoinette. Marie Antoinette lost her head, and the diamond too, in the French Revolution. The diamond was said to have appeared next in Holland. The owner gave it to a Frenchman, and shortly thereafter committed suicide. The Frenchman then brought it to London, where he soon died. Then the diamond came to Henry Hope's attention. He put no stock in the curse and bought the diamond, now cut down to 44.5 carats, for $90,000. From then on, the gem was called *the Hope Diamond*. If there was a curse, it did not affect Hope. After he died peacefully, the diamond was passed to Lord Francis Hope, who went bankrupt and saw his marriage collapse. He sold it to a jewel dealer named Jacques Colot, who committed suicide after selling it to a Russian prince. The prince shot his girlfriend the first night she wore the necklace. He was later stabbed to death. The diamond then came into the posession of a Greek jeweler, Simon Manthadides, who fell off a cliff. Its next owner, Turkish sultan Abdul Hamid, was forced into exile within a year. The Hope Diamond ended up in the hands of Edward and Evalyn McClean, whose family was rocked by tragedy. Edward's father went insane, and Evalyn's father died of complications related to alcoholism. The couple's 10-year-old son was killed by a car, and their daughter Emily committed suicide. Evalyn McClean kept the diamond until her death in 1947, when it was sold to diamond dealer Harry Winston. In 1958, Winston gave the diamond to the *Smithsonian Institution*, where it remains today.

Hopkins, Johns

Johns Hopkins was born in 1795 on the family tobacco plantation in southern Maryland. He was named for his grandfather, also Johns Hopkins. The "s" on Johns came from his mother, Margaret Johns. She married Gerard Hopkins in 1700, and they combined their last names when naming their son Johns Hopkins. His formal education ended in 1807, when his devout Quaker parents decided to free their slaves and put Johns and his brother to work instead. Johns left home at 17 to work with his uncle in Baltimore. When he was 24, he established his own mercantile house. He became an important investor in the nation's first major railroad, the Baltimore and Ohio, and became a director in 1847 and chairman of its finance committee in 1855. The railroad made Hopkins a wealthy man. As the story goes, he fell in love with a cousin, and her father refused to allow them to marry. Hopkins remained a bachelor the rest of his life. In any case, he was left with no heirs. His will indicated that his fortune should be used to found a hospital and a university named the *Johns Hopkins University* and the *Johns Hopkins Hospital.* He died on Christmas Eve 1873, leaving $7 million. At the time, it was the largest philanthropic bequest in U.S. history.

Hormel, George

George Hormel was born in Buffalo, New York, in 1860, but his family soon settled in Toledo, Ohio. As a youth, Hormel worked in his father's tannery before heading to Kansas City to seek his fortune. There he worked as a traveling wool buyer. He did not find the fortune he was seeking, so he moved to Chicago. With only a slight change of direction, Hormel became a hide buyer. But a vacation in 1887 changed his life. That year, while visiting friends in Austin, Minnesota, he learned of a butcher shop that had closed after a fire. Hormel borrowed $500 from his boss and reopened the shop. Next he converted a creamery into a meat market, and by 1893 he controlled most of the meat business in the area. The turn-of-the-century innovation of improved refrigerator cars allowed Hormel to expand outside the area, and the addition of an ice storage facility at the Hormel plant in 1899 allowed the company to process more meat. The business was successful enough to allow Hormel's father and three brothers to join him. Following World War I, his son Jay came on board as well.

In 1935, Hormel added canned chili and *Dinty Moore Beef Stew* to its list of products, and two years later Jay Hormel introduced Spam. Because of their long shelf life without refrigeration, the products were perfect staples during the Great Depression and World War II. At the Hormel Foods plant in Austin, Minnesota, workers today turn out 435 cans of Spam each minute. Americans now consume 3.5 million pounds of Spam per year. Worldwide, Hormel says that 3.8 cans of Spam are consumed every second. Despite efforts by the Hormel company legal department, the name "Spam" has popped into Internet lexicon as a synonym for unsolicited bulk e-mail. According to one source, the Internet use of Spam traces its origin to a famous *Monty Python* sketch in which a cafe customer is offered a choice of "Spam, Spam, egg and Spam, or Spam, Spam, Spam, Spam, Spam, baked beans and Spam or lobster thermidore aux cravettes with a mornay sauce garnished with truffle pate, brandy, fried egg on top and Spam." I will leave any possible connection between that skit and bulk e-mailing to the reader. In any case, representatives for Monty Python have said that the British comedians did not face any legal repercussions for the unsolicited use of the product name because it actually helped increase Spam sales. In 1994, the *Hormel Food Company* rolled out its 5-billionth can of Spam. To celebrate this event, Hormel created a Spam cookbook featuring recipes that might have come from the Monty Python comedy routine. They include Macaroni and Cheese with Spam, Reubens with Spam, Spam Salsa, and Spam Salad with Sesame Dressing.

Horton, Tim

Tim Horton was born in Cochrane, Ontario, in 1930. Horton, a star hockey player for the Toronto Maple Leafs and Buffalo Sabres, in 1964 opened a doughnut store in a converted gas station in Hamilton, Ontario. A year later, a former police officer named Ron Joyce became the shop's manager. Joyce became an equal partner with Horton, who continued to play hockey. *Tim Hortons* was the first in Canada to sell apple fritters, one of the chain's 36 varieties of doughnuts. Following

Horton's death in a 1974 auto accident, Joyce bought out Horton's widow, Lori, for $1 million and a Cadillac Eldorado. Lori Horton later had second thoughts and entered into a bitter legal battle with Joyce. Joyce won out, and in 1995 he sold the company to *Wendy's* for 16.2 million shares in Wendy's International. Tim Hortons is now Canada's largest doughnut chain, with 36 per cent of the market.

Houston, Sam

Sam Houston was born on March 2, 1793, near Lexington, Virginia. After the death of his father in 1807, his mother moved the family to Tennessee. When Houston was about 15 years old, he ran away from home and lived with the Cherokee Indians of eastern Tennessee for nearly three years. Then he enlisted in the U.S. Army, fighting against the Creek Indians under Andrew Jackson. After the war, Houston became a lawyer and later served in the U.S. House of Representatives and as governor of Tennessee. In 1829, after a brief, unsuccessful marriage, he resigned the governorship, returned to live with the Cherokees, and formally became part of the Cherokee Nation. In 1832, he was commissioned by his former commander, Andrew Jackson, who was now president, to negotiate treaties with the Indian tribes in Texas, which then belonged to Mexico. He decided to settle in Texas and became an outstanding figure in its early history. In November 1835, he was chosen as commander-in-chief of the Texan army in the revolution against Mexico. His victory at San Jacinto and capture of the Mexican president, Antonio Lopez de Santa Anna, won the Texans their independence. In 1836, Houston was elected president of the Republic of Texas, beating out *Stephen Fuller Austin*. He served until Texas was admitted as a state. In 1845, Houston was elected senator, serving from 1846 to 1859. He then was elected governor of Texas. He opposed secession from the Union, and in 1861, after the outbreak of the Civil War, he refused to swear allegiance to the Confederacy. He was then deposed. He died at Huntsville on July 26, 1863. The city of *Houston* was named in his honor.

Howard, Oliver Otis

Oliver Otis Howard was born in Leeds, Maine, on November 8, 1830. He graduated from Bowdoin College in 1850 and the United States Military Academy in 1854. After graduating, he remained at the Academy, teaching mathematics until 1861. He later became superintendent. Howard went on to a distinguished military career. He commanded troops in many important engagements during the Civil War. General Howard then became director of the Bureau of Refugees, Freedmen and Abandoned Lands. In this role he was instrumental in securing appropriations from Congress for an institution for the education of newly emancipated slaves and their descendants. Howard served on the original board of trustees of the institution that now bears his name and was president from 1869 to 1873. He died in Burlington, Vermont, on October 26, 1909. The school continued to grow, both in enrollment and in reputation. Today there are approximately 12,000 students at *Howard University*.

Hoyle, Edmond

Edmond Hoyle was born in 1672. He was an English barrister and held office for a time in Ireland. He enjoyed playing whist but found that there was little agreement on the game's rules. He wrote a treatise on the game and his rules became accepted as the last word. He went on to write rule books for many card games. He was responsible for popularizing the term "score," meaning a record of the points in a card game. The term was carried over to other sports. His authority became so widely accepted that the quoting the rules *according to Hoyle* ended any argument. Hoyle died in 1769 at the age of 97. "*Hoyle's Standard Games*" has been reprinted hundreds of times.

Hubble, Edwin

In the early 1920s, many astronomers believed that the Milky Way marked the end of space. A young astronomer named Edwin Hubble changed all of that. Hubble earned a law degree at Oxford before deciding his true avocation was the study of space. He returned to the University of Chicago and earned his doctorate in astronomy in 1917. His career was again delayed when he went off to fight in World War I. Upon his return he took a job at the Mount Wilson Observatory, where he identified the Andromeda nebula 900,000 light years from Earth. Space became much larger, and Earth comparatively smaller. Then, in 1929, Hubble announced his findings on the distances between galaxies. *Hubble's Law* concluded that the farther a galaxy was from Earth, the more rapidly it was moving away. Therefore, not only was the universe immense, it was still growing. In 1990, NASA launched *the Hubble Telescope* in space in honor of the scientist. Unfortunately, the project was plagued by so many problems that the name of one of the nation's greatest astronomers became strongly associated with failure.

Hudson, Henry

On April 19, 1607, navigator Henry Hudson set out to find a northwest passage that would be a shortcut to the East Indies and China. His ship was cut off by ice and he was forced to turn back. A year later he tried again, and was again stopped by the ice. In 1609, he and his crew set out a third time to find the Northwest Passage. They didn't find it. Instead they got as far as Novaya Zemlay, where the crew refused to go any further. So Hudson turned his ship around and headed for the Virginia coast. Following a map that he had gotten from Captain John Smith, he discovered the mouth of a river. It is now called the Hudson River. Hudson traveled down the river for about 150 miles to what is now Albany. About this time, Hudson began to doubt that he would get to China that way. He turned around and headed back to Europe. Hudson made one more trip. In 1610, he sailed directly for what was then called "Davis' Overfall." It is now the *Hudson Strait.* In June 1610, he finally arrived at a great bay. It is now called Hudson Bay.

Hummel, Berta

Berta Hummel was born in Bavaria in 1909. As a girl, she loved to draw pictures of her friends and the Bavarian forests. She earned a degree in fine arts and in 1934 joined the Franciscan

Convent of Siessen, where she was given the name Sister Maria Innocentia Hummel. As a nun, she brought joy to her fellow sisters by drawing sentimental pictures of happy children. Her Mother Superior was so impressed with the artwork that she contracted with the W. Goebel Company of Rodental to make little statues based on Hummel's drawings. Today *Hummel figurines* are among the world's most popular collector's items. Sister Hummel continued to quietly draw and paint sweet-faced children until her death from tuberculosis in 1946.

Huntington, George

George Huntington of Pomeroy, Ohio, was described by one writer as a "horse and buggy doctor." He enjoyed hunting and fishing. His patients were the children of some of the same patients his father and grandfather had treated. In 1827, he wrote about a hereditary disease that he had identified. He believed at the time that it was a local phenomenon. "It exists, so far as I know, almost exclusively on the east end of Long Island," he wrote. The rare disorder is a sort of genetic time bomb. The symptoms of the progressive neurological disorder do not become apparent until middle age. *Huntington's Chorea*, as it is now called in honor of its discoverer, is often referred to in discussions of medical ethics. Current medical science enables doctors to predict which children have inherited the gene, but provides no treatment for the disorder. Children of Huntington's patients thus are faced with the dilemma: is there a benefit in knowing about something that cannot be changed?

Hutton, Edward Francis

When he was 17, Edward Francis Hutton got his first job in the mailroom of a New York mortgage company. He didn't keep the job long. He took an unauthorized vacation and was fired. His next job was as a check writer for the Manhattan Trust Company. (Where can I get a job as a check writer?) He stormed out of that job after the company president criticized his handwriting and suggested he take a night school course. He may have been stung by the criticism, but he took the advice, enrolling in Packer's Business School. When he finished, he and a friend bought a seat on the Consolidated Stock Exchange. He dissolved the partnership a few years later. He had fallen in love with the daughter of a member of the New York Stock Exchange, and the father refused to give permission for his daughter to marry a member of the lesser Consolidated Stock Exchange. Hutton chose the girl over the exchange, and they were married in 1902. While on his honeymoon in California, Hutton realized that there was no direct link from the major West Coast cities to Wall Street. He wasn't able to implement his plan to open a coast-to-coast financial network. Instead he found himself in Cincinnati working with a cousin. Finally he moved back to New York and bought a seat on the New York Stock Exchange. *E. F. Hutton and Company* began trading on October 12, 1903. He was able to execute his West Coast plan shortly thereafter. Hutton paid half the price of construction for a Western Union line from Utah to San Francisco, giving his company the only private transcontinental wire in the country. His brokers in San Francisco could execute their orders much more quickly than competitors. E. F. Hutton became synonymous with the stock exchange on the West Coast. Hutton's wife and son both died before he was 40. He later married the daughter of *C. W. Post*, and traded in his partnership in E. F. Hutton and Company for the chairmanship of Postum Cereal.

I/J

Ishibashi, Shojiro

Shojiro Ishibashi was born in 1885 in Japan. When he came of age, Ishibashi entered the family business, making tabi, the traditional Japanese footwear. In 1923, he patented a rubber-soled tabi, which increased his fortunes. He quickly looked to other rubber products to sell, and in 1928 began producing tires. He was the first Japanese manufacturer to do so. Ishibashi's goal was to sell his products overseas to British and American consumers. He felt he would need an English name for his company. Ishibashi means "stone bridge" in English." As a tip of the hat to fellow rubber manufacturer *Harvey Firestone*, Ishibashi reversed the words and came up with the *Bridgestone Tire Company*. In 1988, Bridgestone bought Firestone. The companies were consolidated in 1990 under a unified organization called Bridgestone/Firestone, Inc.

Jack and Jill

According to the residents of Kilmersdon, England, Jack and Jill were real people. Historian Chris Howell says he has found evidence that in the 15th century there was a young man named Jack who fell down a Kilmersdon hill while fetching a pail of water. The man died of a "broken crown," and his girlfriend, Jill, died shortly thereafter in childbirth. In other accounts, she died of a broken heart after the birth of their son. For years town residents have been claiming the nursery rhyme pair as their own, and Howell believes that 32 phone listings of the surname "Gilson" within a four-mile radius are the descendants of Jill's son, who was raised by the community after his mother's death.

The famous well was sealed 75 years ago because it and the steep hillside path that led to it were considered dangerous. In 1998, the parish council formed a Jack and Jill committee and applied for a 30,000 pound ($49,000) grant to repair the hill and the disused well and install signs welcoming visitors to the home of Jack and Jill.

Jacquard, Joseph Marie

Joseph Marie Jacquard was born in 1752 in Lyons, France. In those days, every piece of cloth had to be made by hand. It was a long, labor-intensive process. Linens were so valuable that household inventories listed them immediately after land-holdings and money. Spinning was considered "women's work" in those days. The task was usually assigned to an unmarried woman in the family. This led to the term "spinster," meaning an unmarried woman. By 1787, a mechanical spinner had been invented, revolutionizing the production of linen. Joseph Jacquard, hoping to do the same for weaving, introduced a mechanical loom in 1801. One might think that eliminating such a tedious process would make Jacquard a popular man, but it had the opposite effect. The Jacquard loom had cost thousands of silk workers their jobs. The inventor was attacked by an angry mob, and barely escaped with his life. Jacquard's fortunes changed when Napoleon bought one of the looms and declared it to be the property of the state. This brought silk prices down, which increased the market for silk. Many of the silk weavers went back to work, using Jacquard looms. In 1819, the once-reviled Jacquard was awarded a gold medal and the Cross of the Legion of Honor. With the Jacquard loom, it was practical for the first time to weave intricate patterns into fabric. The name *Jacquard* came to be applied to elaborate woven designs.

Jacuzzi, Candido

When Candido Jacuzzi, an Italian immigrant, arrived in the United States, he and his brothers began working in aircraft production. They designed a propellor known as the Jacuzzi toothpick, which was used on World War I airplanes. They followed this up with a monoplane known as the Jacuzzi J-7. In 1921, after one of Jacuzzi's brothers was killed in the crash of a prototype airplane, Candido decided to change fields. He began manufacturing hydraulic pumps. His son suffered from rheumatoid arthritis, and so Candido decided to adapt one of his pumps to create a hot water hydromassage for his son. The bath was perfected in the 1950s and the hot tub craze began. The hot tub may have made Jacuzzi's son more comfortable, but success brought little comfort to Jacuzzi. He fled the country in 1969 after being indicted on five counts of income tax evasion. In 1975, while living in Mexico, Jacuzzi suffered a stroke that left him paralyzed. Meanwhile, the Jacuzzi family had begun fighting for control of the company. They finally decided to sell it in 1979.

James I

The future King James I was born June 19, 1566, in Edinburgh Castle, the only son of Mary, Queen of Scots, and her second husband, Lord Darnley. When Mary was forced to abdicate her throne the following year, baby James became king of Scotland. Oddly, he made very few significant decisions for many years. In 1581, James, who had been king in name only, assumed actual rule of Scotland. He became ruler of a Scotland divided by conflict between the Protestants and the Roman Catholics. In January 1604, he convened the Hampton Court Conference to regulate religious matters. Among the grievances discussed at the conference was the need for a good translation of the Bible. In response, the king ordered a new translation. The result was the *King James Version* of the Bible.

Jellinek, Mercedes

Emil Jellinek was a wealthy banker and consul general for the Austro-Hungarian Empire in Nice. He was also a racing enthusiast who wanted to commission a custom-designed automobile. He promised to order 36 of the cars from Daimler automotive works if he could have exclusive rights to sell them. Daimler agreed to the deal, and Jellinek named the cars after his 11-year-old daughter, Mercedes. Were it not for a twist of fate, there might also be a car known as the Maja-Benz today. Jellinek also commissioned an automobile to be named for his other daughter. But the Maja, designed by Ferdinand Porsche, was less than a stellar performer. The Mercedes, on the other hand, became so well known that when Gottlieb Daimler's firm merged with that of Karl Benz, the name Mercedes was retained on the cars. It is said that Mercedes Jellinek never drove any of the cars that bore her name. Tragedy soon struck the Jellinek family. Emil died in prison during World War I, accused of espionage. After two failed marriages, Mercedes died penniless in 1929.

Johnson, Howard Dearing

Howard Dearing Johnson was born in 1897, the son of a cigar merchant. By the time Johnson inherited his father's business, it was heavily in debt. He sold what he could and in 1925 borrowed $500 to open a small patent medicine store in Quincy, Massachusetts. Johnson put in a soda fountain and sold three flavors of ice cream, vanilla, chocolate, and strawberry. Three years later, he added frankfurters, hamburgers, and other easily prepared menu items. The little drugstore became the first *Howard Johnson's Restaurant.* By 1935, there were 25 Howard Johnson roadside ice cream and sandwich stands in Massachusetts. During the next five years, the number grew to more than 100 along the Atlantic Coast through Florida. In 1940, Johnson opened a restaurant on the Pennsylvania Turnpike, the first turnpike restaurant in the country. Howard Johnson's customers had become mostly travelers. The next logical step was to add motor lodges to the orange-roofed highway restaurants. The first *Howard Johnson's Motel* franchise opened in Savannah, Georgia, in 1954.

Johnson, Robert, James, and Edward Mead

The Johnson brothers grew up in Pennsylvania. Robert, the oldest, left home at 16 and traveled to Poughkeepsie, New York, where he became an apprentice for an apothecary. In 1873, he formed a pharmaceutical company with a man named George Seabury. Robert quickly brought his brothers into the company, much to Seabury's chagrin. In 1886, the brothers decided to open their own shop in a former wallpaper factory in New Brunswick, New Jersey. Robert had been hatching a plan ever since he had heard a man named *Joseph Lister* speak in 1873. Lister was a British surgeon who had a then-unique theory that airborne germs caused infection. Robert was greatly influenced by Lister's theories on antiseptic and sterilization. So he designed a sterilized cotton dressing that could be mass produced and shipped in quantity to hospitals. The hospital dressings eventually evolved into the Band-Aid, a brand that sold so well it has become nearly synonymous with "bandage." The Johnson name is also found on *Johnson's Baby Powder* and *Johnson's Baby Shampoo*. Although the company began with three brothers, Johnson, Johnson, and Johnson seemed a bit much for a company name. After a short time, *Johnson & Johnson* had the correct number of Johnsons. Edward disagreed with how the company was being run, so he left to start his own company, called Mead Johnson. When he died, Robert Wood Johnson left the majority of his fortune to a foundation that now bears his name.

Jones, John Luther

Irish-American John Luther Jones was born in Cayce, Kentucky. His friends called him Casey, after the name of his hometown. He became an engineer on the Illinois Central Railroad, where he piloted the Cannonball Express. He was well liked and known for his bravado and tall tales. One April night, Jones made a fatal mistake. As he was taking his train into Vaughn, Mississippi, he miscalculated a sidetrack clearing distance. Realizing that the train was going to derail, he ordered his fireman to jump, but Jones died at the controls. Jones' costly error, and his bravery, might have been forgotten today were it not for his friend Wallace Saunders, an engine wiper, who wrote a song about the wreck.

Joule, James Prescott

James Joule was born near Manchester, England, on December 24, 1818. When his father died, Joule inherited a brewery, but beer was not his calling. He was a home-schooled scientist with a great interest in electricity. In 1838, Joule invented an electro-magnetic engine. Two years later he determined the amount of heat produced by an electric current. He presented his findings to the Royal Society, and the members were sufficiently impressed to name the unit of heat a *joule.* Later he investigated the cooling of compressed gases by expansion. The results of this study were elaborated upon by *Sir William Thomson,* also known as *Lord Kelvin,* to demonstrate the surface condensation property that became known as the *Joule-Thomson effect.*

Julliard, Augustus

Augustus Julliard was born at sea to French parents in 1836. He was reared in Ohio and grew up to be a wealthy banker and textile merchant. He was also a patron of the arts and an active supporter of the Metropolitan Opera. In 1905, the godson of Franz Liszt, Dr. Frank Damrosch, established an American musical academy called the Institute of Musical Art. Woodrow Wilson, then president of Princeton University, spoke at the institute's opening ceremonies. The first-year enrollment was 500 students, five times what the founders had anticipated. Augustus Julliard died in 1919, leaving $20 million to establish the Julliard Musical Foundation. In 1926, the Julliard School and Damrosch's institute merged under one president and one board of trustees. In 1946, the combined institutions' official name was changed to *the Julliard School of Music.*

Juneau, Joseph

In August 1880, Alaskan prospectors Richard Harris and Joe Juneau found pans full of gold in the aptly named Gold Creek. They headed off to find its source, over Snow Slide Gulch into the mother lode of Quartz Gulch and Silver Bow Basin. News of the gold spread quickly, and within a month boatloads of prospectors had arrived. A town sprang up. The town was named for one of its founding prospectors, Joe Juneau. *Juneau* became Alaska's capital in 1906 when the government was transferred from the previous capital. Ten points if you can name that earlier capital. Answer: Sitka.

Justerini, Giacomo

Giacomo Justerini was born in Bologna, Italy. In 1749, he moved to London where, with English partner George Johnson, he set up shop as a wine merchant. The business prospered, so much so that in 1760 George III gave the company a royal warrant. In 1779, Johnson and Justerini added whiskey to their product line. Then in 1831 a man named Alfred Brooks bought the company. The name Justerini was apparently sufficiently well known to warrant keeping it on the bottles, so the company became *Justerini & Brooks*. With the repeal of Prohibition in the United States, the company decided to export its scotch whisky. In 1936, Americans got their first taste of *J&B*.

K

Kamel, George Joseph

George Joseph Kamel was a Moravian Jesuit missionary. For religious reasons Kamel took the name Camellus, the Latin form of his name. In Manila, he opened a pharmacy for the poor. To stock the pharmacy, he grew plants and herbs and became an enthusiastic amateur botanist. He began writing articles about the plants in his garden and sending them to London's *Philosophical Transactions Journal.* One plant that Camellus described was a flowering relative of the tea plant. Today the plant is seen throughout the southern U.S. and in England. It was a Swedish botanist named Linnaeus who read Camellus' accounts and named the plant the *camellia* after its discoverer.

Karchner, Carl

Whenever I have traveled to the West Coast, I have wondered about the curious name of the fast food chain *Carl's Jr.* Why isn't it called Carl Jr.'s instead? I am pleased to say that I now have the answer. It all began when Carl Karchner left his family farm in Ohio to seek his fortune in California. In 1941, Karchner and his wife, Margaret, borrowed $311 on their Plymouth. With that money and the $15 they had in their pockets, they were able to buy a hotdog cart at the corner of Florence and Central in Los Angeles. Soon one cart became two, two became three, and so on until the couple had earned enough to open their first full-service restaurant, which they called Carl's Drive-In Barbecue. In 1950, the first two Carl's Jr. restaurants were opened in Anaheim and nearby Brea. They were called "Carl's Jr." not because they were opened by a Carl Jr. but because they were smaller or "junior" versions of the original drive-in.

Keebler, Godfrey

If fortunes had shifted slightly, you might have heard of a Strietmann elf or a Herkmann elf. Back in the pre-Civil War days, bakeries were, by necessity, local businesses. A horse and buggy could only go so far with baked goods before they became stale. This all changed, however, with the advent of the automobile. In 1927, several bakeries decided to join forces to distribute baked goods on a regional level. The United Biscuit Company of America featured the products of several bakers, including Strietmann of Cincinnati, Ohio, Herkmann of Grand Rapids, Michigan, and Godfrey Keebler, who had opened his Philadelphia bake shop in 1853. By 1944, there were 16 bakeries in the United Biscuit network, stretching from Philadelphia, Pennsylvania, to Salt Lake City, Utah, marketing cookies and crackers under a variety of brand names. To avoid confusion, the network decided to adopt one brand for all its products. Keebler's name was chosen. The Keebler elves, created by a Chicago advertising firm in 1968, helped to make the Keebler company one of the top sellers of cookies and crackers in the country. Trivia question for advertising buffs: What is the name of the chief Keebler elf? Answer: Ernie.

Kellogg, John

John Kellogg was a medical doctor and a deeply religious man. He was deeply concerned with health and health food. He established the Battle Creek Sanitarium in Battle Creek, Michigan, where clients were kept on a strict vegetarian diet. At the time, the typical American breakfast consisted of ham, sausage, eggs, and gravy. Kellogg developed a mashed-grain cereal he called wheat flakes to give his clients for breakfast. John's younger brother, Will Kellogg, was a high school dropout with great ambitions. He joined his brother and developed another cereal he called corn flakes. John and Will soon began to disagree about what should be done with these cereals. John wanted to keep them for his sanitarium and advertise them with catchy slogans. He wrote, "In males, one of the most general physical causes of sexual excitement is constipation. When this condition is chronic, as in habitual constipation, the unnatural excitement often leads to serious results." Will Kellogg had another idea about how to sell breakfast cereal. The brothers' greatest disagreement came over Will's idea for Frosted Flakes. John, who still thought of cereal as health food, was strongly opposed to sugar-coated cereal. When John was out of the country, Will went ahead and released Frosted Flakes. Consumers liked them. After that, John Kellogg turned his attention to his sanitarium as Will gained the majority of Kellogg's stock. Kellogg's Sanitarium is no longer in business. But *Kellogg's Corn Flakes* are still around today.

Kelly, William Russell

William Russell Kelly was born in British Columbia in 1906, the son of a wealthy oil pioneer. Until the family fortune turned and his father lost his millions, they lived in a castle. Kelly's father died in 1928, leaving seven children and no estate. After serving in World War II, young Kelly decided to seek his fortune in the Motor City, Detroit. He rented an office and opened Russell Kelly Office Service, a firm that had clerical workers on the premises to do typing, mailing, and bookkeeping for other companies. One day a customer called and asked if he could have Kelly send him a typist. Kelly agreed to do so, and soon saw a potential new source of income, supplying temporary workers. Word spread quickly, and soon business executives from throughout the region were calling to have one of "*those Kelly Girls*" sent over. Kelly officially adopted the appellation later.

Ketcham, Dennis

Dennis Ketcham was born in 1946 in Carmel, California. His father, Hank, was a cartoonist who worked at home. Dennis inadvertently gained fame at the age of four when he trashed his bedroom instead of taking a nap. His mother, Alice, marched into her husband's studio and announced in exasperation, "Your son is a menace." A cartoon lightbulb appeared over the artist's head, and *Dennis the Menace* was born. By the time Hank Ketcham retired in 1994, the comic strip had 50 million readers. It had spawned a television series and a major motion picture. Although Dennis may have been in storybooks, he did not lead a storybook life. As a boy, he had learning disabilities. His mother was an alcoholic, and his father's work schedule left little time for his son. In 1959, shortly after his mother filed for divorce, Dennis was sent to boarding school. A few months later Alice Ketcham died of an accidental drug overdose at the age of 41. Hank Ketcham remarried and moved Dennis to Switzerland. He had such a difficult time in Swiss boarding school that his father sent him to boarding school in America while he and his new wife remained in Europe. After graduating, Dennis joined the Marines and went to Vietnam. Upon his return, he was treated for post-traumatic stress disorder and drifted from one low-paying job to another. Meanwhile, Hank Ketcham, now a multi-millionaire, was divorced and married a third wife, with whom he had two more children. Dennis was also divorced and had remarried. He was, himself, estranged from his daughter. "I hear from Dennis about once a year, mostly when he needs money," Hank Ketcham told *People* magazine in 1993. Although Dennis says that he wishes his father had written about something other than his childhood, he keeps a large collection of Dennis the Menace dolls and books.

Keys, Ancel

Ancel Keys never stayed in any one city for long. He was born, an only child, in Colorado Springs, Colorado, in 1904. His family moved to San Francisco shortly thereafter. Their timing was less than ideal, however. In 1906, the San Francisco Earthquake rocked the city, forcing the family to flee to Los Angeles. Keys stayed there for most of his childhood. He entered the University of California at Berkeley in 1922, and after a slight delay to take a trip to China, completed his undergraduate degree in 1925. But that was not the end of his academic career. He next obtained a master's degree in zoology and a doctorate in oceanography and biology. A National

Research Council fellowship then took him to Copenhagen to work under Professor August Krogh, a Nobel laureate in physiology. His academic credentials earned him a teaching post at *Harvard*, which he gave up three years later in favor of a position at the University of Minnesota's Mayo Foundation in Rochester. After a year in Rochester, Keys was invited to come to Minneapolis and organize what was to become the Laboratory of Physiological Hygiene. Among Keys's early research projects were subsistence tests for the Defense Department. In 1941, serving as a special assistant to the secretary of war, Keys was the natural choice to develop rations for troops in combat. The rations he developed were known as *K-Rations*, with his name providing the first letter.

Kilroy, James

James Kilroy began working at the Fore River Shipyard in Quincy, Massachusetts, in 1941, shortly before the Japanese bombed Pearl Harbor. He worked on the day shift counting the number of holes the riveters had filled. The riveters were paid per rivet, so the counters would walk through the yard marking each rivet they had counted with chalk so none would be counted twice. If a rivet did get counted twice, the riveter would get paid twice. Many of the riveters would wait until the counters changed shifts and then erase the first set of marks. The shipyard bosses became suspicious, not of the riveters, but of Kilroy. They asked the riveters if the day counter had been doing his job counting the rivets. They of course said no. After that Kilroy took no chances. Whenever he finished counting, he wrote "*Kilroy was here*" next to his markings. Normally, the rivets would have been covered by paint. But since there was a war on there was no time to paint the ships, and they arrived overseas carrying the curious message.

Kinney, George Romanta

George Romanta Kinney was born in Candor, New York. His father died in 1875, when Kinney was only nine. The youngster helped support his family until he was 17, when he moved to Binghamton, New York. There he got a job with the Lester

Shoe Company. By 1888, he was manager. A pair of tragedies in 1890 led Kinney into his own business: the Lester Shoe Company went bankrupt, and Kinney's wife died in childbirth. Kinney bought the leftover inventory of his former employer and opened his own store. He tried displaying his shoes on wallboards in the store. It worked well. He opened a second store later that year, and by 1899 he had eight stores. By the time Kinney died in 1919 there were 48 *Kinney's Shoes.*

Kite, William

William Kite was a circus performer who formed Kite's Pavilion Circus in 1810. He went on to work with Well's Circus and the circus of Pablo Fanque, the first black circus proprietor in England. Also in the circus were the Hendersons, John and Agnes, who walked the tightrope and performed as clowns and trampoline artists. In 1843, Pablo Fanque's Circus Royal put on a program that was advertised as "being for the benefit of Mr. Kite." More than a century later the poster made its way into an antique shop, where it was purchased by Beatle John Lennon. Lennon quoted the poster nearly verbatim in the song *"Being for the benefit of Mr. Kite,"* which appeared on the Sgt. Pepper album:

> "For the benefit of Mr. Kite
> there will be a show tonight on trampoline.
> The Hendersons will all be there
> late of Pablo Fanque's fair
> what a scene."

Klein, Calvin

In 1962, 22-year-old Calvin Klein completed his studies at the Fashion Institute of Technology and began working as an apprentice for $25 a week. Five years later, he was contacted by an old friend, Barry Schwartz, who suggested that Klein join him in opening a grocery store. Klein liked the idea of a partnership, but he didn't want to leave the fashion industry, so he convinced Schwartz to join him. Schwartz put up most of the money, but Klein had the fashion experience, so they named the company

Calvin Klein, Ltd. In the late 1970s, Calvin Klein introduced the first designer jeans. Until then, jeans were primarily work clothes and low-fashion items. Klein introduced a pair of jeans with his name embroidered on the back pocket. A controversial ad campaign featuring the teenaged Brooke Shields cooing "Nothing comes between me and my Calvins" helped sales. Years later a similar campaign, featuring teenaged models answering sexually suggestive questions, backfired, and the ads were pulled.

Kliegl, John and Anton

John Kliegl was born in Bavaria in 1869. His brother, Anton, was born in 1872. Both brothers migrated to the United States. Their first jobs in America were with a stage lighting company in New York. Within a few years they had saved enough to buy out their employer and start their own company. In 1896, they launched the Kliegl Brothers Universal Electric Stage Lighting Company. They didn't simply sell theatrical equipment. They also designed it. They were responsible for many innovative scenic effects for the stage and for the new motion picture industry. Of their designs, the one that had the greatest impact on the cinematic world was a bright carbon arc lamp that allowed directors to make night appear to be day, and to make every day sufficiently bright. The light was called a Kliegl light, and later a *klieg light*. The Kliegl brothers were said to have been responsible for one enduring Hollywood custom. The brightness of the lamps caused actors to have painful eye problems, which they dubbed *klieg eye*. According to the book *Inventive Genius*, "Actors forced to work under the bright lamps created a Hollywood trademark as famous as the Kliegl brothers' invention: the perpetual wearing of sunglasses."

Knox, Charles

After watching his wife, Rose, struggle through the long process of making gelatine, Charles Knox decided to try to make it easier. He began experimenting. By 1890, at the age of 40, Knox had developed the world's first pre-granulated gelatine. This development in itself might not have brought the Knox name to the fore were it not for his talent for advertising. During the presidential campaign of 1900, Knox got permission from the commissioner of highways to hang political banners over the streets of New York with the words "Hopes to Win" under each candidate. Above each candidate it said, "Knox's Gelatine Always Wins." Because Knox had gotten the proper permit, angry local politicians could not force him to remove the banners. Finally one official took matters into his own hands and had the supporting poles chopped down. The story made every newspaper in the state and helped make *Knox Gelatine* a household word. Charles Knox died at age 58, and Rose Knox took over the company, managing it for more than 40 years. She became the first woman to be elected director of the American Grocery Manufacturers Association.

Knox, Henry

Born in 1750, Henry Knox was an artillery commander during the Revolutionary War. In November 1775, Knox transported 55 cannons that had been captured by Ethan Allen to Boston. Washington used the British cannons against the British, driving them out of Boston. Knox fought at the battles of Princeton, Brandywine, Germantown, Monmouth, and Yorktown. After the war, he became commandant of West Point, and later the first U.S. secretary of war. *Fort Knox*, located near Louisville, Kentucky, was named in his honor.

Kohoutek, Lubos

On March 7, 1973, Professor Kohoutek, a Czechoslovakian astronomer at the Hamburg Observatory in West Germany, spotted something between the orbits of Mars and Jupiter. He called the object "Comet 1973F." The comet was about 25 times the size of *Halley's Comet*, and was expected to pass within 13 million miles of the sun. In astronomical terms, this is a close call. Science fiction buffs and media commentators predicted the comet's arrival would spell disaster for the earth. Instead of causing havoc on earth, however, *Comet Kohoutek*, as it came to be known, passed without incident, invisible to all but those with telescopes.

Kraft, J. L.

J. L. Kraft was one of 11 children born to a *Mennonite* family. He began his career behind the counter of a grocery store in Fort Erie, Ontario. In the summer of 1903, Kraft, then 29, left for Chicago with $65 in his pocket. After paying a month's rent, he had enough left over to rent a horse and wagon and a small stock of cheese, which he hoped to sell to local grocers. By 1907, his business had grown enough for him to invite four of his brothers to work with him. Kraft & Brothers, as the company was now called, began importing cheeses from Europe and was able to expand into New York. Kraft's greatest innovation was a method to package cheese so that it could be shipped longer distances without spoiling. When Kraft introduced his pasteurized, blended cheese in 1921, national per capita consumption of cheese rose by half.

Kramer, Kenny

Kenny Kramer is an example of a media-age phenomenon, pure fame unsullied by any noteworthy achievement. A New York bachelor, Kramer is a man long on ideas and short on attention. He prides himself on never having held a regular job. Instead, he has worked as a comedian, a magazine seller, and a drummer. For a while, he made a good living selling his invention—electronic disco jewelry. Among those shaking their heads and saying "What a character!" was Kramer's neighbor Larry David. So when David and his friend Jerry Seinfeld were fleshing out a sitcom based on their lives, Kramer was written in. The success of Seinfeld made "the real Kramer" an unlikely celebrity. Kramer is as surprised as anyone at the media attention. "It was weird reading a story about me in the *Enquirer* with 'quotes' I never said or would never say," he says. "Doing a 20-minute radio interview with Ollie North, that was a bit weird." Kramer also found it "weird" when, in a pop culture footnote waiting to happen, O. J. Simpson trial celebrity Kato Kaelin rushed over to meet "the real Kramer" in the flesh. "I'm getting used to unaccustomed events taking place on a regular basis," says Kramer. Today he makes his living giving guided tours of the real places in New York that inspired the scenes in "*Seinfeld.*"

Kresge, Sebastian Spering

Sebastian Spering Kresge began his career as a beekeeper. He went through a variety of occupations, including bookkeeping, baking, and selling products door-to-door. He traveled across several states, finally landing in Detroit. There he opened his own store, advertising "Nothing Over 10 Cents." By 1916, he had 150 five-and-dime stores. World War I inflation forced Kresge to raise prices to 25 cents. He opened a series of "green-front stores" to sell items at a dollar or less. They were often located next to the "red-front stores," which were five and dimes. The first *K-mart* discount store opened in Garden City, Michigan, in 1962. By the time Kresge died in 1966, there were 670 Kresge stores and 150 K-Marts.

Kroger, Bernard

Bernard Kroger overcame many hardships on the road to financial success. When he was only 13, the family's dry goods store folded, and he was forced to drop out of school and get a job. He worked at a drugstore as a clerk. His mother did not like having her son work on Sundays, however, and Kroger quit. He found himself a job at a farm, working from sun up to sundown and sleeping in a loft in a shed. He contracted malaria, but continued to work until his weight dropped to 100 pounds. He walked the 30 miles back to his Cincinnati home because he couldn't afford train fare. Instead of resting, Kroger found himself a job with the Northern and Pacific Tea Company, where he earned $7 a week—more than he had ever earned before. Sales began to slip, however, and he soon was looking for a new job. He found work with a rival tea company, but discovered the business was poorly managed. He next found himself a job managing a retail store. When he was turned down for a raise, Kroger and a friend decided to open their own store, which they called the Great Western Tea Company. Two weeks later, his delivery horse was killed by a train. Shortly thereafter, Kroger's brother died and he had to pay for the funeral. Then the Ohio River overflowed, flooding the store. Despite all this, Kroger was able to keep the business going and to thrive. By 1902, he had changed the name of his business to the Kroger Company and owned 40 stores. Kroger died in 1938 at the age of 78. By 1952, Kroger sales topped $1 billion.

L

Labatt, John Kinder

In 1833, John Kinder Labatt and his wife moved from Ireland to Ontario, Canada. They bought a farm near London—London, Ontario, that is, not England. There, in 1847, Labatt and a partner, Sam Eccles, invested in the London Brewery. Five years later, Labatt bought out his partner and named the business after himself—John Labatt's Brewery. By the mid-1930s, Labatt was ready to expand his operations beyond the Canadian border. After John K. Labatt died, the family business was carried on by John Labatt, Jr., and his son John S. Labatt. The company released its best-selling beers in the early 1950s. The first light ale, sold for the first time in 1950, quickly became Canada's best-selling brand. A year later, Labatt launched its Pilsner Lager in Manitoba. The beer was nicknamed "Blue" for the color of its label. The nickname stuck, and by 1980 Blue was Canada's best-selling beer, a position it has held ever since.

Lamaze, Fernand

Fernand Lamaze was a French obstetrician. Around 1950 he traveled to Russia where he observed birthing techniques based on the theories of psychologist *Ivan Pavlov*. Pavlov popularized the notion that the brain plays a major role in how pain is perceived. Lamaze witnessed women in labor practicing something called "psychoprofilaxis," or "mind prevention." Basically, the method involved the use of distraction during contractions to lessen the perception of pain. Lamaze returned to France, where he developed his own version of the practice. Without a hint of irony, he called his method, which combined relaxation, breathing exercises, and pushing during contractions, "painless childbirth." We call it, simply, *Lamaze*. The Lamaze organization estimates that 2.2 million deliveries each year employ relaxation and breathing methods popularized in Lamaze classes.

Lamb, William

William Lamb was 26 years old when he became a member of the British Parliament in 1806. His rise to political prominence was delayed slightly by scandalous gossip about his personal life. His wife, Lady Caroline Ponsonby, was less than stable. She was known to abuse her husband physically, and she was not particularly discreet about her extramarital affairs. The most shocking revelation was that Lamb's wife and his mother were both competing for the affections of Lord Byron. Still, Lamb remained with his wife, something that the public could not comprehend. In 1825, he finally separated from Caroline, who died two years later. Around the same time, he took office as chief secretary to Ireland, and when his father died in 1829, Lamb became *Lord Melbourne*. In 1834 and again in 1835, Melbourne became prime minister. In 1837, he became a teacher to the 18-year-old Queen Victoria. That same year, a city in Australia was named after the statesman.

Lamborghini, Ferruccio

Ferruccio Lamborghini was born in 1916 into a family of farmers. In 1949, following World War II, Lamborghini started his first company, Lamborghini Trattori, which converted old military vehicles into tractors. In his spare time, he enjoyed tinkering with sports cars. In 1963, legend has it, he found a faulty clutch in his *Ferrari*, and decided to open his own automobile manufacturing company, Automobili Ferruccio Lamborghini. More likely, however, Lamborghini wanted to compete with the top Italian sports car, and that was Ferrari. His plan was a success. The stylish cars attracted such high profile customers as Grace Kelly and Frank Sinatra. Lamborghini sold his interest in the company in the 1970s and turned his attention to cultivating wine grapes. He died in 1993 at the age of 76.

Langhorne, Irene

Irene Langhorne was the sister of Lady Astor, the first woman to sit in Britain's Parliament. The tall, thin, aristocratic beauty attracted the attentions of a young artist named Charles Dana Gibson. Gibson was born to a rich Roxbury, Massachusetts, family and reared in Long Island, New York. As a boy he demonstrated a keen ability in art, and so he was sent to study at the Art Student's League in Manhattan. In the 1880s and early 1890s, he made a name for himself drawing satirical sketches of the well to do. He later traveled to London, where he met Irene. They married in 1895. Around this time, Gibson began drawing portraits of idealized American women. He based the drawings on his wife. The *Gibson Girl* became the model for a generation of women.

Lay, Herman

Herman Lay was born in 1909. His career got off to an inauspicious start. He dropped out of Furman University, which he had been attending on an athletic scholarship, after only two years. He became a traveling salesman in the South, selling a snack that was then popular primarily in the North. It had been invented in 1853 by George Crum, a feisty Native American who worked as a chef at Moon Lake Lodge in Saratoga Springs, New York. One day a customer at the lodge complained that his french fries were cut too thick, and he sent them back. Crum sarcastically cut the potatoes paper thin, only to discover that the customers loved them. Eventually the snack, then known as "Saratoga Chips," became a specialty of the house. The snack spread throughout the Northeast. When the mechanical potato peeler was invented in the 1920s, the chips became cheaper and easier to make. It was Herman Lay who popularized potato chips in the South. By the end of the 1930s, Lay was able to buy an Atlanta snack food distributor that had fallen on hard times. He changed the name to W. Lay and Company. *Lay's Potato Chips* became the first successfully marketed national brand. In 1961, Herman Lay merged his company with Frito, the Dallas-based producer of Fritos Corn Chips, creating *Frito-Lay*.

Le Begue, Lambert

Lambert Le Begue, or Lambert "the Stammerer," was an cleric in the Netherlands in the 12th century. It was the height of the Holy Wars, and most of the men had left the land. Le Begue formed an order of faithful women who banded together to pray and care for the poor. But unlike nuns, they did not take vows of chastity or poverty. These groups of women were called Beguinanges. Although most of the noblemen had left on a crusade, there were still tradesmen and laborers in the country, and they soon formed their own service groups. The male followers were called Beghards. They lived communally, surviving primarily from donations. The method they used to gather funds survived in the expression *begging*. The women also found a place in the language. It seems that the Beguinanges wore a distinctive style of hat that became a fashion rage among young women. The fashion also gave birth to a dance called *the beguine*, which was immortalized in the song "*Begin the Beguine*." The young women who sported the fancy caps as they danced were sometimes playfully flirtatious. A young woman who was impressed with a certain young man was said to "have a beguine for him."

Lea, John

In the early 1820s, John Lea and his partner, William Perrins, were noted British chemists and pharmacists with a successful surgical supply operation. By 1823, the pair had more than 300 items in their apothecary. It was logical that Sir Marcus Sandys would consult the team to unravel the mysteries of a tasty sauce that he brought back from Bengal, India, where he had served as governor. The chemists analyzed the liquid and came up with a formula. It tasted horrible, so they put it aside. As the story goes, when they tried the forgotten concoction two years later, the flavor had changed. Sandys served the sauce to guests at his Worcester estate, where it became very popular. Soon the surgical suppliers were selling the sauce and shipping it overseas with their other products. *Lea and Perrins* later opened the first chain of drugstores in England, but their names are most closely associated with *Worcestershire sauce.*

Lear, William Powell

Bill Lear was born in Hannibal, Missouri, in 1902. Even though he dropped out of school in the eighth grade, Lear demonstrated early on his skill with electronics. He lied about his age and joined the Navy, where he studied radio technology. In 1929, Lear and a partner, Paul Galvin, developed the first car radios. Galvin named the car radio company Motorola, for "motor" and "victrola." The company was very successful. Basking in his new-found wealth, Lear took up aviation as a hobby. He founded the Lear Avia Corporation in 1934 to produce aircraft navigational equipment. Five years later, he formed and headed Lear, Inc. to manufacture military and aircraft products. Then in 1962 Lear had the crazy idea of producing a small jet aircraft for private use. The timing was right. Today owning a *Lear jet* is perhaps the ultimate status symbol.

Leavenworth, Henry

Col. Henry Leavenworth was commander of the 3rd Infantry Regiment from St. Louis in the mid-1800s. Before Kansas was settled, traffic over the Santa Fe Trail was heavy enough to warrant a detail of troops to protect the region from the Indians. A fort was built and named *Fort Leavenworth.* The fort is the oldest continuously active Army post west of the Mississippi River. In 1866, the U.S. Congress authorized the formation of four Black regiments, and the 10th Cavalry Regiment was formed at Fort Leavenworth. A monument stands at the fort today in honor of the buffalo soldiers of the 9th and 10th Cavalry Regiments. In 1881, the School of Application for Cavalry and Infantry was formed. It is now known as the U.S. Army Command and General Staff College. The region is probably most famous for the U.S. Disciplinary Barracks, the military's only maximum security prison, established in 1875. *Leavenworth, Kansas,* actually has four prisons, three of them civilian, but it is the military prison that is the best known. That Leavenworth is home to about 1,000 inmates.

Lee, Henry D.

Henry D. Lee was born in Vermont in 1849. His first job was distributing kerosene in Galion, Ohio. In 1888, he sold that business to *John Rockefeller* and headed off to Kansas. A year later he had a new business, the H. D. Lee Mercantile Company, which sold groceries, hardware, and other supplies. In 1911, tired of waiting for late shipments of work clothes, Lee decided to make his own. The result, in 1913, was a denim overall called the Union-All. The Union-All quickly became one of Lee's best-selling items. So, in 1924, he followed with denim cowboy trousers called *Lee jeans.* Two years later, the Lee Company made the first jeans with zippers.

Legge, William

In 1754, a Congregational minister and *Yale* graduate, the Reverend Eleazar Wheelock, established a school in Lebanon, Connecticut, for the Christian education of Indian youth. It was then known as "Moor's Indian Charity School," named after Joshua Moor, who had contributed the land. Wheelock needed money to operate the school, so he sent one of his students, an Indian preacher named Samuel Occom, to England and Scotland to find benefactors. Occom raised 10,000 pounds, and a board of trustees was created with the second Earl of Dartmouth, William Legge, at its head. Legge's father, the Baron of Dartmouth, had held several high posts under King James II. But after losing an important battle, the baron was tried for treason, and died in the Tower of London. On December 13, 1769, thanks in part to the efforts of Gov. John Wentworth, a royal charter was approved to establish a college "for the education and instruction of Youth of the Indian Tribes in this Land . . . and also of English Youth and any others." Wheelock had suggested that the school be called Wentworth, but the governor modestly preferred to name it for his friend the Earl of Dartmouth. *Dartmouth College* moved to Hannover, New Hampshire, in 1765.

Leotard, Jules

Leotard was a French trapeze artist in the 1860s. According to his memoirs, his parents hung him from a trapeze to keep him from crying when he was a baby. He was the first to turn a somersault in midair. He was so popular and successful that a song was written about him: "*The Daring Young Man on the Flying Trapeze.*" The tight-fitting outfit that he wore to perform his stunts also became famous. Leotard urged men to adopt the garment. "Put on a more natural garb that does not hide your best features," he wrote. We know the garment today as the *leotard*.

Liddell, Alice

Alice Liddell was born May 4, 1852, the daughter of Dean Henry Liddell of Christ Church Oxford in England. Also at Christ Church was a mathematics instructor, Charles Dodgson. Dodgson wrote logic and mathematics books and was fond of photography. It was in his role as photographer that Dodgson met Alice and her sisters, Edith and Lorina. Dodgson would visit the Liddells and photograph the children. When he visited, he would tell the children stories that he made up. He was especially fond of young Alice. In July 1862, when Alice was 10, he took the girls on a boating trip on the Thames River and passed the time telling a story about Alice's adventures underground. Little Alice loved the story so much that she asked him to write it down for her to keep. *Alice's Adventures In Wonderland* was later published under Dodgson's pseudonym, Lewis Carroll. Alice was not the only real person to appear in Carroll's tales. The Duck was his friend Robinson Duckworth, who came along on many of the afternoon outings. Sisters Lorina and Edith Liddell were immortalized as the Lory and the Eaglet, and the Dodo was drawn from Dodgson himself.

Lifshitz, Ralph

Ralph Lifshitz was born and raised in the Bronx. His father changed the family name to the more euphonic "Lauren" when Ralph was 15. In his high school yearbook, Ralph Lauren listed his career goal as "millionaire." He began his career designing wide polka-dot neckties in an office in the Empire State Building. He kept making the ties wider and wider, and soon he found that shirt collars were not wide enough to accommodate them. So he decided to design new shirts. Then he designed sport jackets with wide collars to go with the wide shirt collars to go with the wide ties. Lauren's first full menswear collection was introduced in 1970. The line, dubbed "elegant and relaxed" by the press, was a huge success. By the early 1980s, the name Ralph Lauren had become so closely identified with elegant fashion that a series of ads ran with only two words of copy: *Ralph Lauren.*

Lipton, Thomas

Scottish-born Thomas Lipton, a hard-working, resourceful lad, went to work to help support his family in 1860 when he was only 10. Over the next five years, he was able to put aside around $26, which bought him passage to New York City with $8 to spare. It was not quite enough to get him lodging, so he struck a deal with a landlord. If he rounded up 12 paying lodgers, he could stay for free. Over the next decade, Lipton worked at various jobs and put aside $500, which he took back to Scotland in 1870. In May 1871, he opened a shop in Glasgow. It sold the regular array of food items. An idea he had brought back from America—aggressive marketing—helped him edge out his competition. He offered entertainment to children to allow mothers the freedom to shop, installed fun house mirrors, and hired cartoonists to make posters for his windows. He even hired someone to walk a pair of pigs through town to his shop to advertise his bacon. In 1881, Lipton captured the attention of the public by creating the "largest cheese ever made." Into the cheese he inserted gold coins. The huge cheese sold at a furious pace to people hoping to get one of the lucky gold slices. After all this activity, Lipton decided to take a much-needed vacation in 1890. En route to Australia, he stopped in Ceylon, where he did some research on tea, the product with which his name would become synonymous. He bought five tea plantations in Ceylon. He then sold the tea in individual packets. At the time, tea was sold in open chests. The packaging paid off. He sold 4 million packets that year. Today Lipton markets more than half the tea sold in America through grocery and convenience stores.

Lister, Sir Joseph

Joseph Lister was obsessed with fighting germs, which he called "invisible assassins." He campaigned for cleaner hospitals and to prohibit surgeons from wearing their street clothes during operations. Many surgeons in the 19th century were doubtful of Lister's theories and continued to use the procedures they had always used. Unclean cotton, collected from sweepings on the floors of textile mills, was used for surgical dressings, and surgeons operated in their regular clothes and wore the blood-spattered outfits in the street to show the world that they were surgeons. Because of infection, the postoperative mortality rate was as high as 90 percent in some hospitals. While some surgeons scoffed at the idea of deadly microbes, others were greatly influenced by Lister. His influence made antiseptic and sterilized surgical dressings common. One of his converts was *Robert Wood Johnson*, a Pennsylvania pharmacist who was inspired to sell individual sterilized dressings for wounds. He also inspired a man from St. Louis, Joseph Lawrence, who invented a mouthwash. Lawrence named his product *Listerine* after the famous germ fighter.

Lloyd, Edward

In 1688, Edward Lloyd opened a coffee house near the London docks. It soon became the favored meeting place of London's insurance salesmen. Lloyd passed away in 1723, but insurance men continued to meet in the coffee house. Lloyd's Coffee House, in fact, became so closely associated with insurance that when a group of brokers decided to open a new meeting place in 1769, they called it "New Lloyd's Coffee House." Eventually they outgrew this location as well, and they decided to finance a new insurance society. The name Lloyd moved along with them, and remains today in the celebrated name *Lloyd's of London.*

Locket, Lucy

Lucy Locket and Kitty Fisher were two famous courtesans in the time of Charles II. Lucy Locket became the character *Lucy Lockit* in John Gay's "Beggar's Opera." Kitty Fisher was immortalized in a song called "*Kitty Fisher's Locket.*" The song had a familiar tune. During the American Revolutionary War, the British simply put new words to it to mock the American soldiers. We know that song today as "Yankee Doodle Dandy." The pair are probably the only prostitutes celebrated in a nursery rhyme. Perhaps you have heard it:

> Lucy Locket lost her pocket
> Kitty Fisher found it
> There was not a penny in it
> But a blue ribbon 'round it.

Logan, James Harvey

James Logan was born in Indiana in 1841. As an adult, he moved to Missouri, where he became a teacher. In the midst of a mid-life crisis in the 1880s, Logan retired and drove an ox team for the Overland Telegraph Company to the West Coast, where he settled into a career as a lawyer. He became a district attorney and later was elected to the Superior Court. But it is because of his hobby that Logan's name is remembered. Logan was an amateur horticulturalist. He experimented with fruit, and in 1881 he planted a row of California blackberries beside a row of Texas blackberries. The seedlings that came from the plants yielded a new kind of berry. It was shaped like a blackberry, but had the color of a raspberry—the first *loganberry*.

Lowell, Percival

Percival Lowell came from a distinguished New England family. His younger brother Abbott was president of *Harvard University*. Lowell himself graduated from Harvard in 1876 with distinction in mathematics. His interest in Mars and its "canals" led him to a career in astronomy. In 1894, he founded an observatory in Flagstaff, Arizona. Its altitude and the dry desert air made it an excellent observation site for the study of Mars, which was then close to the Earth. Lowell devoted the last years of his life to the search for a planet beyond Neptune. He did calculations based on the orbits of Neptune and Uranus, but when he looked at the region of the sky where he expected "Planet X" to be, it was empty. Clyde Tombaugh, a Kansas farm boy without a college education, eventually found the hidden planet. Inspired by science books and articles, he had fashioned a telescope out of home-ground lenses and dilapidated farm machinery, including the crankshaft from his father's 1910 Buick. His drawings of Mars and Jupiter so impressed Lowell that Tombaugh was invited to come to work at the observatory. Lowell did not live to witness the discovery of the planet at the observatory that bears his name. When it came to giving the planet a name, mythological figures such as Minerva and Cronus were considered. Lowell's widow, Constance, at first wanted the planet named Lowell, then changed her mind and asked that the planet be named for herself. Suggestions came in from around the world, and an 11-year-old from England named Venetia Burney was the first to suggest Pluto. Many people believe that it was no accident that the planet's symbol is PL, the initials of Percival Lowell. The discovery of Pluto earned Tombaugh a $10-a-week raise and a scholarship to study astronomy. Stargazing continues today at the *Lowell Observatory*.

Lubin, Sara Lee

In 1935, 32-year-old Charles Lubin and his brother-in-law bought a small chain of neighborhood bakeries in the Chicago area. They were called Community Bake Shops. Lubin was constantly testing new recipes on his wife, Tillie, and his eight-year-old daughter, Sara Lee. After about 100 different cheesecakes, he finally hit upon the perfect recipe. Tillie suggested that her husband name the product after their daughter. The cheesecake was so popular that he renamed his bakery *Kitchens of Sara Lee*. As a teenager, Sara Lee worked part-time in the plant offices, but that was her only professional affiliation with the company that bears her name. In 1953, the Sara Lee company began selling frozen baked goods, which allowed the company to expand into 48 states. In 1956, Sara

Lee was bought by Consolidated Foods Corporation. Sara Lee's name is now featured on more than 100 kinds of bakery products. A marketing survey shows that 98 percent of American consumers are familiar with the name. In 1985, Consolidated Foods adopted the name for their entire operation, "to reflect the consumer marketing orientation." Today *Sara Lee Corporation* has more than $19.7 billion in annual sales. The corporation markets more than 150 brands, including Hanes, L'eggs, and Playtex bras. In fact, the Sara Lee Corporation now sells more underwear than baked goods. Sara Lee Lubin, owner of one of the world's most recognized names, is a computer enthusiast and a grandmother.

Ludwig, Donna

Young Ritchie Valensuela was a student at Pacoima Junior High School. He did the normal things a young teen would do. He enjoyed music and working in the wood shop, and he developed a crush on a pretty girl. The girl was Donna Ludwig. She was a popular student and Ritchie was smitten. He asked her out, and she agreed to go with him to the Rainbow Roller Rink. Unfortunately, as is often the case in teen romance, Donna was not as serious about Ritchie as he was about her. Ritchie was determined to woo her with his musical talent. He built his own guitar and wrote a song to show how serious he was about her. Shortly thereafter, Ritchie changed his name to Valens and recorded a hit single. On one side was "La Bamba." On the other side was *"Donna."* As young Valens' star was beginning to rise, his life tragically was cut short in a plane crash. Donna is now a bank manager in the Sacramento area. She is married with a family; her last name is now Fox.

Lushington, Thomas

Dr. Thomas Lushington was a chaplain and a heavy drinker. His alcoholic adventures earned him such renown that 200 years after his death a pub in London was named after him. The drunken customers who weaved their way out of the Lushington Pub came to be known as *lushes.* There are more synonyms for the word "intoxicated" in the English language than any other. *Webster's Collegiate Thesaurus* lists 66 synonyms. *The American Slang Dictionary* lists over 400. The word "intoxicated" itself comes from a Greek word for the poison used on the tips of war arrows—toxikon. Originally, the word in English also meant to be poisoned. Of the many words for "drunk," my personal favorites are capernoited, nimptopsical, and pifflicated. Next time you've had one too many, try using one of these terms to describe your condition.

M

McAdam, John Loudon

John Loudon McAdam was born in 1756 in Ary, Scotland. When his father died in 1770, young McAdam was sent to New York to live with his uncle. He worked in his uncle's counting house and managed to put away a comfortable sum before returning to Scotland in 1783. He was shocked to see the state of the roads in his home country. He worked as a manufacturer and an auctioneer, but his mind never strayed far from the problem of fixing the nation's roads. In 1806, McAdam became paving commissioner in Bristol and in 1827 was named general surveyor for all British highways. During his years in the paving business, McAdam came up with the idea of paving roads with layers of broken stones, all roughly the same size, placed in three layers over a convex roadbed and crushed into position by traffic. The system came to be known as *macadam* or *macadamized* construction. Roads were built this way for many years, but became less practical as heavy automobiles became the vehicles of choice. Cars tended to jar the stones loose. A binder for roads, made from soft coal tar, came to be known as *tarmacadam*. Tarmacadam was a bit of a mouthful, so people shortened the word to *tarmac*.

McCall, C. W.

C. W. McCall was a one-armed trucker from Missouri. Something about him captured the imagination of an Omaha advertising man named Bill Fries. Fries was hired to write an ad for Old Home Bread. He wrote a series of radio spots featuring a trucker named C. W. McCall, who would flirt with a waitress named Mavis. The commercials sold and earned a lot of bread. In 1974, a record company executive suggested that Fries record a country single based on the Old Home commercials. He decided to give it a shot, and the first single, "Old Home Filler Up," became a local hit. He continued to record trucking novelty songs under the name of McCall. In 1975, during the CB radio craze, the song "Convoy," about a string of truckers talking over the CB, topped both the pop and country charts and earned the artist a gold record.

McDonald, Richard and Maurice

You may know that the owner of McDonald's was named Ray Kroc. So where did the name *McDonald's* come from? Well, once the restaurant was owned by the McDonalds. Enterprising brothers Richard and Maurice McDonald opened the first-of-its-kind fast food shop in San Bernadino, California, shortly after World War II. When they sold it to Kroc in 1961, they gave up the right to use the McDonald's name. In fact, the brothers did try to open another restaurant. They called it "Mac's." Kroc put a McDonald's across the street from Mac's. McDonald's put the McDonalds out of business.

McGinnis, James

James McGinnis was born in Detroit and orphaned at age eight. The unhappy youth ran away from the family who had taken him in and got a job at the Pontiac Hotel. It was there that he met a man named Frederick Bailey, who worked for the Robinson and Lake Circus. Bailey gave the youth a job with the circus and became his role model. James, in turn, adopted the man's name. As James Bailey, he went on to manage the circus. Under his leadership, the circus prospered and grew, buying up other circuses as they failed. On March 10, 1880, the first elephant was born in this country at Bailey's circus. Another showman, *P. T. Barnum*, sent a telegram asking to buy the animal. Bailey refused and began using the telegram in his advertising. Barnum was impressed, and in 1888 the two joined forces to form *the Barnum and Bailey Circus.*

McGuffey, William Holmes

William H. McGuffey was a man who valued learning. He had taught himself to read by memorizing passages in books lent to him by a teacher. He became a Presbyterian minister and roamed Ohio as a traveling teacher before settling as a professor of languages at Miami University of Ohio. The year was 1836, and up to that time there was only one book used in most schools to teach reading and writing. It was *The New England Primer*. The Primer was staid and dull, with few illustrations to capture children's interest. A Cincinnati printer named Winthrop Smith and a teacher named Catherine Beecher approached McGuffey with their idea for a reading book that modern children could relate to. McGuffey designed a textbook that would include subjects from rural children's everyday lives. During the next 21 years, the *McGuffey Reader* became the standard school text. When the *McGuffey Reader* was finally replaced by more modern textbooks in 1900, it had sold 122 million copies. Unfortunately, McGuffey was not a great businessman. He earned a mere $1,000 for the book. The rest of the profits went to the publisher.

Mach, Ernst

Ernst Mach was born in Moravia in 1838. A gifted scholar, he was appointed chairman of mathematics at the university at Graz. Then he went to Prague, where he was chairman of the physics department. He finally moved to Vienna, where he was made chairman of philosophy of inductive sciences. Mach published a number of books on mechanics, philosophy, and psychology. In 1887, he published a paper on the action of fast-moving objects in which he computed their speed in terms of the ratio between their velocity and the speed of sound. The paper remained obscure throughout Mach's lifetime, but as aircraft began approaching the speed of sound, people began to pay attention to the "sound barrier," and his study was revisited. A system for measuring speeds faster than sound was developed. The units were called *Mach numbers*. Mach numbers are relative to the speed of sound. Mach 3 is three times faster than sound, for example, while Mach .5 is half the speed of sound.

Machiavelli, Niccolo

Born to a distinguished family in 1469, Niccolo Machiavelli grew up under the rule of the Medici family. The Medicis remained in power until 1494, when they were ousted by the newly formed Florentine Republic. Machiavelli entered the political arena four years later as an ambassador. Then in 1512 the Medicis rallied. With the help of Spanish troops, they defeated the militia that Machiavelli had organized, thus becoming the city's rulers once again. Machiavelli was captured, tortured, and finally released. Unable to return to politics, he retired to a farm and he took up writing. He wrote several plays and a short novel, but it was a small political science treatise that made his name famous. It was called *The Prince*. Its premise was that political subjects should accept any rules imposed by their leaders and that rulers could retain their power by any means. In later years, political tyrants would use *The Prince* to justify ruthless behavior. Such unscrupulous statesmen came to be known as *Machiavellian*.

Mack, John

John Mack, known to his friends as Jack, was born in 1864 on a farm near Scranton, Pennsylvania. He was one of five brothers born to German immigrant parents. In 1878, young Jack ran away from home to become a teamster. He learned how to operate steam engines and headed to sea, traveling primarily in the Panama Canal region. When he returned, Mack and his brother Augustus bought a carriage-building shop in Brooklyn. They sold few new carriages but were able to stay in business by repairing old ones. As the turn of the century approached, the pair became interested in horseless vehicles. They started tinkering and by 1900 were able to roll out the first Mack motor vehicle—a sightseeing bus. It was the first successful bus in the United States and gained a great deal of publicity. Three more Mack brothers joined the business then to form the Mack Brothers Company. By 1905, they had outgrown their Brooklyn carriage facility, and they moved to Allentown, Pennsylvania, where they changed their name to the *Mack Brothers Motor Car Company*. But Jack Mack did not want to build cars. He wanted to build trucks. By 1911, Mack was the premier manufacturer of heavy-duty trucks, selling 600 of the vehicles a year. In 1997, Mack sold 22,375 trucks in the United States alone. It also sold 2,771 in Canada, and 659 in Australia.

Macy, Rowland Hussey

Rowland Hussey Macy was born into a Quaker family on Nantucket. He became a sailor, traveling on the seas for four years. When he returned to Massachusetts, he was unsure of which direction to take, and he drifted from job to job. In 1844, he ended up in Boston, where he opened a dry goods shop. Five years later, he left his wife and children and joined the California Gold Rush. He did not strike gold, but he did open another dry goods store—Macy and Company. It did not strike gold, either. The business folded and was sold at public auction. Macy returned to Massachusetts and opened yet another dry goods store. Again, the business failed. He decided to try his luck in Superior City, Wisconsin. His luck continued to be bad. His plan was to go into real estate, but his timing was less than ideal—the one-time boom town was no longer booming. So he left Wisconsin for New York City, where he opened a small fancy goods store called Macy's Grand Central Fancy Goods Establishment. He could afford only a storefront far from the main shopping district in a location where several other businesses had failed. Three weeks after he opened, his store was robbed. A few months later, there was a fire. Still, he persevered. The small store added new lines of merchandise and, bit by bit, he was able to expand by buying surrounding stores. By the late 1860s, Macy's was taking in thousands of dollars a day. Macy died in Paris in 1877. He was 55. *Macy's Department Store* lived on.

Maertens, Klaus

Little did Dr. Klaus Maertens know in the 1950s when he sold his first support shoes for older women that he was launching the prototype of anti-establishment punk gear. Maerten's original plan was to design a shoe that would alleviate the pain of a skiing injury. Along with an assistant, Dr Herbert Funck, he crafted an air-cushioned sole from rubber taken from old tires. Within two years the air-cushioned shoes were on the market as the perfect footwear for people with back and foot trouble. The company also designed simple functional boots that were designed to stand up to a tough workday. The line of utilitarian footwear sold very well in Germany. In 1959, the doctors licensed their design to a small British firm, R Griggs. The first of the British versions of the shoes were released April 1, 1960, with an anglicized name: *Dr. Marten's.*

Mallon, Mary

In the early 1900s, Mary Mallon was employed as a cook in summer homes and kitchens of the rich. Her meals were delicious . . . and deadly. Ms. Mallon was a carrier of typhoid fever. In each home where she worked, people came down with the disease. By the time anyone made the connection, Mallon had been the cause of 26 cases of the fever. When Mallon was confronted with the fact that she was a carrier of typhoid, she refused to stop working as a cook, and she was arrested. After years in court, doctors finally agreed to release Mallon, provided she agreed not to work as a cook again. After her release from jail, Mallon took on a secret identity and worked, once again, as a cook. She was hired to work in a hospital kitchen, and once again she caused a typhoid outbreak. Her reputation as a fever carrier earned her the nickname *Typhoid Mary.*

Manischewitz, Dov Behr

Among the first settlers in the new world were European Jews. While some settled in Jewish communities, others struck out on their own as rugged pioneers. In either case, keeping kosher was a challenge in the uncharted land. Until the 1840s, most American Jews bought kosher foods directly from their synagogues. As bakeries went into the matzoh business in the mid-1800s, the debate over whether machine-made matzoh could be considered kosher became heated. Eventually, the chief rabbi of Gleiwitz in Prussia responded to the question.

The rabbi's decision, published in the New York Asmonean on February 28, 1851, was that the use of machinery was lawful. This decision paved the way for Rabbi Dov Behr Manischewitz, a pupil of the noted Rabbi Israel Salanter, to open a kosher bakery. Manischewitz and his family arrived in Cincinnati from Lithuania in 1886. He began as a schochet, or kosher slaughterer, for the Orthodox Jewish community, which had paid his family's passage. A year later, he opened a small matzoh bakery. The bakery filled a great need, and Manischewitz stepped up production with the addition of a machine that produced 50,000 pounds of matzoh a day. Today the *Manischewitz Company*, located in Jersey City, New Jersey, produces 100,000-plus pounds of matzoh a day from October to March. The company has also added products and sells a full line of kosher foods.

Marriott, John Willard

John Willard Marriott, Bill to his friends, was born in 1900 on a Utah farm. He worked his way through the University of Utah selling warm clothing to lumberjacks. Upon his graduation, he decided to go into business himself. But he did not choose the clothing business. On May 20, 1927, he opened a nine-seat root beer stand in Washington, D. C. He next opened a Mexican restaurant, which he named The Hot Shoppe. Several other Hot Shoppes followed, including one near Hoover Airport, where he sold a large quantity of takeout food to departing passengers. In 1937, he stumbled upon the idea of boxing lunches to be distributed on the airplane. In-flight catering was born. In 1957, five years after the Marriott Company sold its first stock, Bill Marriott opened his first hotel.

Mars, Forrest

Forrest Mars was raised in Chicago, the son of a candymaker. One day father and son had a heated dispute. Frank Mars told his son to leave the country and never come back. Forrest did leave America, taking with him the recipe for his father's Milky Way candy bar. He went to England and opened a business selling the candy. He also discovered a British candy called "Smarties" that he thought might do well in America, so he bought the rights to market them back home. He returned to America and started a business with partner Bruce Murrie selling little, round, candy-coated chocolates. They named the candies *M&M's* for Mars and Murrie.

Martell, Anne

In the early 1960s, Anne Martell, known to her friends as Annie, was a coed at Gustavus Adolphus College in St. Peter, Minnesota. One evening a group of friends invited her to a party at the student union. Also at the party were members of the Chad Mitchell Trio, who had just finished playing a concert on campus. Annie didn't dress up for the event. She wore loafers, jeans, and an old plaid shirt, but it was enough to impress the band's new lead singer. He was a Roswell, New Mexico, native who had recently adopted the stage name *John Denver*. Ten months passed before his musical tour brought him her way again. "I was in another concert 15 miles away," he would later tell a reporter. "We'd spoken about two words that first time, but I remembered. I got her phone number, called her, and she raced over to the concert." In 1967, he followed her to Aspen for a Christmas vacation with her ski club. He fell deeply in love, not only with Annie, but with Aspen, which he decided to make his home. The couple were married in June of that year. His bride filled up his senses and inspired many songs, including *Annie's Song*, which topped the charts in June 1974. Unfortunately, the marriage did not last. Annie found the rigors of being a celebrity's wife too draining. In 1983, they were divorced.

Martin, Betty

"*All my eye and Betty Martin*" is an old way of saying "nonsense." No one seems to know who Betty Martin was. In fact, in 1837 author Robert Southey wrote, "Who was Betty Martin, and wherefore should she be so often mentioned in connection with my precious eye or yours?" One explanation is that there was no such person and that the phrase came into existence when a sailor wandered into a Catholic church and thought he heard the Latin phrase "Ah mihi, beate Martin," which means

"Ah! grant me, blessed Martin." But to that explanation Charles Earle Funk, the author of *Heavens to Betsy*, says, "All my eye and Betty Martin!" It seems there is no such Latin prayer in the Catholic Church. So the hunt for Betty continues.

Martin, Henry

In the late 1940s, Henry Martin was a chemist working in Buffalo, New York. While studying perchloroethylene—or "perc" for short—he discovered that it could be used to dry clean fabrics. In those days, dry cleaning was a long process. The chemicals that were used were highly flammable, so instead of shipping them to rural and suburban laundries, the clothes were shipped to the dry cleaners in large cities. Perc, on the other hand, was inflammable and recyclable. This meant that by using perc, dry cleaning could be safely done on the premises. In 1949, Martin staged a demonstration of his process in Manhattan. Dry cleaners were suitably impressed, and soon signs all over the country read "*One Hour Martinizing.*"

Martin, John

Who was the "Martha" of *Martha's Vineyard*? Historians are unsure, but it seems likely that there was no Martha at all. Throughout the 17th century, there was some confusion as to the proper name of the island that lies south of Cape Cod. Half of the inhabitants called it Martha's Vineyard, and the other half called it Martin's Vineyard. Dr. Edward Banks, author of the 1911 book *The History of Martha's Vineyard*, wrote, "Our first book of land records, kept by Mathew Mayhew as Register, has on the title page the statement that it is the Record of Lands 'Upon Martin's or Martha's Vineyard'. . . . In most of the documents before 1700 Matthew Mayhew dodged the issue, and dated the acknowledgments as 'Mart. Vineyard,' which can be read either way." Mart. Vineyard was discovered by an explorer named Bartholomew Gosnold in 1602. Some early historians supposed that it must have been named for Gosnold's mother or sister, but records do not indicate that he had any relatives named Martha. A more likely theory is that it was John Martin, one of the sailors in Gosnold's expedition, who was honored in the name, and that, over time, Martin was so often heard as Martha that the latter became the accepted name.

Martin, Lionel

In 1913, Lionel Martin and Robert Bamford started a company, Bamford & Martin Limited, and built their first automobile, a race car with a top speed of 70 miles per hour. Bamford retired from the company after World War I, and Martin took over as sole owner. He decided to name the new version of the company after a race that was especially famous at the time, the Aston Clinton Hill Climb. The car became known as the *Aston Martin.* To many people, the Aston Martin is best known for its role in the *James Bond* films. Unlike in the Bond films, however, Aston Martins are not equipped with bulletproof coating, smoke-screen capabilities, built-in water jets, or retractable tire shredders.

Maserati, Carlo et al.

Rodolfo Maserati and Carolina Losi had seven sons born between 1881 and 1898: Carlo, Bindo, Alfieri, Ettore, Mario, and Ernesto. Actually, there were two sons named Alfieri. The first died as an infant, and the next son was given the same name. The oldest, Carlo, embarked on a career as a race car driver in 1907. Shortly thereafter he bought a pharmaceutical company that had gone bankrupt and converted it into a mechanic shop. Ettore joined his brother, and the pair manufactured and repaired engines for automobiles and airplanes. Unfortunately, Carlo fell ill and died at the age of 29. In 1914, Alfieri started his own auto business. He was joined by his brothers in the manufacture of race cars. Their cars went on to win several high profile races, and on April 25, 1926, Alfieri introduced and drove the first car to bear the current *Maserati* symbol, which was designed by Mario. Alfieri died in 1939, and the remaining brothers retired from the company that bears their name shortly after World War II.

Mason, Charles

The Mason-Dixon Line, which crosses Maryland, was not originally designed to divide the North from the South, or to separate free and slave states. The line was drawn in colonial times when two families had a dispute over their land grants. The divided families were not the Masons and Dixons, but the Penns of Pennsylvania and the Calverts of Maryland. In 1760, the feuding families called in a pair of surveyors to settle the dispute. The surveyors were Charles Mason and Jeremiah Dixon. Not only did Mason and Dixon chart the territory, they physically marked it with milestones. By 1767, they had marked 244 miles.

Mason, John Landis

John Mason was born in New York in the 1830s. In 1857, he opened his first metalwork shop and was granted a patent a year later for a glass jar with a screw top. In 1859, he began manufacturing glass jars bearing the legend "Mason's Patent Nov. 30th 1858." Soon people were referring to any jar with a screw-top cap as a *Mason jar*. The invention failed to make Mason a millionaire, however. Although he was inventive, he was not good with money, and he gave up most of his patent rights. He died in 1902 in a poor house in New York City.

Masson, Paul

The California wine industry owes its existence, in part, to a devastating disease called phylloxera that attacked European vineyards in the 1870s. In 1878, a 19-year-old named Paul Masson was one of the many who left the French wine country for California. He worked his way through Santa Clara College at the vineyard of Charles LeFranc. By the 1880s, the California wine market was full of French expatriots, and competition was fierce. LeFranc's business was one of the wineries that survived and prospered. When Masson married one of LeFranc's daughters, the business officially became the LeFranc—Masson Wine Company. It wasn't until his father-in-law died, however, that Masson put his own name on a bottle of wine. It was *Paul Masson Champagne*, introduced in 1892. Business boomed until Prohibition loomed. When it went into effect, Paul Masson managed to stay in business as one of only six wineries in the United States licensed to make wine for sacramental purposes.

Mausolus

Mausolus was the king of Caria, an ancient country in Asia Minor. When he died, his widow, Artemisia, was so distraught that she toasted him each day with a drink that contained some of his ashes. In 353 B.C., Artemisia erected a tomb for him at Halicarnassus. The tomb was over 100 feet high, and was surrounded by statues and filled with riches. After two years of drinking her husband's remains, Artemisia joined him in the Great Beyond. The building survived into the 12th century and was counted among the Seven Wonders of the World. Although the first *mausoleum* no longer stands, portions of it are preserved in the British Museum in London.

Maverick, Samuel

American cattleman and politician Samuel Maverick engaged in revolutionary agitation that helped lead to Texas' independence. He was a member of the convention that established the Republic of Texas and became mayor of San Antonio in 1839. But it was not his achievements that made Maverick's name famous. It was his disorganization. Maverick owned a large cattle ranch. He didn't brand his cattle, and many of the calves would get loose and run free. When people saw stray calves, they called them *mavericks*.

Mayer, Oscar

Oscar F. Mayer emigrated from Germany to Detroit in 1873 when he was 14. Shortly thereafter, the Mayers moved to Chicago, where the young man got his first job in a meat market. In 1883, Mayer, then 24, decided to open his own butchery. Mayer's business boomed. By 1888, he had to move to a larger building. The business, now known as Oscar Mayer and Company, employed 43 people, including "five wagon salesmen, one pig-head and feet cleaner and cooker, and two stablemen to take care of delivery horses." The reason we know Oscar Mayer's name today is probably because of his penchant for advertising. Most meat packagers at that time did not put brand markings on their products. In 1929, Mayer started labeling his weiners. But the person who did the most to make Mayer's name a household word was the author of the "Oscar Mayer Weiner Song." It and the bologna song (the one that starts "My baloney has a first name . . .") ensured that generations of Americans would be singing the butcher's name.

Mayo, William

William Worrall Mayo was born near Manchester, England, on May 31, 1819, and moved to the United States in 1845. After earning a medical degree at Indiana Medical College, he opened a practice in Lafayette. In 1854, Mayo moved to Minnesota before finally settling in Rochester, New York, in 1863. Two decades later, Mayo's two sons had also become doctors, and they joined him in his practice. A tornado struck Rochester in 1883. With no hospital in the area, it was a challenge to care for all of those who were injured. The Sisters of St. Francis asked Mayo to head the medical staff of a new hospital, which they would build. When the hospital was finally completed in 1889, none of the other doctors in the area was willing to work there. Since the Mayos made up the entire medical staff at the facility, it was logical to name it *the Mayo Clinic.*

Maytag, Fred

Fred Maytag was born in 1856 on the family farm in Newton, Iowa. He began his career as a 10-year-old supplying coal to schoolhouses. In 1880, Maytag left the farm and became an agricultural supply salesman. By 1893, he had become co-owner of the Parsons Band Cutter and Self Feeder Company. The company's main stock in trade was buggies, which were fast being replaced by automobiles. The company needed to expand its product line, so Maytag invented a gas-powered machine that would wash and wring out clothes. He began marketing his invention in 1907. In 1909, Maytag bought out his partners and renamed the business *the Maytag Company.* Soon Newton, Iowa, was boasting that it was the washing machine capital of the world.

Meijer, Hendrik

People who live in the American Midwest are probably familiar with the name Meijer. Meijer's is the type of store where you can stop in at 3 A.M. and pick up a dozen eggs, a pint of milk, a pair of jeans, or a new microwave oven. Today the chain has more than 145 stores in Michigan, Ohio, Indiana, Illinois, and Kentucky. The superstore began life as a barbershop in the early 1930s. In 1934, Hendrik Meijer, the son of a Dutch immigrant, couldn't find anyone to rent the space adjoining his Greenville, Michigan, barber shop. So he purchased $338.76 worth of merchandise on credit and opened his own grocery store. By 1950, the family business, now headed by Meijer's son Fred, had grown into a small chain of hometown supermarkets. In 1962, the stores had grown large enough to warrant being called *Meijer's Thrifty Acres*.

Mellinger, Frederick

Frederick Mellinger began his career as a buyer for a mail order firm. In 1946, after a disagreement with his bosses, Mellinger decided to start his own mail order business on Fifth Avenue in New York. He wanted to sell something that captured the imagination. After some consideration, he decided on women's intimate apparel. "I love women," he once explained. "I love their curves. I love looking at them. That's how it all started in 1946. Where were the satin and lace nightgowns and slips that went with every mental picture I had of girls who turned me on when I was in the Army?" A year later he moved to Hollywood, where he found a tiny room near the main post office. The Hollywood location would forever after be associated with Mellinger, whose business became known as *Frederick's of Hollywood*.

Mennen, Gerhard

Gerhard Mennen came to America from Germany in 1871 and became a New Jersey surveyor. Mucking through the bogs and underbrush led to a case of malaria, which forced Mennen to quit. While he was recovering, he developed an interest in medicine. When he was well again, he took a job in a drugstore and studied pharmacy in the evenings. In 1877, when Mennen was only 22, he bought a drugstore in downtown Newark. The first product he developed was Mennen's Sure Corn Killer for the feet. It sold well, and Mennen developed a second product, Borated Talcum Infant Powder, which he began selling in 1889. The secret to Mennen's success, however, was not his corn killer or talcum powder but his advertising. Mennen had one of the largest advertising budgets of his time. He used 50 cents of each dollar earned to advertise the Gerhard Mennen Chemical Company. Mennen died in 1901 at the age of 45. His wife ran the company for the next 10 years, making Mennen a leader in the sale of skin lotion and shaving cream.

Mentzer, Josephine Esther

Josephine Esther Mentzer was born in Queens, New York. She grew up above the hardware store owned by her father, a Hungarian immigrant. It was a teacher in school who gave her the romantic-sounding nickname Estee. Inspired by her uncle, a skin specialist, she tried her hand at making face creams, which she shared with her friends at school. In 1930, Estee married a man named Joseph Lauter. Lauter was an Austrian immigrant whose name had been changed by immigration officials. The couple used the occasion of their marriage to legally change both of their names back to the original Austrian spelling of "Lauder." *Estee Lauder* never stopped creating face creams. By 1993, one out of every three cosmetics and perfume products sold in department stores were manufactured by Estee Lauder.

Merrill, Charles

After graduating from the University of Michigan in 1907, Charles Merrill moved to New York, where he got a job in the financial office of a textile group. Two years later he was on Wall Street working for a commercial paper house. Merrill was hired in the new bond department that the business was developing. One day, while he was relaxing at the Y.M.C.A., he met a *Johns Hopkins* graduate who was selling soda fountain equipment. The man's name was Calvert Lynch. The two became good friends, and Merrill found Lynch a job with his firm. In 1914, Merrill decided it was time to take a shot at a business of his own. His plan was to sell securities, especially in the emerging chain store business. He convinced his friend to join with him. *Merrill Lynch and Company* was the result.

Mesmer, Franz

Dr. Franz Mesmer was born in 1733. He earned his medical degree at Vienna at the age of 33. Six years later, he began to research magnetism. He believed that magnets could control the human body. He used magnets as possible cures for all varieties of ailments. He later began to use his hands to experiment with animal magnetism. A French government commission was displeased with Mesmer's experiments, and his prominence declined until he was virtually forgotten. His name, however, survives today in the verb *to mesmerize.*

Michelin, Andre and Edouard

Andre Michelin was born in 1853. After finishing his engineering degree at the Paris Central School in 1877, he entered art school as an architecture student. He later spent five years in the cartography department of the Ministry of the Interior, then set up a metal framework business in Paris. His brother, Edouard Michelin, was born in 1859. He studied at the Paris School of Art. In 1889, he left his arts career to manage a company founded by his grandfather, Aristide Barbier, and his cousin Nicolas Edouard Daubree. The company had been founded in 1832 as a farm machinery and pump manufacturing business. They soon became interested in the industrial possibilities of vulcanized rubber, which they used in their factory for seals, belts, valves, and pipes. When Edouard Michelin became manager of the company, assisted by his older brother, he changed its name to *the Michelin Company.* The popular mascot, the Michelin Man, was also created by the Michelin brothers. During a visit to the 1894 International Fair in Lyon, they found themselves in front of a stack of tires. The shape of the stack reminded them of a man, and thus the mascot was born. The

Michelin Man's name is Bidenbum, by the way, and the first Bidenbum was drawn by a poster artist named O'Galop in 1898.

Miller, Frederic

In 1854, 30-year-old Frederic A. Miller arrived in the United States from Germany. He was an established brewer, and he arrived with a plan to open a brewery in America. He found New York to be less than ideal, and set out on a trek across the country to find the perfect location. In 1855, he settled in Milwaukee, where there was abundant water and grain. He sold the beer he made at his small brewery to taverns at $5 a barrel. Tavern customers bought the beer at three to five cents a glass. Throughout his life, Miller started each morning, as he wrote in his journal, "touring the brewery energetically," which must have been annoying to the brewers who were not morning people. Frederic Miller lived to be 63 years old. After his death, his sons took over the brewery, which they renamed *the Frederic Miller Brewing Company.*

Milne, Christopher Robin

Christopher Robin Milne was born, according to *The Times of London,* "in a genteel street of bay-windowed cottages where fuchsias and geraniums flourished in fastidious front gardens." His father was a playwright and novelist, but he became most successful with the stories he wrote about his son. The two most famous are *Winnie the Pooh* and *The House at Pooh Corner.* Christopher Robin did have a stuffed bear named Pooh, and he did remember playing "pooh sticks" as a boy. But as he grew up, he found it hard to remember which of his childhood memories were real and which his father had invented for his books. While A. A. Milne was most famous for writing about his only son, according to Christopher Milne the writing took the place of spending time with him. As a young boy, Milne spent most of his time with his nanny in a nursery on the top floor of the house. Three times a day the nanny would formally bring him downstairs to see his parents. When he was old enough, Milne was sent to a boarding school. Winnie the Pooh was already tremendously famous, and Milne was often teased by other students. Throughout his adult life, Milne tried to distance himself from his famous name. He opened a bookstore in London, but found that customers came in on a regular basis to meet "the real Christopher Robin." "I'll write about him and see how he likes it," Milne once said of his father. In the 1940s, that is exactly what he did. He published a series of three autobiographies. Eventually, Milne decided to use his name to advantage, selling autographed copies of his father's books for Save the Children. Christopher Robin Milne died in April 1996. And Winnie the Pooh's best friend, Christopher Robin? He will probably live forever.

Miranda, Ernesto

In 1966, the U.S. Supreme Court overturned Ernesto Miranda's conviction for rape, ruling that his confession had been illegally obtained because Miranda was not made aware of his constitutional rights. As a result of this ruling, police now recite a specifically worded list of the arrestee's rights, which we know today as *Miranda rights*. Ernesto Miranda did not fare as well as his name, however. He was tried again for rape and went to jail. When he got out, he made a living for a time selling autographed copies of Miranda cards. When this did not prove to be sufficiently lucrative, he augmented his income with various crimes. He died in 1976, stabbed to death in a gambling quarrel.

Mitchell, Nellie Porter

Australian operatic coloratura soprano Nellie Porter Mitchell was born near *Melbourne*. In 1887, using the stage name Nellie Melba (for her hometown), she debuted in Brussels in *Rigoletto* by the Italian composer Giuseppe Verdi. In 1888, she began a 38-year association with Covent Garden in London. In 1893 she made her American debut at the Metropolitan Opera House in New York City. She joined the Manhattan Opera Company and was later made a Dame of the British Empire. She was quite the celebrity in her day, and the public took note of many things about her, including her eating habits. Dame Melba was fond of food, but often tried to diet.

When she went off her diet, she was especially fond of a dessert that came to be known as *peach melba*. When she had devoured too much dessert, she would return to her diet and snack on *melba toast*.

Mobius, August Ferdinand

Home schooling works. Case in point? August Ferdinand Mobius, who was taught at home until he was 13. He went on to study law and then mathematics, earning a doctorate. In 1816, he became professor of astronomy, mathematics, and mechanics at Leipzig. In 1848, he became the director of the university's observatory. There he wrote a volume on astronomy, geometry, and the mechanics of space, but it was a simple twist in a piece of paper that would earn Mobius a place in the dictionary. In 1858, he discovered that if you take a strip of paper, twist one end 180 degrees, and glue the two ends together, it will appear to have one continuous surface. The *Mobius strip* was made famous by Dutch artist M. C. Escher. It could have been known as a "Listing strip," by the way. A mathematician by the name of Johann Listing independently discovered the phenomenon around the same time.

Mocha Dick

Mocha Dick was a whale. A really big whale. He was reported to measure 110 feet by 57 feet. Sailors attributed to the creature the sinking of seven ships, including most famously *The Essex*, which went down in 1819. That same year, Herman Melville was born. The boy grew up hearing sailors' tales of the great whale that fought and won hundreds of sea battles. Melville read tales of the whale in *Knickerbocker Magazine*, and the stories captured his imagination. He changed the whale's name only slightly when he wrote his tales of Moby Dick in 1850. The real Mocha Dick was finally defeated in August 1859. The old whale was weary and gave up with little struggle. But he achieved a kind of immortality. As one writer said of the animal, "Readers of *Moby Dick* know that he swims the world unconquered, that he is ubiquitous in time and space."

Molson, John

In 1772, when Lincolnshire, England, native John Molson was only eight, his parents died, and he was sent to live with his grandfather. His circumstances did not change for the better. At 17, he became ill with an unknown malady. His doctors thought a change of scene was in order, so at the height of the American Revolution he headed to sea on a ship bound for Canada, a dangerous proposition, indeed. At one point, Molson and his fellow passengers had to transfer to another ship. Once he had arrived in one piece, Molson discovered that the primarily French Montreal had many vinters but no working breweries. Sensing an opportunity, Molson went into business with a brewing friend. By 1785, Molson had become the sole owner of the brewery.

Moncke, Charles

According to the 1946 book *A Book About a Thousand Things*, Charles Moncke (pronounced Monkey) was a London black-smith who invented a wrench. The wrench came to be called the monkey wrench. Other linguists have pointed out, however, that "monkey wrench" is an American term, and that the British call the device a "spanner." Dr. M. M. Matthews, the author of *American Speech*, believes that an American employee of the Springfield, Massachusetts, company Bemis and Call invented a moving jaw for the wrench. His name, according to Matthews, was Monk, and people soon started calling his invention the Monk wrench. The term evolved into *monkey wrench.*

Monroe, Rose Will

When Rose Will Monroe died in 1997, a headline read: "Rosie the Riveter dies at age 77." This was only partially true. When Monroe started working as a riveter on military aircraft at the Willow Run plant in Ypsilanti, Michigan, "Rosie the Riveter" was already a popular figure from a song by Kay Kyser and a famous war poster. Filmmaker and actor Walter Pidgeon went to the factory to find a "real life" Rosie to star in newsreels and promotional films for war bonds. In much the same way,

Microsoft recently went on a search for the "real Dot Com" and found a woman named Dorothy Comm. Unlike Dot Comm, who had never used a computer, Rose Monroe was a genuine Rosie the Riveter in almost every way. She even bore a striking resemblance to the character on the poster. The *Encyclopedia of American Economic History* credited the Rosie the Riveter movement with helping to increase the number of working women to 20 million in four years of war, a 57 percent jump from 1940. Following the war, most "Rosies" were laid off and expected to return to the kitchen. In this way, Monroe differed from Rosie. She kept working. She drove a taxi, operated a beauty shop, and started her own home construction firm called Rose Builders.

Montessori, Maria

Maria Montessori, born and educated in Rome, was the first woman in Italy to graduate with a medical degree. Later, she became interested in the problems of mentally handicapped children and joined a psychiatric clinic. She opened her first "children's house" in 1907, developing a system of education for children three to six years of age based on freedom of movement, considerable choice for pupils, and the use of specially designed activities and equipment. *Montessori schools* were also later developed for older children throughout the world.

Montezuma

Montezuma was the name of two kings of the Aztecs. Montezuma the First ruled from 1440 to 1464, and used his great power to extend the Aztec Empire throughout central Mexico. Montezuma the Second was born in 1480 and became king in 1502. He began his career by defeating the nearby Tlaxcaltecas. But in 1519, the Spanish arrived, led by Cortes. Montezuma believed that Cortes was the god Quetzalcoatl, whom prophecy said would return. So he welcomed the Spanish with open arms. It was a mistake. The Tlaxcaltecas, who were still miffed about being defeated, joined forces with the Spanish. The Spanish imprisoned Montezuma and killed those who remained loyal to him. The Aztec people revolted against the Spaniards, and the death toll was high. Montezuma pleaded with his people to stop the violence. Montezuma was killed in 1520, either by the Spanish or by Aztec revolutionaries. The once proud Aztec Empire crumbled, and Mexico became New Spain. But Montezuma had his revenge against the European settlers in a term that endures today.

Montgomery, Bernard

Born in London in 1887 and educated at the Royal Military College, Bernard Montgomery entered the British Army in 1908 and served in World War I as a captain. During World War II, he was appointed commander of the British Eighth Army in Africa. His army defeated the German-Italian forces in Egypt and in Libya. As commander-in-chief of the British armies on the Western Front, he served under the Supreme Commander of Allied Forces, Gen. Dwight D. Eisenhower, from December 1943 to August 1944, when he was promoted to field marshal in command of English and Canadian troops. Apparently, Montgomery insisted that his troops have a full English breakfast before they fought, thus, the origin of the expression *the full Monty.* This tidbit came by way of a noted expert on Montys, Eric Idle of the British comedy team *Monty Python.* Although I knew that there was no Mr. Python behind the group's name, I had reason to believe that there was, in fact, a Monty. The name "Monty Python's Flying Circus" evolved from many sources. The "flying circus" was contributed by the British Broadcasting Corporation. John Cleese added the python to the mix, but Bob Python's Flying Circus didn't sound quite right. (I would have suggested Peter Piper's Peck of Pythons, but no one asked me.) This is where Monty enters the picture. As Idle tells it, at his local pub there was a small man in a suit and bow tie who would always come in and ask, "Has Monty been in yet?" "It is true that [this] Monty was Montgomery," Idle explains. But he says that he chose the name because it "has a kind of bad agent ring to it."

Moog, Robert

Robert Moog of Flushing, New York, began his career manufacturing theremins. A theremin is an electronic instrument that creates an eerie buzz. (It created the buzz of the Green

Hornet on radio and the strange effects in the Beach Boys' "Good Vibrations.") Moog was an electronics whiz from an early age. He first earned degrees in physics from Queens College in New York and electrical engineering from Columbia University. Then he received a Ph.D. in engineering physics from *Cornell University*. In 1954, he founded the R. A. Moog Company. Over the next 10 years, the company designed new electronic synthesizers in collaboration with composers Herbert A. Deutsch and Walter (later Wendy) Carlos. Carlos used an early Moog synthesizer to record "Switched on Bach," which became the biggest-selling classical album of all time and made the Moog synthesizer the talk of the town. The only problem with the instrument was that it was a huge, switchboard-like apparatus that was expensive and difficult to move. In 1970, Moog introduced the mini-moog, a stream-lined version of the electronic keyboard. The synthesizer was now within the reach of young pop musicians, who took advantage of the technology to its fullest. The name Moog did not stick with the term synthesizer, however. These days you usually hear the word "Moog" in a sentence that sounds like this: "I had this far out LP of Moog music that I played all the time on my hi-fi."

Moore, Dinty

Yes, there was a real Dinty Moore. In fact, there may have been more than one. During the Great Depression, the Roosevelt Administration came up with a plan to buy livestock from farmers and then turn it over to several meat-packing companies, including *Hormel*, to produce canned meat for the nation's poor. The experiment ended after only nine months. Hormel was left with 500,000 cans. Company president Jay Hormel, son of founder *George Hormel*, decided to make the leftovers into canned beef stew. The product was so successful that Hormel had to buy up the surplus canned meat from other packers to meet the demand. Hormel needed a name for the product, so in 1935 the company bought the rights to the name Dinty Moore from a Minnesota grocer, C. F. Witt and Sons. It is unclear whether the grocer previously sold a stew or meat product by that name, or how he came to choose the name.

What is known is that the name was also being used for a character in the popular comic strip "Bringing Up Father." Since the products were not in competition with each other, it was decided that there would be no confusion. But who was the Dinty Moore of the comic strip? A New York City restaurateur came forward, claiming that it was he who had inspired the character. He sued Hormel for stealing his name, but he lost the case when George McManus, creator of the comic strip, insisted that the character came from a St. Louis bellhop by that name. Was it the comic strip character, and indirectly the St. Louis bellhop, who inspired C. F. Witt to use the name Dinty Moore, or was his Dinty Moore the New York restaurateur? Perhaps there was a third Dinty Moore who has never stepped forward to take credit.

Morris, Phillip

Phillip Morris was a merchant in Victorian London. When British soldiers returned from the Crimea with a taste for Russian cigarettes, Morris did his best to oblige. He hired cigarette rollers from Russia, Turkey, and Egypt. They worked 10 hours a day, turning out 3,000 hand-rolled cigarettes every day. He advertised this business as "Phillip Morris, Esq. Tobacconist and Importer of Fine Seegars." The smokes became popular with England's well to do. The company began exporting its products to the United States in 1827. By 1902, the New York Phillip Morris Corporation was organized. One of its first brands was Marlboro. The Victorian merchant's name became known in America, thanks in large part to a pair of advertisers and a bellhop at the New Yorker Hotel. Those who are old enough to remember cigarette advertising on radio and television will probably recall the slogan "Call for Phillip Morris!" That slogan got its start in 1933 when ad men Milton Biow and Kenneth Goode strode into the New Yorker Hotel and asked a bellhop, 22-year-old John Roventini, to page "Phillip Morris." He walked through the hotel shouting, "Call for Phillip Morris!" It got the attention of the people in the lobby and of the advertisers. They immediately hired Roventini to repeat his call across the nation.

Morse, Samuel Finley Breese

It is believed that *Alessandro Volta* constructed the first primitive working telegraph in the early 1700s. In 1829, Joseph Henry built the first practical telegraph, but since he believed that inventions belonged to all mankind, he did not patent it. In 1844, a portrait painter named Samuel Finley Breese Morse applied for a patent for the telegraph. He neglected to mention Henry's contribution, and went down in history as the inventor. Morse's name survives today in the code that he devised to send messages over the telegraph. It just goes to show that the person who gets the credit may not necessarily be the person who comes up with the idea. It may be the person who telegraphs it to the world.

Mulligan

We may not know Mulligan's first name, but what we do know is that he was a golfer, probably an amateur. He had this habit of making up excuses to take a second shot. The term *to take a Mulligan* has been applied to the practice of taking a second shot without penalty. This is allowed only in casual play, as it is against the rules of the game. The problem with identifying Mr. Mulligan is not that no one has come forward to point him out, but that too many people have. As the folks at Mulligan Software, a company that makes items for golfers, explain, "The players at every famous golf course in the world claim they used to have a member named Mulligan or some variant of the name, like 'Mel Egan.'" A more creative explanation is that the term evolved from players who declared, "Hit 'em all again."

Murphy, Edward

In 1949, Capt. Ed Murphy was a development engineer for Wright Field Aircraft Laboratory working on a malfunctioning transducer, part of Air Force Project MX981 experimental crash research. As Murphy worked, he said of the technician who had done the wiring, "If there is any way to do it wrong, he will." Murphy's project manager, George Nichols, dubbed the statement *Murphy's Law*. A couple of weeks later, Col. J. P.

Stapp, the head of the project, held a press conference in which he referred to Murphy's Law, which by then had been changed to "Anything that can possibly go wrong will."

Murphy, William Lawrence

William L. Murphy was born in Stockton, California. Around the turn of the century, he moved to San Francisco. Like many a young bachelor, he lived in a one-room apartment. After making room for a bed, there was not much floor space left. He wanted to be able to have another person visit without walking sideways, so he began experimenting with a bed that would fold into the wall. He applied for his first patent in 1900, and went into business. He called his company the Murphy Door Bed Company. In 1918, Murphy invented the pivot bed, which turned on a door jam in a dressing closet and then lowered into a sleeping position. Many pivot beds are still in use today. Murphy beds were used to comic effect in old films and early television shows, but the invention of the sofa bed and the use of the Japanese futon have made them relatively uncommon in homes today. The company still exists, however. In January 1990, the Murphy Door Bed Company officially changed name to *the Murphy Bed Company*.

N

Nestle, Henri

In 1857, 46-year-old Henri Nestle decided to leave the life of a traveling salesman behind and open his own company selling liquid gas for the street lamps of his hometown, Vevey, Switzerland. Nestle soon became preoccupied, however, with a problem that plagued the people of that time. In the 1850s, one in four new-born children did not live through the first year. Nestle wanted to change this. He felt that the solution was nutritious food that mothers who could not breast feed could give to their babies. To create his product, Nestle concentrated milk using an air pump and "a new process" that he invented. Initially, most of the food was sold by doctors. Later, thanks to many medical endorsements, Nestle was able to take his product directly to the public. Nestle sold his baby food business in 1873, and had no more contact with its operations until his death in 1890. The champion of infant nutrition had no children of his own, and left no heirs. Of course, that wasn't the end of the Nestle story. Nestle, the company, went on to produce the first condensed milk in Europe and the product that made Nestle a household word—the first milk chocolate.

Newman, Alfred

Alfred "Pappy" Newman was a noted film composer. He was responsible for the scores of literally hundreds of movies, including A*irport, The Man Who Shot Liberty Valance*, and *The Hunchback of Notre Dame*. He won nine *Oscars* in the process. He also composed the 20th Century-Fox theme. His brother Lionel Newman also won an Oscar for his *Dr. Doolittle* score, and nephew Randy Newman continued in the family tradition, writing award-winning music for such films as *Toy Story.* (Randy Newman also played the singing bush in *Three Amigos.*) When writers were putting together "The Henry Morgan Radio Show," they named one of the characters Alfred Newman after the composer. A few years later some cartoonists were looking for a name for their mascot, a character borrowed from a turn-of-the-century dental advertisement. *Mad* magazine first dubbed the toothless, grinning redhead Malvin Koznowski, but then decided instead to steal a name from "The Henry Morgan Radio Show." The "What, Me Worry" kid became known as *Alfred E. Newman.*

Nicot, Jean

Jean Nicot was 29 years old in 1559 when he was sent from France to Portugal to negotiate the marriage of six-year-old Princess Marguirte de Valois to five-year-old King Sebastian of Portugal. When Nicot returned, he brought tobacco plants. The queen mother, Catherine de Medici, became an instant tobacco convert. The plant was also an instant success with the Father Superior of Malta, who shared tobacco with all of his monks. More and more of the fashionable people of Paris began to use the plant, making Nicot a celebrity. At first, the plant was called Nicotina. But *nicotine* later came to refer only to the active ingredient of the plant.

Nobel, Alfred

Alfred Nobel was born in Stockholm in 1833. As a boy, he moved to Russia. There he was taught at home by a private tutor until he was 16. He began working in his father's munitions factory when he was only a boy. When nitroglycerine was discovered in the 1850s, Nobel was eager to find uses for it. He returned to Sweden and began working in an explosives research laboratory with his brother Emil. Some of the explosives there worked far too well, and in 1864 the lab blew up, killing Emil. Despite the tragedy, Nobel kept experimenting with explosives. In 1867, he invented dynamite. The invention brought him fame and fortune. He did not want to be remembered solely as the man who invented an explosive, so Nobel used his money to endow a prize each year for a person who has bestowed a great benefit on mankind. The most notable of the prizes funded by the dynamite fortune is *the Nobel Prize for Peace.*

Nolan, Philip

Lt. Philip Nolan really existed. The story built around the character by that name in *The Man without a Country,* however, was fiction. Everett Hale used the real naval officer's name in his fictional tale of a man who announces, "Damn the United States! I wish I may never hear of the United States again!" He is condemned to sail on a Navy ship the rest of his life without ever hearing the name of the United States again. This never happened to Nolan, who was a loyal officer. Hale later regretted using the real man's name in the story and wrote a book called *Philip Nolan's Friends* to correct the mistake. But it was too late. Some history books today recount Philip Nolan's personal story as though it had actually happened the way Hale wrote it.

O

O'Hanlon, Virginia

Francis P. Church was working on the New York *Sun* in 1897 as an anonymous editorial writer. Since Church, the son of a Baptist minister, had a background in religion, most of the letters to the *Sun* that dealt with sticky theological issues went to him. In December 1897, he received a letter written by eight-year-old Virginia O'Hanlon. O'Hanlon said that her friends were telling her that there was no Santa Claus. She asked the *Sun* if this was true. Church's reply, which contained the line "Yes, Virginia, there is a Santa Claus," became perhaps the most famous editorial of all time. The *Sun* reprinted it each year until it went out of business in 1949. Virginia O'Hanlon went on to become a teacher in the New York City school system, later becoming a principal. Throughout her life she received a steady stream of mail about her Santa Claus letter, and she replied to each one. Virginia O'Hanlon Douglas died on May 13, 1971, at the age of 81.

O'Jay, Eddie

In 1957, a group of students from McKinley High School in Canton, Ohio, decided to form a band. As the Mascots, they recorded several singles for King Records. They caught the attention of Cleveland disc jockey Eddie O'Jay. O'Jay gave the fledgling band advice and support. "He taught us the business and how to be gentlemen," said band member Eddie Levert. In their mentor's honor, the band was renamed *The O'Jays*.

Oakley, Annie

Phoebe Anne Oakley Mossee was born in Darke County, Ohio. At the age of six, she began using a rifle to help provide food for her family. As a young woman, she was one of the best-known professional game hunters in the country. In 1885, she shortened her professional name to Annie Oakley, and began performing in Buffalo Bill's Wild West Show. Because of her ability to throw a playing card into the air and shoot it full of holes before it fell to the ground, "Annie Oakley" came to mean a free pass or meal ticket. A playing card riddled with bullet holes resembles a perforated ticket or punched meal ticket. The expressions are rare today, but both were popular early in the 20th century. She was also the model for the protagonist in the musical comedy "Annie Get Your Gun" by Irving Berlin.

Oberlin, John Frederick

John Frederick Oberlin was an Alsatian pastor. He was loved by his parishoners and respected by his community, because he worked to better his churchgoers materially as well as spiritually. He was known in his time as "the pastor of Steinthal." Two missionaries, John J. Shiphed and Philo P. Stewart, were among those inspired by Oberlin. In 1833, they decided to found a college "to train teachers and other Christian leaders for the boundless, most desolate fields in the West," which was, at that time, near Cleveland, Ohio. They named the school Oberlin Collegiate Institute, in the pastor's honor. The school was coeducational from the beginning, with 29 men and 15 women students. The institution also accepted students regardless of race, and was one of the chief stations of the "Underground Railway" that was set up to help slaves escape to free states. Journalist Steve Bryant wrote of the institution, "Oberlin College probably contributed more to the education of Blacks before 1866 than any other college in America." In 1850, by an Act of the Ohio Legislature, the "Oberlin Collegiate Institute" became "Oberlin College."

Odonne, Lorenzo

Young Lorenzo Odonne was diagnosed in early 1984 as a victim of ALD, an incurable degeneration of the brain. Although doctors told his parents, Augusto and Michaela, that he was beyond help, they were unwilling to give up the struggle. After trying many therapies, the Odones began reading medical texts and searching on their own for solutions to Lorenzo's problem. What they discovered was an oil that stopped the progression of ALD. The treatment came to be called *Lorenzo's Oil* and was documented in a 1992 movie. Although the oil halted the progression of ALD, damage was already done. Lorenzo, now a young adult, still requires constant medical care, but he continues to make gradual progress. The Odonnes continue their quest for a treatment that will reverse the damage caused by ALD.

Ohm, Georg Simon

Georg Ohm was born a locksmith's son in 1787 in Erlangen, Germany. He received a doctorate in physics at age 22 and took a position teaching mathematics at the Jesuit college in Cologne. He was not appreciated by his peers, and he resigned. After Ohm sent the King of Prussia a copy of a book that he had written, the King invited him to teach at the Royal Konsistorium in Cologne. There, in 1827, the same year that *Alessandro Volta* died, he published a pamphlet that defined the basic law of electrical resistance—current equals volts devided by resistance, or $I=V/R$. The formula is known as *Ohm's Law*. His discovery did not electrify his colleagues, and he remained largely unappreciated. In 1841, the British Royal Society gave Ohm a medal for his discovery, and he was awarded a chair in physics at the University of Munich in 1852. He died in 1854. It was 39 years after his death that the International Electrical Congress voted to adopt Ohm's name for a unit of electrical resistance.

Olds, Ransom E.

Ransom Olds was born in Geneva, Ohio. In the late 1800s he began to experiment with horseless carriages. His first successful steam-propelled, three-wheeled vehicle was completed in 1885. Olds then began work on a gasoline-powered car. Although Henry Ford had driven a gasoline-powered vehicle before Olds, it was Olds who in 1890 started the first auto company in what would soon be known as the Motor City, Detroit. The *Oldsmobile* was the first popular American car. It sold for an affordable $650. The song "In My Merry Oldsmobile" soon became a big hit, helping Olds to sell 425 of the vehicles in the first year. About 12,000 Oldsmobiles were produced between 1902 and 1904, when Olds sold his interest in the company. By 1905, the Olds Motor Works was producing 6,500 cars a year.

Onan

According to the Bible, Judah knew his wife and she begat Er, and then Onan. Er was slain by the Lord because of his sinful ways. So Judah instructed his second son to marry Er's widow, Tamar, and to know her so that she might beget a child. The child would then be raised as Er's heir. Onan didn't think that was fair. Instead of complying with his father's wishes, Onan "spilled his seed on the ground." For failing to fulfill his duty, God slew Onan, too. In Victorian times, religious leaders interpreted this to mean that masturbation was a sin in the eyes of God, and *onanism* became synonymous with that sin.

Orfalea, Paul

While Paul Ofalea was a college student he earned himself the name "Kinko." He insists the nickname refers to his kinky red hair. After he graduated, Kinko borrowed enough money to open a small photocopy shop near the University of California at Santa Barbara. The shop was located in the corner of a building that also housed a hamburger stand, which allowed him to cut a hole in the connecting wall and order lunch without leaving the store. This innovation demonstrates his love of efficiency. The decision to keep *Kinko's Copy Shops* open 24 hours a day to serve those who need to make copies at 3 A.M. allowed the company to grow until it seems like there are Kinkos on every suburban corner.

P

Packard, David

David Packard was born September 7, 1912, in Pueblo, Colorado. Even before completing his master's degree in electrical engineering, Packard worked as an engineer with the General Electric Company in Schenectady, New York. In 1938, he returned to California. There he met up with William R. Hewlett, an old friend from his days at *Stanford University*. Hewlett had developed a design for a resistance-capacitance audio oscillator while he was in graduate school. The pair set to work manufacturing the oscillators from a small garage in Palo Alto, earning $538. Today the *Hewlett-Packard* company is the nation's second largest computer maker after IBM. The garage workshop is an official California state landmark known as "the Birthplace of Silicon Valley." Packard died in 1996 at age 83. He left his entire estate, valued in the billions, to a charitable trust.

Packard, James Ward

In 1890, James Ward Packer and his brother, William Doud Packard, opened the Packard Electric Company, which made incandescent light bulbs and other electrical products. In the late 1890s, James Packard became frustrated with his motor car, a Winton, which kept breaking down. So he started to build his own car in a corner of the Packard Electric Company's subsidiary plant, the New York and Ohio Company. He rolled out his first vehicle in 1899. He named his automotive venture the Ohio Automobile Company. It was renamed the Packard Motor Car Company in 1902. In 1907, Packard moved the company to Detroit. Packards were luxury vehicles, the favorites of the rich and famous. James Ward Packard died in 1928, four years after the Winton company went out of business. Interestingly, when the Great Depression struck, luxury cars kept selling. The only people who could afford new cars were those who bought automobiles made by such manufacturers as Packard, Pierce-Arrow, and Cadillac. In 1937, the Packard organization enjoyed its best year, selling nearly 110,000 cars. A prominent auto historian wrote in 1953, "As long as there is a man left to own one, there will be a Packard for him." This unnamed author was a better historian than a prognosticator. In October 1954, Packard merged with Studebaker. Two years later, after an especially bad year, Packard closed its doors for good.

Pantaleon

Pantaleon came from Nicomedia in Asia Minor. He was reared as a Christian, but suffered a lapse of faith. He then became the personal physician to Emperor Galerius Maximanus. After rediscovering his Christian faith, Pantaleon turned instead to treating the poor for free. He became known as the "Holy Moneyless One." His habit of giving away medical care proved to be his undoing. Other physicians, who felt he made them look bad and took away business, reported him to Emperor Diocletian, who had made it his business to stamp out Christianity. Pantaleon was condemned to death. He survived attempted executions by liquid lead, burning, drowning, wild beasts, the wheel, and the sword before finally being beheaded. In his death, he became a sainted martyr, the patron of doctors and Venicians. In was in Venice in the 15th century that the Commedia dell'arte adopted his name for one of its characters— a comic player who wore a distinctive style of breeches. When the Italian performers brought the character to England, English speakers called both the character and his garment *pantaloons*. That term has since become shortened to *pants*.

Papanicolaou, George Nicholas

Born in Greece, George Papanicolaou earned a medical degree at Athens and a doctorate in biology at Munich. Just before the outbreak of World War I, he came to America. He worked at New York Hospital and then at *Cornell Medical College*. In the 1920s, Papanicolaou pioneered the use of cervical tissue smear samples in detecting uterine cancer. The medical community did not immediately applaud his efforts. But in 1942, the scientist wrote a monograph with gynecologist Herbert Traut called "Diagnosis of Uterine Cancer by the Vaginal Smear." The monograph won many converts in the medical field. Worldwide, the test has become the standard for cervical cancer screening, and over 170 million women are tested annually at 20,000 clinical laboratories. Dr. Papanicolaou today has the honor of having given his name, or at least part of it, to his famous test—*the pap smear.*

Parker, George

George S. Parker was born in 1867 in Salem, Massachusetts, the third youngest son of a merchant. He, his brothers, and friends formed a small club to play checkers, chess, and dominoes. Although there were a few board games in those days, most of them were designed to teach religious values. Parker was more interested in a game about another kind of values—monetary. He created a game called "The Game of Banking." The object was to become the richest player on the board. The members of the club enjoyed the game so much that they suggested Parker try to sell it. He took his game to two book publishers, but they did not see any value in it. His friends were sure it would be a hit, however, so they lent him $50 to produce 500 copies of the game. He then traveled throughout southern New England selling his creation. He sold all but a few of the games, and returned home $100 richer. He used that money, less the $50 he owed his buddies, to found the George S. Parker Company. By 1888, the company had 29 different games, most of which were designed by Parker. The business was so successful that Parker convinced his older brother, Charles, to leave the oil business and join the company. They were soon joined by another brother, Edward, and the company was renamed *Parker Brothers.* Interestingly, one game that George Parker never much liked was Monopoly. A man named

Charles B. Darrow invented the game during the Great Depression, and he pitched it to Parker Brothers. Parker passed on it, saying that no one would buy a game that took more than 45 minutes to play. As George Parker had done years earlier, Darrow decided to sell the game on his own. He did so well that Parker Brothers was forced to reconsider. They released Monopoly in 1935, and were soon selling more than 20,000 copies a week. George Parker was convinced that it was a fad, and on December 19, 1936, he ordered the company to stop producing the game. He reconsidered that decision, too.

Parker, Matthew

Matthew Parker, a devoutly religious scholar, served as chaplin to Anne Boleyn and Henry VIII. In 1559, he became the Archbishop of Canterbury. He introduced many reforms to the Anglican Church, causing some resentment among both Catholics and Protestants. He was blessed with a rather long nose, and people began to accuse him of sticking it into other people's business. And so he was popularly dubbed *Nosey* Parker. The term has been applied to inquisitive souls ever since.

Parkinson, James

English surgeon and paleontologist James Parkinson was the author of the first article on appendicitis in 1812. He also wrote the page-turner *Organic Remains of a Former World* and many other highly technical medical texts. In 1817, he became the first to identify a chronic progressive nervous disease marked by tremors and a mask-like facial expression. He called it "paralysis agitans." Most people, however, call the disorder *Parkinson's Disease*. One little known fact about Parkinson is that in 1794 he was questioned about his suspected part in an attempt on the life of George III. The king was said to have been targeted to be assassinated by a poisoned blow dart during a performance at a London theatre. The investigation revealed no such plot by Parkinson, and he was exonerated.

Pasteur, Louis

In 1864, French chemist Louis Pasteur discovered a way to sterilize milk and make it last longer before souring. Before experimenting with milk, he had already achieved success in sterilizing beer and wine. Pasteur himself did not reap the financial rewards of his invention. He did not believe in patents and placed his discovery in the public domain. It was not until 1881 that the word *pasteurization* was adopted for his process. When Pasteur died in 1859, pasteurization had not made him a rich man.

Patti, Adelina

Adelina Patti was born in Madrid to Italian parents and grew up in New York City. She made her first concert appearance at the age of seven. Her formal operatic debut took place in New York City in 1859. Her London debut won her recognition as one of the greatest singers of her day. Cylinder recordings show Patti's voice to have had an extremely wide range. In 1896, an 18-year-old named Henry Armstrong wrote a piece of music. Although he was skilled in writing tunes, he was not so skilled at lyrics, so he asked a friend, Richard H. Gerard, to provide words to his tune. He called the song "Sweet Rosalie." The pair took the song from publisher to publisher, but found no takers. Gerard began to think that maybe he should change the title. As he pondered the matter, he walked past a poster announcing the farewell concert tour of Adelina Patti. "That's it!" Gerard decided, and immediately changed the title *Sweet Adeline.*

Paul, Les

Les Paul was born on June 9, 1916, in Waukesha, Wisconsin, where a seven-mile stretch of highway is now called Les Paul Parkway. Paul became a musician, and with his wife, Mary Ford, had such hits as "Vaya Con Dios," "How High the Moon," "Nola," and "Lover." Of course, being the man behind "How High the Moon" would not have earned Paul a place in the Rock and Roll Hall of Fame. But Paul was not only a fine musician. He was also good with electronics. By 1940, tired of the feedback from plugged-in acoustic guitars, he started building his own electric guitar. With a 4-by-4-inch piece of pine and a guitar neck, he created an instrument he called "the Log." It was the first solid-body electric guitar. He offered "the Log" to the

Gibson Guitar Company, but was turned down. Company officials finally changed their minds 10 years later after *Leo Fender* began producing a solid-body electric guitar. It was better late than never, and *the Les Paul guitar* is now Gibson's biggest seller, one of the most widely used electric guitars ever made.

Pavlov, Ivan Petrovich

Ivan Petrovich Pavlov was a priest's son, born in Rayazan, near Moscow. He thought of following in his father's footsteps, but instead enrolled at St. Petersburg University, where he studied science and physiology. After receiving a medical degree from the Medico-Chirugical Academy, he remained on staff at the institution and did scientific research. In 1902, Pavlov began his most famous research, applying his physiological training to psychology. In his experiments, he showed that if a dog heard a bell every time he was shown food, his digestive enzymes would eventually start flowing whenever a bell was rung. His study of conditioned reflexes was so influential that he received the Nobel Prize in 1904. He was recognized as a great scientist in Russia, despite the fact that he disagreed with communism. Today the adjective *pavlovian* is applied to any predictable, conditioned response.

Peel, Robert

Robert Peel was born in 1788 in England, the son of a successful mill owner. In 1809, he obtained a seat in Parliament, and in 1812 he became the Irish secretary. He established the first successful police force in Ireland. In 1828, he did the same for London in his role as home secretary of that city. The members of the first police force were popularly called by the name of the man who organized them. They were sometimes known as *peelers*, and sometimes as *bobbies*. After giving Britain the bobby, Peel continued his political career. In 1834, he founded England's Conservative Party, and became the first Conservative prime minister. He established a national banking system, advocated free trade, and battled for Irish relief after the 1845 famine. He retired in 1846 and died four years later.

Penn, William

Quaker William Penn left England and established a colony based on free thought in the New World. Penn's father was Admiral William Penn, and he had some influence with King Charles II. The king gave a 48,000-square-mile tract of land in the colonies to William Penn, Senior, as repayment for a sizeable loan. The land began in the east at the Delaware River and ran from the Maryland line up to Lake Erie. Penn wanted to name the region Sylvania, which means "woods." King Charles admired Admiral Penn and insisted the area be named in his honor. The younger Penn, being an humble Quaker, was not pleased with the idea. He even tried to bribe the official secretaries into changing the name on the papers. But the king was the king, and if he wanted the land to be called Pennsylvania, it would be called *Pennsylvania*.

Penney, James Cash

James Cash Penney was born on September 16, 1875, on a small farm outside Hamilton, Missouri, the son of a Baptist minister. After graduating from high school, Penney became a clerk in a dry goods store. The position paid him $2.27 a month. His health began to fail and he moved Colorado, where he believed the fresh air would help his condition. There he bought a butcher shop. Penny's biggest account was a local hotel, and his meat cutter explained that to keep the hotelier's business, Penney would have to provide the chef of the hotel with a bottle of bourbon every week. Penney refused, the hotelier went to another butcher, and the shop closed. In 1898, Penney went to work for a dry goods store operated by Guy Johnson and Thomas Callahan. They were impressed with Penney's hard work and offered him the opportunity to join them as a partner in opening a new store. Penney managed to save $500 and to borrow the remaining $1,500 he needed to buy in. He and his family moved into a small apartment over the new shop in Kemmerer, Wyoming. He called his store *The Golden Rule*. Penney's business thrived, and in 1907 he was able to buy out his partners. At the end of 1912, there were 34

Golden Rule Stores, with sales of more than $2 million. In 1913, the chain changed its name to the *J. C. Penney Company, Inc.*

Pepper, Kenneth

Kenneth Pepper was a Virginia pharmacist in the 1880s. He had a beautiful daughter and an assistant named Wade Morrison. To Pepper, this was a recipe for disaster. When Morrison took a liking to Miss Pepper, her father suggested that Morrison find employment elsewhere. Morrison moved to Waco, Texas, and opened his own drugstore. Morrison's drugstore invented a new soft drink syrup. As the drink became popular, Morrison decided to name it after the man who had made it all possible, *Dr. Pepper.*

Pepperdine, George

George Pepperdine of Los Angeles became quite comfortable financially as the result of the success of the Western Auto Supply Company, which he had established and developed. A devout member of the Church of Christ, Pepperdine decided in 1937 to use his wealth to establish an institution of higher learning. The institution would have as its mission "to help young men and women prepare themselves for a life of usefulness in this competitive world and to help them build a foundation of Christian character and faith which will survive the storms of life." For its first three decades, George Pepperdine College was a small undergraduate institution. In 1970, the institution added graduate and professional schools and became *Pepperdine University.* Today Pepperdine has about 6,500 students.

Perkins, Ivan

Ivan Perkins was born in Fraser, Colorado. He moved to Alaska in the 1930s to supervise kitchens at a gold mine. Later, he got a somewhat less exotic job as a troubleshooter for the *Fleischmann Yeast Company.* During World War II, he worked as the superintendent of a commercial bakery. In 1948, he decided to try his hand at a bakery of his own. He opened Perkins Bakery, which sold packaged mixes for cakes, pie crusts, biscuits, and pancakes in grocery stores. In 1958, Perkins and his brother Matthew founded the Perkins Pancake

House in Cincinnati, Ohio. The restaurant was so successful that two years later they decided to sell franchises. According to the Cincinnati *Enquirer*, that made Perkins "one of the first people in the country to franchise a business." Today the Perkins chain boasts 468 restaurants in the U.S. and Canada.

Perrier, Louis

Dr. Louis Perrier of Nimes, France, was the director of the Establissement Thermal d'Euzet-les-Bains and the Sociétédes Eaux Minerales, Boissons et Produits Hygieniques de Vergeze, which is a long way to say that he was interested in water and its therapeutic uses. In 1894, the doctor leased a natural spring called Les Bouillens, or "Boiling Water." Perrier studied the water for years before teaming up with a partner, Englishman Sir John Harmsworth, in 1903. Together, they bought the spring. In 1904, Harmsworth bought out his partner and founded Compagnie de la Source Perrier (Perrier Spring Company) with an entirely British management team. Harmsworth ran the company until he died in 1933. Following the war, the company was sold by his heirs.

Perry, Antoinette

Antoinette Perry, the only child of an affluent Denver attorney, was born June 27, 1888. As a girl, she studied piano and voice, and was sent to New York's exclusive Miss Ely's School to prepare for a concert career. Her heart, however, was always in the theatre. In 1905, at the age of 16, she made her stage debut in Chicago in a play called "Mrs. Templeton's Telegram." By age 20, Perry had already become a stage star. Over the course of her lifetime, Perry became not only a noted actress, but also a director and philanthropist. She became active in the American Theatre Wing, helping to form the American Theater Wing War Service, which held benefits to raise money for the British war effort. When she died at age 58, the members of the American Theatre Wing were determined that some type of memorial be established to honor her. They decided on a series of annual awards for distinguished acting and technical achievement. They named them the *Tony Awards*.

Peugeot, Armand

In 1890, in Valentigney, France, a group of relatives launched a farm equipment manufacturing business called Les Fils du Peugeot Fréres, or the Sons of the Peugeot Brothers. Armand Peugeot introduced a gasoline-powered engine to the family business, and a year later became the second automobile manufacturer in France. Armand's brother, Robert, decided to make his own car, and in 1906 set up rival Lion-Peugeot. The sibling rivalry died after a short time, and the lion was adopted as the symbol of the reunited *Peugeot Company*.

Philbert

Philbert was born in Gascony, the noble son of King Dagobert's official. In A.D. 636, he retired to the monastery of Rebais. Then in A.D.. 654 he founded the abbey of Jumieges. Later Philbert founded the Noirmoutier abbey, where he died in A.D. 685. Following his death, Philbert was made a saint. His day of sainthood falls on August 20. August 20 is the height of the nut harvesting season, so Norman nut farmers named their crop philberts—later translated into English as *filberts*. The association with nuts spawned some filbert slang as well. Early in the century a popular song, "Gilbert Filbert, Colonel of the Nuts," led to the expression "Gilbert Filbert," meaning an overly fashion-conscious man. "Cracked in the filbert" is British slang meaning, well, nuts. While we're discussing nuts, it seems a good time to mention that the hazelnut was not named for someone named Hazel, but from the Old English word for the color of the shell.

Phillips, Frank

Frank Phillips grew up in Creston, Iowa. In 1903, a friend told Phillips about newly discovered oil fields in what is now Oklahoma. Two years later, Phillips and his brother L. E. moved to the area in search of oil. The first well they drilled struck oil, but it soon dried up. They dug two more wells—both dry. Their fourth attempt was the charm. They dug 81 wells after that, and all of them produced oil. When the United States entered World War I in 1917, oil prices surged, and the

Phillips brothers incorporated the Phillips Petroleum Company and opened their first gas station. Someone suggested they name it Phillips 66, but that idea was initially rejected. A company official later was riding on Texas Route 66 in a car that was road testing the new Phillips gasoline. "This car goes like 60 on our new gas," the company official said. "Sixty nothing," the driver replied. "We're doing 66!" They needed to make a decision on the name that day, and *Phillips 66* seemed as good as anything else.

Phillips, Henry

Henry Phillips was a Portland, Oregon, businessman with a penchant for gadgets. Realizing that carmakers needed a screw that could be driven with more torque and that would hold tighter than slotted screws, he developed a recessed cross screw that could be used easily with an automated screwdriver. The screw establishment was unimpressed. "The manufacture and marketing of these articles don't promise sufficient commercial success to warrant interesting ourselves further," wrote a representative of the American Screw Company. Phillips was undaunted, and when World War II broke out, industrialists needed to turn out large quantities of jeeps and other machines very quickly. The *phillips screw*, and of course the *phillips screwdriver*, caught on. Interestingly, the Phillips Screw Company never manufactured a single screw or screwdriver. It simply licenced the rights to manufacture the products. By 1919, the phillips screwdriver had become so ubiquitous that Phillips was stripped of the patent. He died in 1988 at age 68.

Pierce, Oscar

In 1931, Margaret Herrick reported to work as a librarian at the Academy of Motion Picture Arts and Sciences. The Academy had been presenting awards to films for only four years at the time. The 10-inch-tall, 7-pound, gold-plated statue that the Academy awarded had no name. One of the statuettes was sitting on Herrick's desk one day, and she remarked that it reminded her of her Uncle Oscar. People around the office began calling the statue *Oscar*. The name stuck.

Pillsbury, Charles

In 1869, Charles Pillsbury went to work for his Uncle John. John Pillsbury had snatched victory from the jaws of defeat after an 1853 fire destroyed his hardware store and all its inventory. His quick recovery so impressed his peers that he was offered the presidency of Farmers & Mechanics Bank. He went on to become a prosperous banker with diverse business interests, including land, railroads, timber, and a sawmill. By 1869, he was ready to expand again, this time into milling flour. He called on his nephew to join him. Charles and his father, George, purchased a one-third interest in a failing Minnesota flour mill. Charles Pillsbury installed a new purifier in the broken-down mill and amazingly made a $6,000 profit in the first year. He used the profits to start his own business, C. A. Pillsbury and Company, in 1872. During the 1920s and 1930s, the company expanded its line of products to include pancake mixes, cereal, and bakery items. But it is the giggling advertising icon Poppin Fresh, *the Pillsbury Doughboy*, that may be most responsible for making the name a household word. He was created in 1965, and by 1968 more than 87 percent of Americans were familiar with the character. He even has his own Web page at www.doughboy.com. According to Pillsbury, Poppin Fresh usually ranks number 1 on the list of America's most popular food product characters, beating out such contenders as the Jolly Green Giant. The Green Giant is Poppin Fresh's adopted brother, by the way. Pillsbury bought Green Giant in 1979.

Pike, Zebulon Montgomery

In 1806, a military contingent commissioned by President Thomas Jefferson to explore the country west and southwest of St. Louis spotted a high range they called the Mexican Mountains. Towering above the others was one notable peak, which Zebulon Pike, the captain of the team, wrote "appeared like a small blue cloud." It took more than a week for the team to reach the foothills and begin climbing the mountain. The conditions were punishing. The temperature was 4 degrees below zero, and the team decided to leave the mountain unclimbed and continue their expedition. In July 1820, the summit of the mountain was finally reached by a group headed by Dr. Edwin James. Because of his leadership, the mountain was named "James' Peak." In the 1830s, however, some prominent people began to refer to the mountain as *Pike's Peak* for its discoverer, and in the 1850s the name was officially changed.

Pinkerton, Allan

Born in Glasgow, Scotland, Allan Pinkerton came to the U.S. and settled near Chicago in 1842. While engaged in business as a barrelmaker in 1846, he captured a gang of counterfeiters and was consequently elected county sheriff. He enjoyed crime fighting so much that in 1850 he organized Pinkerton's National Detective Agency to investigate railroad theft. The agency recovered a large sum of money stolen from the Adams Express Company and uncovered a plot to murder Abraham Lincoln. During the Civil War, Pinkerton organized the U.S. Army's secret service. By the late 1800s, the agency's work on behalf of the railroad companies evolved. Then the Pinkerton Agency was called upon to quash union activity. In 1892, workers from the Carnegie Steel Company's Homestead, Pennsylvania, plant went on strike after the company cut their wages. The Pinkerton detectives who were brought in to stop the strike were sneeringly called pinks, and eventually, *finks*.

Pitt, William

William Pitt the Elder was a controversial figure. Called "the Great Commoner," Pitt believed in constitutional rights for the common man. He led the British in the Seven Years War, and although he opposed American independence, he worked to change the harsh colonial policies of King George III and his ministers. In November 1758, during the French and Indian War, General John Forbes ousted the French from what was then called Fort Duquesne. He renamed the fort Pitts-bourgh. The next day he sent a letter to the fort's namesake: "I have used the freedom of giving your name to Fort du Quesne, as I hope it was in some measure the being actuated by your spirit that now makes me master of the place." According to George Stimpson, the author of *A Book About A Thousand Things*, Pittsburgh is one of the most frequently misspelled placenames in the United States. It is not surprising, since even the experts have had trouble making up their minds on the matter. In 1794, the town was incorporated as the "Borough of Pittsburgh." When it was incorporated as a city in 1816, it was spelled "Pittsburg." In 1891, the United States Geographic Board listed the spelling as "Pittsburg," but after residents of the city petitioned the board, the spelling was changed to "Pittsburgh" in 1911. Pittsburgh, with an "h" is the accepted spelling today.

Poinsett, Joel Roberts

Joel Poinsett, an intelligent but sickly boy, was born in Charleston, South Carolina, to wealthy parents. After getting his education in Europe, Poinsett dropped out of medical school to travel. In the course of his travels, Poinsett met Napoleon, Queen Louise of Prussia, and the Russian Czar, who sent him on an official tour of southern Russia from which only he and two others returned. In 1809, President Madison sent Poinsett to South America, where he served as the consul to Buenos Aires, Chile, and Peru. He became a controversial figure when he supported Chilean revolutionaries. He returned to America during the War of 1812. For a time he joined the establishment. He became a member of the South Carolina legislature and a congressman. In 1825, however, Poinsett was appointed the first American minister to Mexico. Here his revolutionary spirit was revived. He was asked to leave by the government he helped to overthrow, and then again by the government that replaced it. Poinsett didn't discover the red-leafed flower that he sent home. In fact, it had been introduced into the United States earlier. But Poinsett was so well known for his fiery spirit that the colorful flower came to be called the *poinsettia*.

Poisson, Antoinette

Antoinette Poisson was born of middle-class stock, but she was so beautiful and charming that she became "maitraisse declare" of France. That is to say, she was King Louis XV's official mistress. The king gave his lover the title "Marquise de Pompadour." Because of her low birth, she had many detractors in the royal family and among the nobility of France. During her time at Versailles, she was highly influential, virtually ruling what was then the most powerful nation in Europe. Madame de Pompadour conferred pensions, appointed generals, and selected ambassadors. She also was instrumental in establishing the École Militaire. In addition, she supported the arts, encouraging many of that country's most notable sons: Voltaire, Diderot, and Montesquieu. She died at age 42, reportedly in grief over the Seven Years War. It is interesting that this highly influential woman is remembered today for her hairstyle, *the pompadour*.

Popeil, Ron

Perhaps you recall the amazing television products of the mid-1960s and the 1970s. If not, let me refresh your memory: "It slices, it dices, it chops, it juliennes! Not available in stores!" The Veg-O-Matic, the Pocket Fisherman, Mr. Microphone, Seal-A-Meal, and Mr. Dentist were all products of *Ronco*. The Ron of Ronco was Ron Popeil, a salesman who apparently had never heard the word subtle. Popeil began his sales career in his father's company, Popeil Brothers. His job was to demonstrate such products as the Chop-O-Matic at state fairs across the country. In 1964, Popeil formed Ronco in order to bring his pitch to television. He had to fit his entire spiel into 30 or 60 seconds, and he accomplished this by mechanically editing out the pauses between sentences and speeding up the tapes. It cost $550 to produce the first Veg-O-Matic commercial, and it was worth every penny. Nine million Veg-O-Matics were sold. Ronco continued to sell directly to television viewers until 1984, when its CleanAire machine sold so poorly that Popeil was forced to declare bankruptcy.

Porsche, Ferdinand

Ferdinand Porsche was born in 1875, the son of a tinsmith. As a young man, his main hobby was building electric motors. He even built an electric generator for his family home in

Maffersdorf, Bohemia, making his family one of the first in his neighborhood to be wired for electricity. In 1898, he joined the firm of Jacob Lohner and Company, where he created carriages for the royal Austrian House of Hapsburg. He left in 1905 to work with Austro-Daimler, the largest automobile maker in Austria. During World War I he used his design skills to build tanks for the Austrian military. In 1924, he left Austro-Daimler and joined Daimler in Germany. He worked his way up until he was designing vehicles for a head of state, in this case, Adolf Hitler. The first vehicles to sport the name Porsche were, in fact, Third Reich tanks. Did you know that the Volkswagen Bug is a Porsche creation? It's true. While Porsche was designing military vehicles, he was given an assignment to design a car for the masses, then called the Volksauto. The result of his design was the best-selling car in history, the Volkswagen Bug. Porche later became even better known for his sports cars.

Post, Charles William

Charles William Post grew up in Illinois, and after a brief stint in the Springfield Governor Guards, he and a friend headed west to seek their fortunes. They opened a hardware store. After only a year, Post sold his half of the shop and moved back to Illinois, where he got married. He promptly left his bride behind for a career as a traveling salesman. In 1880, Post manufactured an improved seed planter, and a year later he formed Illinois Agricultural Works to sell the machines. He patented several farm machines. Business was good. Post was 27 years old, and so exhausted from all his hard work that his health began to deteriorate. After a nervous collapse in 1890, he went to the Battle Creek, Michigan, sanitarium of *John Kellogg* to recover. Kellogg had started a veritable breakfast cereal revolution in Battle Creck. In 1901, in fact, 40 companies were incorporated in the city to manufacture wheat flakes. Kellogg's health sanitarium was nationally known, but it could do nothing for Post. After nine months, Dr. Kellogg pronounced his case hopeless. Mrs. Post would not believe it. She took her ailing husband to a practitioner of Christian Science. He recovered under her care. He published a book called *I Am Well* about his recovery and started his own rival health food business. His first product was a coffee substitute, *Postum*. Three years later, he perfected Grape Nuts. Many other cereals were to follow.

Procter, William

Shortly after William Procter opened his new woolen goods shop in London, it was robbed. He was left with nothing but an empty building. Instead of rebuilding in London, Procter packed his things, and he and his wife, Martha, headed to America. They planned to go west and seek their fortune. They never made it to the West Coast, however. Martha was stricken with cholera, and the couple's travels ended in Cincinnati, where she died. Without his wife, Procter lost his will to travel any further. He opened a small candle shop. His fortunes changed soon after. He met a woman named Olivia Norris, and the two were married in 1834. Olivia had a sister, Elizabeth, who was also married that year. The brides' father, Alex Norris, suggested that Procter go into business with Elizabeth's new husband, an Irish immigrant soapmaker named James Gamble. On August 22, 1837, the brothers-in-law formalized their business relationship by pledging $3,596.47 each to build a combined soap- and candle-making operation. In a little more than a decade, their sales would top $1 million annually. *Procter & Gamble* is now one of the leading consumer goods manufacturers in the world. It has more than 300 different brands, operations in more than 70 countries, and about 103,000 employees worldwide.

Pulitzer, Joseph

Born in Hungary in 1847, Joseph Pulitzer moved to the United States in 1864. After serving in the Union Army during the Civil War, Pulitzer got a job as a reporter for the St. Louis *Westliche Post*, a German-language daily newspaper. He became so well known that he ran for the Missouri state legislature—and won. He continued in politics until 1878, when he decided to buy the St. Louis *Dispatch*. He merged his paper with the rival *Post*, creating the *Post-Dispatch*. He ran the paper until 1883, when he moved to New York and bought the New York *World.* This was the heyday of "yellow" journalism, and Pulitzer went head to head with newspaper giant William Randolph Hearst, who published the *Journal.* The two newspapers competed for sensational headlines and photographs. In his will, Pulitzer left $2 million to Columbia University for the establishment of a school of journalism and to award annual prizes for excellence in the field. The *Pulitzer Prize* is today the highest award in journalism.

Pullman, George

George Mortimer Pullman was the president and chief designer of Pullman Palace Carriage Works of Illinois. In 1863, his company produced the Pioneer train car. The Pioneer was oversized and overly luxurious. It was too tall to pass under bridges and was put aside as a failed experiment. In 1865, however, President Abraham Lincoln was assassinated, and each state offered its finest railway cars for his funeral train. The Pioneer was included, and praised by dignitaries. The publicity helped make Pullman a rich man. The name Pullman at first was applied only to train cars made by the Pullman company, but it was soon associated with any luxuriously fitted railway car. For a time, the very rich had their own personal Pullman cars, a sign of luxury much like a personal *Lear jet* is today. Pullman himself was reputed to be a ruthless businessman. One of the things he required of his employees was that they relocate to a company town called *Pullman.* There is also a town in Washington State named for Pullman. The citizens of the town named it in his honor in hopes that he would pay for libraries and other gifts. When they invited him to the naming ceremonies, Pullman sent a thank you note and a check for $50, the sum total of his gifts to the town.

Pyrrhus

Pyrrhus, the second cousin of Alexander the Great, was the king of Epirus, a district in ancient Greece. He succeeded to the throne in 307 B.C., later lost it, but regained it in 295 B.C. Early in 280 B.C., at the request of the people of Tarentum, a

Greek colony in southern Italy then at war with the Romans, Pyrrhus sailed for Tarentum with a force of 25,000 men and 20 elephants. His army defeated the Roman legions, but in the process most of his finest officers were killed or wounded. Pyrrhus declared, "One more such victory and I am undone!" Hence the phrase a *pyrrhic victory*, defined in *Webster's Dictionary* as "costly to the point of negating or outweighing expected benefits."

Q/R

Quisling, Vidkun Abraham

Vidkun Quisling was born in Norway in 1887. In 1933, soon after Hitler became chancellor of Germany, Quisling organized the Norwegian Fascist Party to aid the Germans in their invasion of his country. In return for his assistance, he was named the Fuhrer of Norway, and was responsible for reconstructing it as a Nazi nation. Two days before Nazi Germany collapsed in May 1945, however, Quisling and several members of his cabinet were arrested by the Norwegian Resistance. He was charged with treason and executed on October 24, 1945. His name has come to be synonymous with *traitor.*

Raffles, Sir Thomas Stamford Bingley

Thomas Raffles established the Zoological Society of London and served as its first president. He was also a colonial administrator in the East Indies. He fell out of favor, however, when he attempted to free slaves in that region. After his death, Raffles' wife had to pay the costs of his mission to found Singapore. The world-famous Raffles Hotel in Singapore is named in his honor, but he is better known in horticultural circles as the discoverer of a giant flower that was later named the *rafflesia.* Whether he was honored by the appellation is unknown. The common name of the plant is the "stinking corpse lily." The flower is a parasite that grows on vines and gives off the stench of rotting meat in order to attract carrion flies to pollinate it.

Rand, William

In Chicago in 1858, William Rand, a printer from the East Coast, met Andrew McNally, a printer who had recently arrived from Ireland. The pair teamed up and opened a print shop. Their biggest clients were the railroads, which needed large quantities of tickets and timetables. In 1868, the company officially became *Rand McNally and Company*. Their first book was a business directory of Chicago. Next they published a railway guide. Their business was slowed, temporarily, by the Great Chicago Fire of 1871. They were able to salvage only two ticket-printing machines, but that was enough to allow them to reopen for business only three days after the fire. A year later, the company printed its first maps. By using the latest methods of wax engraving, the company was able to correct railroad maps more quickly than their competitors and thus dominate the market. Rand retired in 1899, and McNally died in 1904, before road maps became Rand McNally's main source of business.

Redenbacher, Orville

Orville Redenbacher studied agronomy, a branch of agriculture dealing with field-crop production and soil management, at Purdue University. Using his agronomic skills, Redenbacher and a partner named Charles Bowman developed a hybrid popcorn that made plumper kernels. The hybrid popcorn was more expensive, so no company would buy it. Redenbacher believed it would sell, and so he and Bowman began marketing the product themselves. Orville was right. Consumers loved it. In 1976, Redenbacher and Bowman sold the company to Hunt and Wesson, but the company kept the agronomist as a spokesman. Redenbacher died the last day of 1995.

Renault, Louis

Not to be confused with the Louis Renault who won the 1907 *Nobel Peace Prize*, this Louis Renault was a French mechanic who began tinkering with bicycles and tricycles at an early age. He moved from cycles to making cars in his garden shed in

Boulogne Billancourt in 1888. He designed and built the first gearbox for an automobile at the age of 21. His brother Marcel was business-minded, and he suggested they produce the vehicles commercially. In 1898, along with another brother, Fernand, they founded Freres Renault Billancourt. The first year they produced 60 cars. Automakers made their names back then in auto racing, and it was Marcel who took up the gauntlet. He drove a Renault at speeds approaching 60 miles per hour and won the high profile Paris-Vienna Race in 1902. This was the foundation of Renault's reputation. Marcel died a year later in a 1903 race from Pairs to Madrid. Louis Renault oversaw operations at Renault until the end of World War II. Following the war, Renault was charged with collaboration with the enemy, imprisoned, and within a month was dead. His business was taken over by the French government.

Reuben, Arnold

Arnold Reuben was the owner of a celebrated New York delicatessen of the 1940s and 1950s. His establishment was known for its elaborate sandwiches named for celebrity regulars. For example, a tasty combination of cream cheese, white currant jam, tongue, and sweet pickles on whole wheat was known as the Frank Sinatra, for reasons only Reuben could understand. One day, the story goes, he put together a grilled combination of sauerkraut, corned beef, and Swiss cheese on sourdough pumpernickel. Or maybe he didn't. The Reuben has also been credited to Reuben Kay, a wholesale grocer in Omaha who may have invented the sandwich for a weekly poker group. My first thought on hearing both stories was that Arnold Reuben probably should get the credit, because a Reuben is just too messy to eat during a poker game. But Reuben named his sandwiches after celebrities. If he had invented the sandwich, wouldn't he have called it a Tony Bennett? You make the call.

Reuter, Paul Julius von

The year was 1850. Paul Julius von Reuter was in charge of delivering financial news and stock prices across the gap in the European telegraph lines between Aachen and Brussels. He accomplished this by using 40 carrier pigeons. According to a certain news service, Reuter's pigeon post delivered the news in just two hours, well ahead of his competitors. In 1851, the same year that the New York *Times* began publication, the pigeon post was transformed into a "news service." Julius Reuter died February 25, 1899. *Reuters* is now the world's largest news agency, with more than 1,900 journalists in 163 countries. The company has a presence in 91 countries and employs over 15,000 people. Every second, Reuters transmits more than 27,000 pages of text, which is substantially more than your average pigeon can carry.

Reynolds, Richard

Richard Reynolds began his career working his way through law school at the tobacco company of his uncle, *R. J. Reynolds*. After 10 years with the company, Richard Reynolds decided to open his own business. He moved to Bristol, Tennessee, where he began producing a cleaning product called Spotless Cleanser. Just as he was making a dent in the market, his factory burned to the ground. Undeterred, Reynolds rebuilt, just in time for World War I, when his cleanser was declared a "nonessential product." He was forced to change gears and find a product that was "essential." He chose waterproof barrels made without steel. When the war ended, Reynolds went back to his uncle with a plan to manufacture foil cigarette packaging. R. J. Reynolds loaned his nephew the money to form the U.S. Foil Company. Soon, under a new name, the *Reynolds Metal Company*, the plant was producing more tin foil than any other company in the country. In the mid-1930s, Reynolds was shown a new type of foil made from aluminum. He recognized its potential and set up a new plant to make aluminum foil. Aluminum foil all but replaced tin foil, and *Reynolds Wrap* became a staple in almost every American home.

Reynolds, Richard Joshua

Richard Joshua Reynolds was born in 1850 and grew up in a place called No Business Mountain in Virginia, which was home to the family's tobacco plantation. He began his career peddling chewing tobacco in the mountains of Virginia, Tennessee, and Kentucky. Obviously, this was not the most efficient means of distribution, so Reynolds set out to find a location close to a railroad. He was 24 when he arrived in Winston, North Carolina, in 1874 with $7,500. He used the money to buy a lot next to the railroad tracks and built a two-story wooden factory. He began production with 12 seasonal workers. By 1890, he had 35 factories turning out 9.6 million pounds of chewing tobacco a year. In 1900, Reynolds was able to buy out his biggest competitors, *P. H. Hanes & Company* and *Brown & Brothers*. By 1905, the year of his marriage to Katharine Smith, the 55-year-old Reynolds had become one of the wealthiest industrialists in the United States. Reynolds may have been one of the big names in the American cigarette industry, but he hated smoking. He would not allow smoking in his house. He preferred chewing tobacco. An interesting note: It was Joshua Reynolds of the R. J. Reynolds family who invented that 1970s pop culture item, the mood ring.

Rhodes, Cecil

Cecil Rhodes was the fifth son of the vicar of Bishop's Stortford in Hertfordshire, England. The vicar wished for his son to follow in his footsteps, but Rhodes had other dreams. He wanted to go to Oxford College. His disappointed father sent Rhodes to join an elder brother who was growing cotton in South Africa. There Cecil earned a fortune in the diamond mines, and was able to return to England and realize his dream. He graduated from Oxford at age 28. He then returned to the African continent and planned the Federation of South Africa under British rule. As Prime Minister of British South Africa, Rhodes was instrumental in organizing and developing a new African territory, which came to be called *Rhodesia*. He never forgot his college dreams. When he died, he left a gift of over six million pounds to Oxford College for the establishment of the *Rhodes Scholarship*.

Richter, Charles

Charles Francis Richter was born in 1900 near Hamilton, Ohio. He went on to work as a seismologist at the California

Institute of Technology. In 1927, he and partner Beno Gutenberg created a scale of earthquake magnitude, a measure of the earth's movement as recorded on seismographs. On the *Richter scale*, an earthquake with a magnitude of 1.5 is the smallest earthquake that can be felt. At 4.5, an earthquake causes slight damage. An earthquake with a magnitude of 8.5 is devastating. On January 17, 1994, a powerful quake measuring 6.6 on the Richter scale rocked California. Among the damaged items were some of Charles Richter's personal possessions.

Rickenbacker, Adolph

Adolph Rickenbacker was born in Switzerland, and emigrated to America as a young man. Known to his friends as "Rick," he was a relative of World War I flying ace Eddie Rickenbacker. In the early 1900s, Adolph Rickenbacker owned and operated a tool and die shop in Los Angeles. In 1920, a Hawaiian steel guitar player named George Beauchamp set up a factory next door with his partner, John Dopyera. The pair were among the first to experiment with electrifying instruments. After a few years, however, they found they could not work together and the partnership dissolved. Dopyera left to form the Dobro Corporation. In 1931, Beauchamp created the magnetic pickup that transformed the vibrations of the strings into electrical impulses. This allowed him to build a Hawaiian steel guitar with built-in pickups. To manufacture the instrument, dubbed the "Frying Pan," he turned to his next-door neighbor, Adolph Rickenbacker. They named their new company Ro-Pat-In Corporation. They very quickly traded that name in on the snappier Electro String. They decided that since the flying ace had made "Rickenbacker" a famous name (and Rickenbacker was easier to pronounce than "Beauchamp), they would call the instruments *Rickenbackers*. Both Rickenbacker and Beauchamp died before the 1950s, when rock and roll brought the electric guitar to the fore. The Beatles used Rickenbacker guitars, an endorsement so valuable that a British advertisement in the 1960s called the company's latest model the "Beatlebacker."

Ricketts, Howard T.

In 1906, American pathologist Howard Ricketts discovered a genus of microorganisms carried by ticks, fleas, and lice. *Rickettsia* are larger than bacteria and smaller than viruses. They are the cause of typhus and another disorder now called *rickettsial pox.* This disorder should not be confused with rickets, a disease caused by defective nutrition that affects the growing bones of children. One 17th century writer, John Aubrey, attributed the name of this disorder to a man named "Ricketts of Newberye, a practitioner of physick." Aubrey wrote, "The disease being new and without a name [and] He being so famous for the cure of it, they called the Disease the Ricketts." This is probably not true, however. Modern scholars believe that rickets comes from the Greek "rhachitis," meaning "inflammation of the spine."

Rigby, Eleanor

The famous lonely person of the Beatles song "Eleanor Rigby" was a Paul McCartney invention . . . or was she? McCartney wrote the melody to "Eleanor Rigby" before the words came to him. The original name he gave to the woman picking up rice in the church where a wedding had been held was Daisy Hawkins. But McCartney realized that she should be an older woman. Somehow he came up with Eleanor and combined it with the name Rigby from a sign for Rigby & Evans Ltd. Interestingly, the name Eleanor Rigby was spotted on a tombstone in the graveyard of the church where John Lennon and Paul McCartney first met, while playing at a church social. Perhaps the name made an impression on the McCartney mind and there was an Eleanor Rigby after all.

Rimbaud, Arthur

The French poet Arthur Rimbaud wrote some of the most remarkable poetry and prose of the 19th century. He has been identified as one of the creators of free verse. He is less known as the name behind one of the pop culture icons of the 1990s. In the 1980s, a young pacifist named David Morrell was inspired to write a novel by two news stories: one about Vietnam veterans, the other about a group of hippies who had been mistreated by the police. The novel was the story of a Vietnam veteran who was driven over the edge when arrested and mistreated by a small-town sheriff. When Morrell was trying to name his character, a memory from his French class came to him. Arthur Rimbaud became the celebrated American vigilante *Rambo.*

Ringling, Al, Alf, Otto, Henry, Gus, Charles, and John

August and Marie Ringling had seven sons and a daughter named Ida. The family grew up in McGregor, Iowa. Not much happened in Iowa in the 1860s, so when a traveling circus passed through in 1868, the boys were inspired. In 1870, they sewed themselves a tent, trained a goat named Billy Rainbow, and put on their own circus. They earned $8.37 for their efforts, but this was not to be the end of the boys' circus careers. The show grew and grew, taking on more performers and becoming a real traveling caravan. Eventually, brothers Gus and Henry opted out of the circus life. When circus legend James Bailey died in 1906, the Ringling Brothers negotiated to buy the Barnum and Bailey Circus. In 1907, the *Ringling Brothers Barnum and Bailey Circus* was created. The last of the Ringling Brothers died in December 1936.

Ripley, Robert

Robert Ripley had a penchant for stretching the truth. Although he was born LeRoy Ripley on December 26, 1890, throughout his life he said that he was born on Christmas day. Each time he filled out a passport application, Ripley got a year younger. He first reported that he was born in 1891, then 1892, and finally 1893. He unofficially adopted the name Robert as a young man. In 1913, the teller of tall tales was employed as a sportswriter. On a slow December day in 1918, he put together a series of sketches of people accomplishing odd sports feats, such as running 100 yards backward in 14 seconds. He called the collection "Champs and Chumps." It was a hit, and he soon branched out to include non-sports topics. After a year, the name of the cartoon was changed to "Believe it or Not." In the 1930s, Randolph Hearst bought the syndication rights. In its heyday, Ripley's cartoons had a worldwide readership of 80 million people.

Robbins, Irvine

As a teenager, Irvine Robbins worked at his father's Tacoma, Washington, dairy. Robbins grew up, moved to California, and opened his own ice cream shop in Glendale. Meanwhile, his sister Shirley had grown up, fallen in love, and married. The man of her dreams was a Chicago native who had been a Navy post exchange operator. During his stint in the Navy, Burt Baskin made ice cream for soldiers in World War II. When the war ended, he opened his own ice cream shop in Pasadena, California. After a year of running separate ice cream businesses, the two brothers-in-law, *Baskin and Robbins*, decided it was time to join forces.

Robert, Henry Martyn

The son of a minister, Henry Robert graduated from the United States Military Academy at age 20. He served as a Union soldier during the Civil War, attaining the rank of brigadier general. After the war, he returned to the Academy as an instructor, and headed up the department of military engineering. It was there that he began work on a manual of parliamentary procedure. "Where there is no law, but each man does what is right in his own eyes, there is the least of liberty," Robert wrote in his book. *Robert's Rules of Order* quickly became the authority on procedure for clubs, corporate boards, and lawmaking bodies.

Rockfeller, John D.

John D. Rockefeller was educated in the public schools of Cleveland, Ohio. He became a bookkeeper in Cleveland at the age of 16. He went into business with Samuel Andrews, the inventor of an inexpensive process for the refinement of crude petroleum. By 1878, Rockefeller had control of 90 percent of the oil refineries in the U.S. and, soon afterward, a virtual monopoly of the marketing facilities. Rockefeller then formed First Corporate Trust, which was declared an illegal monopoly and ordered dissolved by the Ohio Supreme Court in 1892. Rockefeller also established the Standard Oil Company of New Jersey, remaining its president until he retired in 1911. At its peak, Rockefeller's personal fortune was estimated at almost $1 billion. The total amount of his philanthropic contributions was about $550 million. His charitable contributions included *the Rockefeller Foundation* and the Rockefeller Institute for Medical Research, now *Rockefeller University*. In 1889, chef Jules Alciotore of Antoine's Restaurant in New Orleans concocted a stuffed-oyster dish that he advertised was "as rich as Rockefeller." The name Oysters Rockefeller stuck. *Rockefeller Center* in New York was named for John D. Rockefeller, Jr., who supervised the construction of the complex in the early 1930s.

Roget, Mark

Dr. Mark Roget was a physician, doctor, man of medicine, and healer. In fact, he was a bit of a prodigy, a genius, a phenomenon. He graduated from Edinburgh Medical School at age 19. He made his living practicing and teaching medicine. He was one of the founders of the Manchester Medical School and was the first to hold the Fullerian Professorship of Physiology at the royal institution. He had quite a few hobbies, including the study of electricity. He wrote treatises on electricity and electromagnetism and tried to build a calculating machine. He was fond of chess, and he designed a pocket chessboard for himself. In 1805, he began work on another hobby. He was inspired by classifications in natural history and decided to apply similar classifications to words. In 1852, Dr. Roget completed a catalog of words with similar meanings. *Roget's Thesaurus* was instantly recognized as a valuable reference book. It was a great success, accomplishment, and triumph. After his death in 1869, Roget's son and grandson continued the tradition by gathering material, terms, expressions, utterances, and communications for the famed reference book.

Roosevelt, Theodore

Just in case you missed this particular tidbit in your history class, Teddy Roosevelt was once the president of the United States. While visiting Mississippi to settle a border dispute, Roosevelt was taken on a hunting expedition. The organizers of the hunt pinned a bear cub to the ground so that the President could not miss the shot. Roosevelt refused to shoot the cub, and the incident became the focus of a widely circulated political cartoon. One person who saw it was a Russian immigrant named Morris Mitchom, who owned a toy shop. When he saw the cartoon, he decided to make a special stuffed bear, which he placed in the window with the cartoon and a sign reading "Teddy's Bear." Mitchom contacted the President to make sure that he didn't object to the toy. Roosevelt replied, "I don't think my name is worth much to the toy bear cub business." Roosevelt was wrong. From then on, *teddy bears* were an almost essential part of childhood.

Rorschach, Hermann

Klecksography. That is the word for art made from inkblots. The exercise was especially common in schools in Hermann Rorschach's native Switzerland. Rorschach enjoyed the activity so much that his fellow students called him "Kleck," or "inkblot." Little did they know that the moniker would continue to follow Rorschach's name throughout his life, and even beyond. As a medical student, Rorschach studied under psychiatrist Eugen Bleuler, who had taught Carl Jung. At the time, the world was buzzing with the theories put forth by Viennese physician Sigmund Freud. In studying Freud's work on dream symbolism, Rorschach was reminded of his youthful inkblot hobby. He began to experiment. He tested people's reactions to a series of inkblots to see if they could be used as a tool to uncover unconscious desires. *The Rorschach inkblot test* was almost immediately adopted by Freudian psychologists. Although many psychologists question the test's value today, it is still the most widely used projective psychological test in the world.

Roslyn

Roslyn's last name has been lost to history, but what is known is that she lived in New York in the late 1800s. She once had a sweetheart, Logan Bullett, who decided to go west to seek his fortune. He was not the type to do anything halfway, so he didn't stop heading west until he was in Washington State. There Bullett became the vice president of the Northern Pacific Coal Company, and he designed a town to house the people who would come to work in the mines. He named it *Roslyn* in honor of the sweetheart he'd left behind. Roslyn, founded in 1886, at one time contained some of the most extensive coal fields on the West Coast. Although the last of the coal mines closed in the late 1960s, Roslyn retains vestiges of its 1920s popularity, when the population peaked at 4,000. When the creators of the televison series "Northern Exposure" were looking for a town to double as the fictional Cicely, Alaska, they chose the old-fashioned simplicity of Roslyn. The opening scene of the series shows a moose walking past a building-side advertisement for Roslyn's Cafe. In the pilot episode, Maurice, the astronaut, comments that the sign painters made a mistake and had to squeeze the "'s" in later. In reality, it was squeezed in because the sign actually advertises the "Roslyn Cafe." Roslyn even became a character in the show. She was portrayed as one of the founders, along with a woman named Cicely, of the fictional Alaskan town.

Royce, Frederick Henry

In 1904, Frederick Henry Royce bought a used car. It was a French Decauville, and it didn't run well. Royce had grown up poor and trained himself as a mechanic. Always a hard worker, Royce decided that instead of fixing up his old clunker, he would simply build himself a new car from scratch. He did just that. By 1906, Royce's homemade car had caused enough of a stir to catch the attention of a wealthy man named Charles Rolls. Rolls was a vehicle hobbyist. He loved to race motorcycles, cars, and even balloons. Upon inspection of Royce's invention, Rolls decided to go into business with him. *The Rolls-Royce Company* was formed in March 1906, but Charles Rolls lived to enjoy only four years of its success. After flying with Wilbur Wright, Rolls decided to buy an airplane for himself. In 1910, he crashed the plane and was killed. Royce lived until 1933. That same year the radiator emblem of the Rolls-Royce changed from red to black. Although company legend has it that the emblem was changed to black to commemorate Royce's death, Royce actually ordered the change himself shortly before he died. He felt that the red emblem clashed with some of the colors on the cars.

Rubik, Erno

Erno Rubik was born in a hospital air raid shelter in Budapest. He went on to become a mathematician and teacher. Always looking for ways to help demonstrate math concepts, he came up with a cube-shaped puzzle. *Rubik's cube* swept Hungary. Two million were sold. The rights to the puzzle were purchased by the Ideal Toy Corporation in 1980. The cube was a worldwide phenomenon, and Rubik became the first self-made millionaire in communist Hungary. Rubik's cube has over 43 quintillion combinations. No wonder you couldn't get it!

Rushmore, Charles

You might assume that Mt. Rushmore was named for the person who sculpted the presidential figures in the rock face. But the sculptor's name was John Gutzon de la Mothe Borglum. (Can you imagine a Mt. Gutzon de la Mothe Borglum?) If not the sculptor, you might assume that it was named for the man who commissioned the work. But that was South Dakota historian Doane Robinson. Then who was Mt. Rushmore named after? It was named for a lawyer, Charles Rushmore. Rushmore was riding along the mountain range with a guide. He asked the guide what the range was called. The guide answered, "It never had a name, but from now on we'll call the damn thing 'Rushmore.'"

Rutgers, Henry

Col. Henry Rutgers, who lived from 1745 to 1830, was a Revolutionary War hero. After the war, Rutgers became a prominent and wealthy member of the Dutch Reformed Church in New Jersey. In 1825, the pastor of the church was also the president of a struggling college. It had been founded in 1766 under a charter granted by King George III, and was named Queens College in honor of Queen Charlotte, his majesty's consort. The pastor believed that if he renamed the institution for Rutgers, the rich man would surely leave a hefty bequest to the institution. Rutgers' generosity was not as great as the pastor had hoped. He is known to have given $5,200 to the institution that bears his name. It survived anyway.

S

Sacher-Masoch, Leopold

Leopold von Sacher-Masoch was the son of the local police chief, born on January 27, 1836, in Lemberg, then part of the Austro–Hungarian Empire, now known as Lvov, Ukraine. He studied at the universities of Prague and Graz, married, and raised a family. He was a teacher for a while before becoming a novelist. His novels contained the recurring theme of people deriving sexual pleasure from being abused, a source of pleasure many have speculated he shared with his characters. He so often wrote on this theme that a 19th century Viennese professor of psychiatry, Richard von Krafft-Ebing, named the disorder *masochism* after the author. Although "sado-masochism" sounds similar to Sacher-Masoch, the term "sadism" was derived from another man's name.

Salisbury, James H.

An English physician born in 1823, James Salisbury promoted a diet that would make most modern nutritionists squirm. He suggested his patients eat ground beef for breakfast, lunch, and dinner. The large beef patties he recommended were fortified with eggs, milk, and bread crumbs and covered with brown gravy. He believed that such a diet would cure hardening of the arteries, colitis, anemia, and tuberculosis. During his life, the good doctor had many followers, most of whom probably died of heart attacks. Although this particular health movement did not last long, *Salisbury steak* is still popular.

Salmon, Daniel E.

In 1876, Daniel E. Salmon became the first person to earn a doctor of veterinary medicine degree from *Cornell University*. In 1884, the U.S. Department of Agriculture established a Bureau of Animal Industry, and Salmon was hired to head it. In 1892, Salmon's team, by quarantine and slaughter of affected animals, completely eradicated a cattle disease known as pleuropneumonia. It was the first instance of the total eradication of a disease in history. Salmon was also the first to distinguish hog cholera from swine plague. But it was an 1885 discovery that propelled Salmon's name into the lexicon. That year he discovered the first strain of the organism we now call *salmonella*. Shortly after his discovery, Salmon launched the federal meat inspection program.

Sanders, Harlan

Harlan Sanders was born near Henryville, Indiana. As Colonel Sanders he started selling chicken in the late 1950s. Indiana Fried Chicken apparently didn't have the right ring to it, so Kentucky became the Colonel's new home state. Sanders didn't have much to say about the secret recipe of *Kentucky Fried Chicken*. He once called the "extra crispy" version "a damn fried dough ball on a stick."

Sanford, John Elroy

John Elroy Sanford was born in St. Louis on December 9, 1922. By the age of 13, he made his mark by offering audiences gritty off-color humor. It was "the humor heard in the ghettos," he once said. "They didn't pull no punches, and they didn't want to hear about Little Boy Blue and Cinderella. So I gave them what they wanted." At the age of 16, he left home to join a New York street band. There he earned the nickname "Red" for his complexion. He completed his professional name by adding the last name of baseball star Jimmie Foxx. Honing his comic skills in the 1940s, Redd Foxx became one of the nation's funniest nightclub comics, although his racy language limited his exposure. His 50 off-color "party" records reached a larger audience, selling more than 20 million copies. In the 1960s, he toned down the language in his act enough to allow him to appear on television variety shows, and eventually to star in his own television situation comedy in 1971. In naming the show, Foxx chose his real name, and "*Sanford and Son*" became a television hit.

Sawyer, Mary Elizabeth

Mary Elizabeth Sawyer owned a little lamb. It followed her to school one day, which was against the rules. So she hid the lamb under her shawl, under her desk, but everywhere that Mary went the lamb was sure to go. When it followed her to spelling class, it was discovered and thrown out by the teacher. It made the other children laugh and play to see the lamb at school, and it made one of the children, named Rawlston, write a rhyme. Rawlston, sadly, died shortly after the incident, but Mary's Little Lamb and Rawlston's poem about it live on. Sawyer, who by then had the married name of Tyler, went on to sell pieces of wool from the little lamb at 10 cents each to raise money for the Old South Church in Boston.

Sax, Adolphe

Adolphe Sax was born in Belgium in the early 19th century. He was one of the eleven children of Charles Joseph Sax, a well-known musical instrument craftsman. According to Willard Espy, author of *O Thou Improper, Thou Uncommon Noun*, the young Sax was particularly accident prone. "He was struck on the head by a brick, swallowed a needle, fell down a flight of stairs, toppled onto a burning stove, and accidentally drank sulfuric acid," he reports. Amazingly, Adolphe grew up to learn his father's trade. In 1835, he combined the reed of a clarinet with a bent conical metal tube and then added finger keys to the whole thing. In 1846, he patented this creation under the name *saxophone*. He invented other instruments by the way, although they were less famous. They were called the sax-otrompa and saxhorn.

Schick, Jacob

Iowan Jacob Schick was a lieutenant in the U. S. Army. He retired from service in 1910, but reenlisted in World War I. During his hiatus from military service, he was a miner in Alaska and British Columbia. One winter, Schick weathered temperatures of 40 degrees below zero. When it is that cold, using water to shave is painful. While a lesser man might have simply grown a beard, Schick began devising a way to shave painlessly without water. Inspired by the repeating rifle, he came up with the Magazine Repeating Razor. In 1926, he tried to market the razor. It was not a stunning success, and he sold the rights to the product in 1930. A year later, Schick was back in business, this time manufacturing the first electric shavers. By 1936, Schick had sold a million of them. So had a lot of other people. Schick died in 1937 in the midst of a lawsuit over patent violations. The Court of Appeals in New York ruled that Schick's electric razor patent was not valid. The judge was later found guilty of accepting bribes in the case. In the end, it was the company Schick sold that made him a household name. In 1946, Eversharp, Inc. acquired the Magazine Repeating Razor Company and renamed it the *Schick Safety Razor Company*.

Schmitt, Louie

One day Harry Reeves and Jim Carmichael were working on the Donald Duck cartoons. Carmichael was reading a paper when Reeves stopped into his office for suggestions on what to call Donald Duck's new nephews. Carmichael glanced at his paper. On the front page were stories about politicians Thomas E. Dewey and Huey P. Long. He suggested Huey and Dewey. Just then a friend of Carmichael's, Louie Schmitt, passed in the hall. "How about Huey, Louie, and Dewey?" Carmichael asked.

Scholl, William

Billy Scholl was born in La Porte, Indiana, one of 13 children. He began his career as an apprentice to the local shoemaker. Hearing customers complain of foot pain, he was inspired to go to school and become a foot doctor. He moved to Chicago, where he worked his way through Chicago Medical School as a salesman. At age 22, Scholl completed his medical training. By this time, Dr. Scholl already held more than 300 patents for foot treatments, arch supports, and other foot-comfort devices. His first commercial product was an arch support called the Foot-Eazer. It was only the first of many foot-related products he devised. In 1907, he patented the name *Dr. Scholl*. He later founded the Illinois College of Chiropody and Orthopedics, which was later renamed *the Scholl College of Podiatric Medicine.*

Schuchert, J. William

"Windy Bill" Schuchert was the manager of the Chester, Illinois, Opera House. He was a short man with a fondness for hamburgers. This habit was noted by a young projectionist by the name of Elzie Crisler Segar. Segar went on to create the comic-strip character Popeye. All of the "*Popeye*" characters were based on the people of his town. A local grocer, Dora Paskel, was the prototype for Olive Oyl. A local tough guy, Frank Fiegel, was the model for Popeye. And J. William Schuchert donated his first names (with a little alteration) to the character J. Wellington Whimpy. Popeye and his pals became so well known in England that hamburgers were popularly referred to as whimpies. A major fast-food chain in that country is Whimpy, which advertises, "Come in for a great Whimpy meal."

Schweppe, Jacob

In Switzerland of the 1700s, a young man of 12 was considered to be old enough to join the working world. When Jacob Schweppe was that age, his parents decided that he was not strong enough to work on the family farm, and they turned over his care to a traveling tinker. The tinker turned him over to a silversmith, and the silversmith in turn sent him to Geneva to be a jeweler. While he was working as a jeweler, Schweppe developed a unique hobby. He was fascinated with Joseph Priestly's experiments with gas and water, so he built a compression pump and carbonation system of his own. He gave the results of his experiments to neighbors and patrons of his shop. Enough people liked the bubbly water that he decided to try selling it. When carbonated water sales outpaced his jewelry business, Schweppe's beverage company was born. Jacob Schweppe ran the company until 1799, when he retired. In 1824, his daughter sold the last of the family's share of *Schweppes*. The new owners kept the name.

Schwinn, Ignaz

Ignaz Schwinn was born in 1860 in Hardheim, Germany. His father died when he was only eleven, and he was forced to leave school and become a mechanic's apprentice. After completing his apprenticeship, Schwinn traveled from town to town repairing the primary mode of mechanical transportation at the time—the bicycle. At night he would work up designs for bicycles of his own. He showed some of these designs to a wealthy customer, who was sufficiently impressed to back the designer financially. In 1895, Schwinn teamed up with a man named Adolf Arnold, and they formed Arnold, Schwinn and Company. The company grew dramatically, and in 1908 Schwinn bought Arnold out, becoming the sole owner of Schwinn and Company.

Scott, Dred

Dred Scott was born a slave in 1795 on a Virginia plantation. During Scott's lifetime, he was the property of several slaveholders. His last owner found him to be incompetent and let him go. The former slave could not find a job, and so he returned to the son of his first master. Henry Blow agreed to support Scott, and also went to court to win him his freedom. Blow argued that since Scott had lived for four years in Wisconsin and Illinois, both free states, he was a free man. The resulting legal battle went all the way to the Supreme Court. In what was called the *Dred Scott Decision*, the court ruled that slaves were not citizens, and that living in a free state did not entitle a slave to freedom. The landmark decision accelerated the onset of the Civil War. Scott himself was legally awarded to Blow, who freed him and his family.

Scott, E. Irvin and Clarence

The year was 1879. E. Irvin and Clarence Scott arrived in Philadelphia from Saratoga County, New York, and together they opened a company that produced a product that was only spoken of in whispers. Imagine the scene: a small East Coast dry goods store . . . a polite gentleman walks in . . . he eyes the shelf with a certain product . . . walks around a bit, picks up a box of soap, just for appearances, and finally grabs a product in a plain brown wrapper. The product? Toilet paper. The Scott brothers' company was one of the early producers of the product. In earlier times, people used corn cobs or old newspapers in their privies. Since they were selling an unmentionable product, the *Scott Paper Company* saw no need to shout about it. Instead, they sold the toilet paper to merchants who would sell it either with no brand label or with a label of their own. It took a pair of eyes from another generation to change this view. It was Irvin's son Arthur Hoyt Scott who urged the older Scotts to advertise their products. They began labeling their toilet paper "Waldorf Tissue," which was advertised as "soft as old linen." By 1907, the ScotTissue company was well known. In that year, a shipment of long tubes of tissue, which were cut down to size at the factory, was deemed defective. It was too tough, not at all like tissue. The company was stuck with a railroad car full of paper it couldn't sell. Again, Arthur had an idea. Why not cut the paper into towel-sized sheets and sell it as "paper towels." The product was offered to the public as SaniTowels. At first, they mostly were sold for use in public buildings, but as the price dropped, people were able to buy them to use in their homes. In 1931, the company changed the name of the product from SantiTowels to ScotTowels.

Scott, Winfield

Gen. Winfield Scott was an officer in the U.S. Army for half a century, serving under every president from Jefferson to Lincoln. A native of Virginia, he joined the Army in 1809. He was a brigadier general in the War of 1812, distinguishing himself at the battles of Chippewa and Lundy's Lane. He then fought in the Black Hawk War and in the campaign against the

Seminole and Creek Indians. Scott briefly turned his attention from war to peace, serving as a peacemaker in the Anglo-American dispute over the Canadian border in 1838. He was appointed general-in-chief of the Army in 1841 and commanded troops in the Mexican War. He was nominated for president by the Whig Party in 1852, but was defeated by Franklin Pierce. His fame is said to have inspired the expression "*Great Scott!*"

Sears, Richard Warren

In 1886, Richard Sears managed the railroad office in tiny North Redwood, Minnesota. Back then, the town consisted of only three houses. Wholesalers in those days would ship on consignment, and if the product remained unclaimed, the freight agent would have the opportunity to buy it at a greatly reduced price. Sears got his start this way selling watches. He then took his $5,000 profits and left the railroad business. His advertisement for a watchmaker was answered by a man named Alvah Curtis Roebuck. The pair went into business together, selling their wares via a mail order catalog for a company called *Sears & Roebuck.*

Sellers, Isiah

Isiah Sellers was an old Mississippi River pilot who wrote stories about his adventures for the New Orleans *Picayune.* The stories were self-congratulatory and always began, "My opinion for the benefit of the citizens of New Orleans." Sellers signed the articles "Mark Twain." But he was not THAT Mark Twain. A man named Samuel Clemens wrote a column in a rival paper that parodied Sellers. Sellers was so hurt by the parody that he stopped writing completely. In 1863, Clemens went on to write for the Virginia City, Nevada, *Enterprise.* While trying to decide on a pen name he learned of Sellers' death. Samuel Clemens adopted his old rival's pen name, Mark Twain, a name now known to every school child.

Sequoyah

Sequoyah was born around 1770 in the Cherokee village of Taskigi (later to be called Tuskegee by the white settlers who would take it over). He was a craftsman and storyteller. Sequoyah observed that the white men wrote their ideas down and compiled them in books, and thus thought was preserved. He said that if he could keep thoughts on paper it would be "like catching a wild animal and taming it." Sequoyah sequestered himself in the woods and in 12 years devised a written Cherokee language. It consisted of 86 characters, representing all the sounds in spoken Cherokee. Within a matter of months, almost the entire tribe had learned to read and write. Sequoyah came to be revered by his people. He went on to represent the Cherokees in Washington and to organize them into the Cherokee Nation. Shortly after his death the genus of redwoods that boasted the tallest trees in the world was named after him.

Shannon

In 1976, Beach Boy Carl Wilson suffered a loss. His beloved Irish setter, Shannon, was killed by a car. A songwriter and founding member of Sha Na Na, Henry Gross, had often opened for the Beach Boys on their concert tours. He visited Wilson shortly after the dog's death and was touched by the tale. He went home and wrote a song in Shannon's honor. Gross offered the song to the Beach Boys to record, but they were not interested in a dead-dog song, so Gross recorded it himself. The public, not realizing it was a tribute to a lost canine love, made *Shannon* a gold record. It sold 1.5 million copies and made it to number 6 on the *Billboard* charts.

Sherwin, Henry

Henry Sherwin was born in 1842 in Vermont. He quit school at 13 and took a job in a store, sleeping upstairs during his off hours. By 1859, the young man had saved enough money to go to Cleveland, where he became a successful bookkeeper for a grocery store. He soon left that job for moral reasons— he didn't want to be part of a grocery that sold alcohol. In 1870, Sherwin became part of a paint component business called Sherwin, Dunham and Griswold. It was called the paint "component" business because in those days people bought pigments separately and mixed the paints themselves. Henry Sherwin thought that his company could improve business by selling pre-mixed paint. His partners thought he was crazy, and dissolved their partnership. Sherwin still believed in his ready-mixed paint idea, so he called on a friend named Edward Williams, whom he knew to be an excellent salesman. Sherwin was right. Consumers did want to buy pre-mixed paints, and *Sherwin-Williams* is now synonymous with paint.

Shrapnel, Henry

Henry Shrapnel was born in 1761 in Bradford-on-Avon. He became a British soldier and served in Gibraltar, the West Indies, and Newfoundland. In 1784, as a second lieutenant in the British Royal Artillery, Henry Shrapnel had an idea that would change the nature of war and give the British an edge over Napoleon at Waterloo. He spent his own money to develop a new type of shell that would be filled with musket balls and gunpowder. The canister would explode in flight, spreading deadly metal fragments for hundreds of yards. The soldier was never paid for his invention, nor reimbursed for his expenses in developing it. His only payment was immortality in the form of the word *shrapnel.*

Simons, Menno

Menno Simons was born in 1496 in Witmarsum, the Netherlands, which was then under Spanish rule. In 1524, he was ordained as a Catholic priest. Soon after, he heard about a religious group known as the Anabaptists. They had received much publicity when a member of the group, Sikke Feerks, who had been baptized as an infant, was executed for being baptized again. Simons read all he could about the movement, and he found many of their beliefs to have merit. When he heard members of the group singing hymns as they were taken before the Spanish Inquisition in 1536, he was so moved that he left the Catholic Church and joined them. He was baptized, and quickly became an influential leader. Throughout his life, Simons traveled and preached. Wherever they went, he and his followers faced persecution. Their descendants are today called *Mennonites*. Worldwide, there are currently at least 500,000 practicing Mennonites.

Singer, Isaac

Isaac Merrit Singer ran away from his Oswego, New York, home in 1825, when he was only 12 years old. He joined a band of traveling players and remained an actor until he was 24. Then he decided to "get a real job." He worked at a machine shop, but continued as an actor part time. In 1850, Singer headed to Boston with a device he had created to carve wood-block type. It never caught on. But while he was in Boston, Singer became interested in another device—the sewing machine. Such machines were rare, and those that did exist were large and unreliable. He borrowed $40 from a friend and started working on his own version of the machine. In 1851, Singer received a patent for the device. It attracted the attention not only of tailors, but also of Elias Howe, often credited as the inventor of the sewing machine. Howe had patented his machine in 1846. He sued Singer, but they soon settled. Under their agreement, Singer and Howe pooled their patents and each received five dollars from every sewing machine sold. Singer was not sentimental about his machine. "I don't care a damn for the invention. The dimes are what I'm after," he once said. Singer's business partner, a man named Edward Clark, was responsible for another innovation—the installment payment plan. This payment option made sewing machines affordable for the first time in many homes. In 1863, Isaac Singer was surrounded by scandal. The public learned that he had fathered 24 children by at least 5 different women. Clark was so shocked by the revelation that he ended his partnership with Singer. Isaac Singer had too much money to be worried. He moved to England, where the scandal did not reach him. He lived there until his death in 1875. The scandal had little effect on sewing machine sales, however. Mahatma Gandhi is said to have called the Singer sewing machine "one of the few useful things ever invented." Adm. Richard Byrd found them so useful that he carted six of them all the way to the Antarctic. At its peak, Singer was producing 3 million sewing machines a year. In the mid-1970s, however, the number of people in America who sewed, or even repaired, their own clothes dropped sharply. The modern Singer company stopped selling sewing machines in 1986. Today it sells aerospace electronics.

Singh, Noonien

In the fall of 1941, a young man named Gene Roddenberry volunteered for the U.S. Army Air Corps. He was sent to the South Pacific. He was in combat at Guadalcanal, flying B-17 bombers out of the newly captured Japanese airstrip that became Henderson Field. While in the South Pacific, he met a pilot named Noonien Singh. After the war, Roddenberry began a career as a writer, eventually creating a television program called "Star Trek." By this time, Roddenberry had lost touch with Singh, but he hoped the program's visibility might attract his old friend's attention. He named a villain on the show Khan Noonien Singh. The character of Kahn was later spun off into a Star Trek film, "The Wrath of Kahn," but Roddenberry still received no word from Singh. Years later, when Roddenberry began production on a second "Star Trek" series, he tried again. This time he named the android character's inventor Noonien Soong. Neither Noonien caught Singh's attention, and the war buddies were never reunited.

Skidmore, Lucy

Lucy Scribner was born Lucy Skidmore. She had been married only four years when her husband, J. Blair Schribner, died in 1879. In her grief, her health deteriorated, and she left New York City for Saratoga, New York, which was famous for its medicinal waters. The treatment was apparently effective, and she became a permanent resident. In 1903, she opened the Young Women's Industrial Club of Saratoga in the parsonage of the Presbyterian Church. The curriculum at the school was designed to give young women a combination of technical and artistic skills. In 1911, the school's name was changed to the Skidmore School of Arts. Today *Skidmore College* has an enrollment of approximately 2,100 men and women.

Skinner, Eugene

Eugene Franklin Skinner was born in Essex, New York, on September 13, 1809. At age 14, he moved to a farm in Green County, Wisconsin. As a teenager, Skinner decided to see the world. He headed west, getting as far as Illinois. While a resident of that state, he was elected to several positions, including county sheriff. On November 28, 1839, he married a woman named Mary Cook. Unfortunately, after a few years Skinner's health began to deteriorate. He decided that perhaps another journey would cure him. So in May 1845, Skinner and his family joined a company going to California. The company spent the winter at *Sutter's Fort* and in the spring continued on to Oregon. In June of that year, Skinner built a small cabin on the west side of Ya-Po-Ah, later known as Skinner's Butte. There he founded Eugene City, Oregon, on June 6, 1853. The city was incorporated in 1862 and later changed its name to simply *Eugene.*

Skryabin, Vyacheslav Mikhailovich

Vyacheslav Skryabin was born in Kukarka, Russia, on March 9, 1890. As a student in Kazan during the Revolution of 1905, he took an interest in politics. He joined the Bolsheviks in 1906. It was then that he adopted the pseudonym "Molotov." Three years later, Molotov was arrested and exiled to the north of Russia for two years. In 1912, he and Joseph Stalin founded the Communist Party newspaper *Pravda.* Exiled to Siberia in 1915, he escaped a year later and helped to plan the 1917 revolution. His role in the revolution helped Molotov to rise rapidly in the party. In 1921, he became secretary of the Central Committee of the Communist Party. Three years later, he supported Stalin in his bid for power after Lenin's death. In 1926, he was made chairman of the Council of People's Commissars, a post he held until 1941 when Stalin assumed it himself. Molotov next became the Soviet foreign minister from 1939 to 1949 and 1953 to 1956. It was the Finnish Resistance that named the gasoline-filled bottles they hurled at the Russian tanks *Molotov cocktails.*

Smirnoff, Peter

The name Smirnoff is known to Americans today primarily because of creative advertising. Peter Smirnoff was a Russian distiller of some note. By 1886, Smirnoff's vodka was so well respected that he became the distiller of the court of Czar Alexander III. By 1900, he was producing a million bottles a day. Then history caught up with the Smirnoff family. The Czar was overthrown, and anyone associated with him was in grave danger. A fourth-generation member of the Smirnoff family, Vladimir Smirnoff, managed to escape to France, where he opened a new distillery. A former Smirnoff supplier, Rudolph Kunett, had made it to America, and when he learned that Smirnoff had gone into business in France, he bought the rights to manufacture the drink in the United States. In 1934, he imported the first Smirnoff vodka. No one liked it. Even the many Russian immigrants turned up their noses at it. Kunett tried marketing whiskey instead, but it too failed. When Vladimir Smirnoff died in 1939, Kunett felt the time was right to give up on vodka, and he sold the business to G. F. Hublein and Company. There were 2,000 full bottles left in the factory when Kunett sold it, but there were no vodka corks left. So they used the leftover Smirnoff's whiskey corks. The bottles were then shipped off to the south. The salesman accompanying them was curious about this colorless whiskey and sampled it. Right away he came up with a slogan to advertise the product: "Smirnoff's White Whiskey, No Taste, No Smell." He sold out right away. *Smirnoff's* is today the best-selling liquor in the United States.

Smith, Lyman Cornelius

Lyman Cornelius Smith was fascinated with the possibilities of a new machine he was working on. He and his brothers Wilbert, Monroe, and Hurlbut were Syracuse, New York, gunmakers in the mid-1800s. In 1887, Smith convinced his brothers to join him in the manufacturing of a new device—the typewriter. The first crude writing machine had been built in 1868 by Christopher Latham Sholes of Milwaukee, Wisconsin. E. Remington & Sons improved it and released the "Sholes & Glidden Type Writer." It typed only capital letters. By 1878, the "No. 2 Type Writer" had both capital and lower case letters. Smith wanted to create a typewriter that would allow a typist to use both upper and lower case letters without shifting. The first Smith Brothers typewriter, the "Smith Premier Typewriter No. I," was introduced in 1889. In 1903, the Smiths became the *L. C. Smith & Brothers Typewriter Company*. In 1926, they merged with Corona Typewriter Company, and *Smith-Corona* was born. The company introduced the first portable electronic typewriter in 1957. Smith-Corona continued to prosper until the 1990s, when the typewriter was largely replaced by computers. With typewriters a dying breed, the company filed for bankruptcy protection in 1995. The company still exists, but it no longer sells the product that made it famous.

Smithson, James

In his lifetime, chemist and mineralogist James Smithson never set foot in the United States. He was an Englishman, born in France, to widow Elizabeth Macie. His father was the Duke of Northumberland, Hugh Smithson. When he died, James Smithson mysteriously bequeathed his entire estate to the United States for the establishment of an institution "for the increase and diffusion of knowledge among men." After eight years of congressional argument, the *Smithsonian Institution* was established. More than 20 million people visit its buildings every year. And Smithson, who never visited the nation in his life, now resides in death in a tomb in one of the Smithsonian buildings. A white zinc carbonate was also named in his honor. It is called *smithsonite*.

Smucker, Jerome Monroe

Jerome Smucker was descended from Swiss immigrants. The original family name was "Schmucker." In America, the name was changed first to Smoker. But Jerome's father, Gideon, strongly opposed smoking, and so the name was changed again to Smucker. In 1879, Jerome Smucker opened a cider mill near his Orrville, Ohio, home. He sold his cider for a penny a gallon. Like most cider mill operators, Smucker sold other products made from apples, including apple butter. To increase the popularity of this product, Smucker peddled the butter door to door to neighborhood housewives. Sales of the apple butter grew steadily until in 1915 he sold more than

$59,000 worth of it. This convinced Smucker to invest in better machinery for making and canning the apple butter. In 1923, apple butter sales were so good that Smucker decided to expand his product line and sell other types of preserves. *Smucker's* jams and jellies began selling nationally in 1942.

Sopwith, Thomas

Thomas Sopwith was a self-taught pilot. He apparently had a good teacher, because in 1910 he won the De Forest Prize for the longest flight from England to continental Europe. He won England's first aerial derby two years later. That same year, he founded the Sopwith Aviation Company. The company made the planes used by the Royal Flying Corps in World War I. The warplanes were named for animals. There was the Sopwith Cuckoo and the Sopwith Pup, but they never gained the fame of the Sopwith Camel, which brought down 1,300 enemy pilots. Fans of the comic strip "Peanuts" will remember that World War I flying ace Snoopy flew an imaginary Sopwith Camel into his battles with the Red Baron.

Stanford, Leland, Jr.

Leland Stanford was born in 1824 in New York State. He studied law and opened a law office in Port Washington, Wisconsin. His brothers soon convinced him to come with them to California, where he prospered as a railroad builder. In 1861, he was elected governor of California. As governor, he was in a position to give land grants to the Pacific and Central Pacific Railway Companies, of which he was a shareholder. The result was that he became quite wealthy. But his actions did not damage his political career. He became a United States senator and served for eight years. In 1884, Stanford suffered a personal tragedy when his beloved son, Leland Stanford, Jr., died at the age of 15. A simple tombstone would not be a fitting memorial for the boy, his father decided. Instead, he founded Leland Stanford, Jr., University on his San Francisco ranch. He left an additional $2.5 million to *Stanford University* in his will.

Stanley, Edward

Edward Stanley was the 12th Earl of Derby. The title of Earl of Derby has been held by the Stanley family since 1485. The first Earl of Derby was Thomas Stanley, the stepfather of Henry VII. He was given the title as a reward for deserting Richard III at the Battle of Bosworth, thus helping Henry rise to the throne. The title of the earldom was not taken from the town of Derby, but from West Derby in Lancashire. It was there that Thomas' grandfather, Sir John Stanley, was, as Shakespeare once wrote, "spacious in the possession of dirt." There were many earls of Derby of distinction, including the 14th earl, another Edward Stanley, who was prime minister three times. This particular earl was not one of them, however. Stanley served in Parliament, but for the most part, he preferred a life of leisure, including horse racing. It was because of his sponsorship of the first Epsom Downs that we call some horse races derbies today. The black, bowl-shaped hat that Americans call a derby (the British prefer the term *bowler*) takes its name from the race. When such hats were manufactured in America for the first time, they were advertised as the type of hat that was worn at the *derby*.

Stanley, Frederick Trent

Frederick Trent Stanley was born in 1803 in Connecticut. He began his career selling locks that he and his brother William had made. Business was marginal, and when the Panic of 1837 struck, it went under. To get away from all the people he owed, he moved to Mississippi for a time, but returned to Connecticut in 1843. He brought with him enough money to buy a former armory to house the Stanley Bolt Manufactory. Stanley sold his bolts from a horse-drawn wagon. In 1852, with the help of five friends, he was able to expand operations. He renamed the company *the Stanley Works*. In its first year, the company lost $361. By 1995, however, sales exceeded $2.6 billion. Today Stanley is one of the world's most recognized brand names for tools and hardware, with over 50,000 different products.

Steinweg, Heinrich

Heinrich Engelhardt Steinweg was born on February 15, 1797, the youngest of 12 children. By the time he was 15, Steinweg had lost all of his brothers and his father to the Napoleonic Wars. His mother died of exposure while hiding from soldiers, and Steinweg was left alone. He, too, was drafted into the army in 1815. He survived his military service, and despite a complete lack of musical training began a career as an instrument maker. His first creation was a zither. In 1818, he found a job at an organ builder's shop. Legend has it that he built his first piano in his kitchen and presented it to his bride, Juliane Thiemer, as a wedding gift. They later had seven children. In 1849, as the political climate in Germany became unstable again, one of their sons, Theodore, emigrated to America. A year later his father followed. On March 5, 1853, Steinweg opened a piano factory that he christened with an Americanized version of the family name: *Henry Steinway and Sons.*

Stetson, John Batterson

John Batterson Stetson was born in New Jersey in 1830. As a young man, he worked as an apprentice for his father, a milliner. This work was not adventurous enough for young Stetson, who headed west in a quest for clean air and better prospects. Working as a trapper, he looked for ways to keep the harsh sun off his face. He used his millinery training and sewed pelts together to produce large, wide-brimmed hats that could double as a bowl for water if needed. The hats were very popular among the Western pioneers. When he returned to the East Coast in 1865, he established the John B. Stetson Manufacturing Company of Philadelphia with $100. By the time of his death, the factory was producing 2 million 10-gallon hats a year. Today we know these hats as *Stetsons*, but at one time people referred to them as "the Boss of the Plains Hat" or "John Bs."

Stouffer, Abraham and Mahala

Mr. and Mrs. Stouffer opened a small lunch counter in Cleveland in 1922. The menu was not grand—it had three different sandwiches, apple pie, buttermilk, and coffee. The counter earned the couple enough to open a real sit-down restaurant, which they named the Stouffer Lunch. The restaurant was popular enough to allow the Stouffers to open branches in Detroit, Pittsburgh, and New York. After World War II, Wally Blankinship, a manager at one of the Stouffer's Cleveland eateries, began freezing the restaurant meals for customers who wanted to cook them at home. The frozen meals were in such demand that a store next to the restaurant started to carry them. When the Stouffers saw how popular the dishes were, they decided to give the frozen-food business a try. In 1954, they launched *Stouffer Foods Corporation*, and the rest is frozen-food history.

Stover, Russell

In 1921, Russell Stover, a superintendent for an Omaha ice cream company, met Christian Nelson. Nelson was a failed entrepreneur who was earning $20 a week racking balls in a pool hall. He had hoped to make his fortune selling a chocolate-covered ice cream bar, which he called the "I-Scream" bar. Stover liked the idea and agreed to form a partnership with Nelson. Stover's first act as a partner was to change the bar's name to "Eskimo Pie." With the new name, it was a stunning success. There was only one problem. Copycats around the country began selling their own "Eskimo Pies," and Stover and Nelson spent most of their time and money in court trying to defend the rights to their patent. Stover soon tired of the battle and sold his half of the company to his partner. With the money, he opened a candy store in Denver and was soon a success selling boxed chocolates.

Stradivari, Antonio

Antonio Stradivari was born in Cremona, Italy. He worked as an apprentice to violin craftsman Niccolo Amati until Amati's death in 1684. Stradivari began to experiment with the structure of the violin. He created an instrument with a slightly longer body and flatter arch than previous violins. He earned a reputation for excellence that has not diminished over the years. He continued crafting violins until he was 93, more than a thousand violins in all. His creations, called by a Latinized form of his name, are marked with a Maltese cross and the initials A. S. Collectors have been known to pay as much as $1 million for a genuine *Stradivarius.*

Strauss, Levi

During the gold rush a young entrepreneur saw an opportunity to strike gold—not from the ground but from the '49ers themselves. He traveled to California to sell canvas tents to the prospectors. When he got there, however, he discovered that prospectors had a greater need for sturdy clothing than for tents. Strauss constructed work pants from the canvas and called them "waist high overalls." The secret to Levi's success, however, was not entirely in the strong fabric he used, but in an innovation from a Jewish tailor who had migrated from Latvia. Jacob Davis heard complaints from a prospector by the name of Alkali Ike, who was always ripping his blue jeans at the seams. Davis solved the problem by sewing rivets into them. He wrote to Strauss with his suggestion, and for $68 Strauss bought the patent. In 1872, Davis wrote to Strauss suggesting that they split the patent. "The secratt of them Pents is the Rivits that I put in those Pockets," Davis explained. Strauss was unmoved by the request.

Stuckey, William

William Stuckey began his career in 1931 as a pecan peddler. He bought his pecans with $35 borrowed from his grandmother. He then sold them door to door. Stuckey prospered in the pecan business. In 1936, he sold $150,000 worth. The pecan proceeds allowed him to open a candy store in Eastmand, Georgia. After World War II, he began building candy and nut shops along the country's new highways. He then added gas pumps so travelers could fuel up and buy a pecan roll for the road. He built 29 of the shops in 8 years. Stuckey sold his business to Pet, Inc., in 1964. They kept the name *Stuckey's.*

Sucatus, Magonus

Magonus Sucatus was Welsh-Italian, born in the 5th century in Roman-occupied Britain to a Roman officer and his Welsh wife.

In the year 395, Sucatus traveled to Gaul to begin theological studies. He wanted to bring religion to the godless people of backward Ireland. He was ordained as a bishop in 432 and given the name Particus, or Patrick. Patrick was not the first Christian missionary sent to Ireland. That honor went to Saint Palladius. Patrick is most noted for driving the snakes out of Ireland, but scientists say there were no snakes there to begin with, so it probably wasn't that hard to do. Patrick used the native clover to teach the concept of the Holy Trinity, although the Druids of Ireland had used the plant as being symbolic of the regenerative powers of nature. When Patrick was canonized, church officials weren't sure whether he was born on March 8 or March 9. So they decided to honor him on the 17th—the sum of the two dates. Thus, despite the fact that St. Patrick was not Irish, did not drive the snakes from Ireland, and was distrustful of the Irish heathens, he is now the patron saint of the Irish and Irish-Americans. Perhaps that is why his feast day is celebrated by drinking large quantities of beer and telling tall tales.

Sutter, John

John Sutter was not a man blessed with good luck. He was born of Swiss parents in a small German town. After serving as a Swiss guard in the French campaign against Spain, he got a job as a clerk for a cloth merchant. Things seemed to be going well for Sutter in 1826 when he married his sweetheart and started his own cloth and yarn business. The business went bankrupt. In 1834, Sutter left his wife and four children to try his luck in America. First, he sailed to Missouri to try his hand at exploring the Missouri River. His boat was wrecked, and once again Sutter lost everything. In 1839, he found himself in a region that was then part of Mexico. He built a settlement and a fort he modestly called *Sutter's Fort*. He built a blacksmith shop, a tannery, and a sawmill. In 1846, the Bear Flag Revolt transferred the area of Mexico he lived in to the United States. Sutter's luck appeared to have changed. His business was booming, and he had built a second sawmill about 40 miles east of his fort. In January 1848, Sutter's partner, James Marshall, discovered gold at *Sutter's Mill*. One would think that the discovery of gold on your land would be a great stroke of luck, and at first it seemed to be. Sutter sent for his family in 1849, as the '49ers began crossing the land in search of gold. Soon Sutter's land was overrun by prospectors and people hoping to cash in on the prospectors. Sutter spent years in court trying to prove his claim to the land, but the Supreme Court ruled that it was invalid. Sutter, whose name became synonymous with gold, was forced once again into bankruptcy. In 1885, he died, despondent and broke.

Suzuki, Michio

Around 1910, in the small seacoast village of Hamamatsu, Japan, Michio Suzuki opened a company to build weaving looms. Suzuki was a man blessed with an eye for quality and innovation and an ability to adapt quickly to changing circumstances. His company quickly rose to prominence. Suzuki's textile loom displaced the previously dominant British and Dutch products, and he was awarded the Blue Ribbon Medal by the government of Japan for his contribution to the growth of the nation's economy. By the mid-1930s, Suzuki was looking for a new product to help the company grow. In 1937, he decided that the new product would be the automobile. By 1939, the company had built its first compact cars. Suzuki's automobile production stopped during the early 1940s since passenger cars were not essential to the war effort. Suzuki tried focusing on the loom business, but there was not enough demand for new textiles. To stay in business during such difficult times, Suzuki built whatever he could sell, from farm tools to musical instruments. After the war, he returned to textile production. Then the cotton market in Japan collapsed. He decided to return to vehicle production, but instead of building automobiles, he produced a motorized bicycle called the "Power Free." By 1954, Suzuki was producing 6,000 motorcycles per month and had changed the name of the firm to *Suzuki Motor Company, Ltd.*

Suzuki, Shinichi

Born in 1898, the son of a violin manufacturer, Shinichi Suzuki believed that the best and most effective way to learn music is to be exposed to it from a very early age. In 1946, the violinist established a music institute in his hometown of Matsumoto. Two years later, it became known as the Talent Education Institute. The name referred to Suzuki's philosophy that musical "gifts," or "talents," are not inborn but nurtured. In teaching a child music, he believed he was creating a medium for the child's emotional and spiritual growth. His method involved teaching children at a very early age, so that music would become second nature, like one's native language. Suzuki called his method the "mother tongue" method, but most people today call it the *Suzuki method.* Suzuki's institute now has branches all over the world and more than 300,000 students.

Swafford, Sherrie

In 1983, Sherrie Swafford was dating a musician, Steve Perry, who was working on a solo album. One evening, Swafford sat in on a song-writing session with Perry and fellow musicians Craig Krampf and Bill Cuomo. After a few hours, she got tired and went to bed. After she left, an idea for a new song came to Perry. The trio finished the song around five o'clock in the morning. It was called "*Oh, Sherrie.*" The song, an ode to everlasting love, became Steve Perry's biggest solo hit. It hit number 3 on the *Billboard* charts in April 1984. Swafford played herself in the accompanying music video. She never did become Sherrie Perry, though. They broke up shortly after the single was released.

Swanson, Carl

Carl Swanson was the perfect example of the American Dream at work. He arrived in America as a Swedish immigrant with no money and speaking no English. He settled in Nebraska, where he started a small grocery business. It grew to be one of the largest turkey processors in the country. When brothers Gilbert and Clarke Swanson took over the company, they had a lot of business, but only once a year—at Thanksgiving. To try to sell more turkey, the brothers made a turkey pot pie. The pot pie was so successful that the Swansons were able to sponsor a television show, "Ted Mack's Amateur Hour." On the night of the premiere, the Swansons invited a group of friends over to watch the show. When they saw their friends eating in front of the television set, they were inspired. They were already working on a series of frozen dinners in aluminum trays. Why not market them as dinners to eat in front of the television? In 1952, they released a frozen turkey dinner to the public. On the box was a television set and the words *Swanson TV Dinner*.

T

Tafari, Ras

In the early 1900s, a charismatic Jamaican leader named Marcus Garvey earned himself a loyal following with his prediction that a black king would be crowned and that he would be the God of the black race. In 1930, Prince Ras Tafari of Ethiopia became emperor and took the name Haile Selassie. Garvey's followers saw this as a fulfillment of Garvey's prophecy. His followers, once known as Garveyites, came to be known as *Rastafarians*. Rastifarians believe that Selassie, who died in 1975, is a deity and that he will guide them back to the promised land of Africa. They use marijuana (ganja) as a sacrament, just as Christians use bread and wine. They also adopted the Nazarite law, which prohibits the cutting of their hair, and so they are seen wearing long dreadlocks. Many mainstream Americans have been introduced to the outward symbols of the movement through its music, reggae.

Tasman, Abel Janszoon

Abel Tasman was born in the Netherlands in 1603. Around 1632, he entered the service of the Dutch East India Company. He was later chosen as second in command for an exploratory voyage in the north Pacific. In 1642, Anthony Van Diemen, the governor-general of the company, nominated Tasman to investigate the possibility of a Pacific Ocean passage to Chile. On November 24, 1642, he discovered an island, previously unknown to all but its inhabitants. He named it *Van Diemen's Land*. It was still called by that name during the days when England used Australia as a prison colony, and so there are many folksongs from the time which refer to being transported to Van Diemen's Land. (The Irish rock band U2 even did a song by that name in the late 1980s.) People back then assumed, however, that Van Diemen's Land was a part of the main continent. In 1855, the island's name was changed to *Tasmania*. Many Americans know of Tasmania primarily because of the *Tasmanian devil*. In *Warner Brothers* cartoons, it is a large, brown creature with fangs that travels by turning itself into a mini-tornado. The actual Tasmanian devil, or *Sarcophilus harrisii*, is about the size of a badger and has no tornado-like capabilities. Once the little devils roamed the land down under, but because they killed large numbers of livestock and poultry, they were widely hunted and now exist only in Tasmania. A fellow marsupial, the *Tasmanian wolf*, is believed to be extinct.

Tesla, Nikola

Tesla was an eccentric inventor who had a clean fetish and used 18 towels after every bath. He would test his inventions by running electricity through his body. He claimed to be in contact with aliens and some have even suggested that he was from outer space. When he died, at age 87, he held 700 patents, including one for the first electric power plant. He developed ideas for radar and radio-controlled rockets. In the International Measurement System, a unit of magnetic-flux density is now known as the *tesla*. The hard rock band Tesla also took its name from the scientist.

Thespis

Thespis was a Greek poet, born in Attica. In his day, most dramatic performances consisted of a choir that sang and danced the stories of the gods. The choruses recited passages in unison. The theatrical form known as tragedy developed out of a chorus singing and dancing in honor of Dionysus, god of transformation. The word "tragedy" itself comes from the Greek *tagoidia*, meaning "goat song." Whether there were actually singing goats is left to the imagination. It was around 530 B.C. that Thespis decided to add to his chorus a single performer who would speak a prologue. It is believed that Thespis spoke the prologue himself, which would make him the first actor. He is also said to have introduced the use of face painting and masks to disguise the performers. The poet also gave the world the word *thespian,* meaning "actor." In 534 B.C. Thespis won a prize for his "goat song" in Athens. He was awarded, fittingly, a goat.

Thomas, Wendy

Wendy was the nickname of one of three children born to Dave and Lorraine Thomas. The couple met when they were both working at a Hobby House restaurant in Fort Wayne, Indiana. Dave Thomas was then 15 years old and living on his own. He was an orphan and grew up in boarding houses. Now he was living at the YMCA, and working in the restaurant's kitchen. Lorraine was a waitress. Thomas, who never finished high school, worked in a series of restaurants, including a stint as a Kentucky Fried Chicken manager. Then, in 1969, Dave Thomas decided to take a shot at his own fast food chain. On November 15, 1969, he opened his first restaurant in downtown Columbus, Ohio. He named it for his third daughter, Wendy. Today there are more than 4,800 *Wendy's* restaurants in the United States. Dave Thomas has become a national celebrity by appearing in television commercials. At the age of 60, he finally earned his high school diploma. After studying with a tutor for three months, he passed the General Education Degree test and attended the graduation ceremonies at Coconut Creek High School in Florida. He wore a cap and gown, took his wife of 45 years to the senior prom, and was voted Most Likely to Succeed.

Thompson, William

William Thompson was born in Belfast on June 26, 1824. In 1846, he became professor of natural philosophy at the University of Glasgow. There he established the first physics laboratory in Great Britain and presented groundbreaking lectures and scientific papers. His experiments on the mechanical properties of heat, inspired by the work of *James*

Joule, greatly improved the steam engine. The two great laws of thermodynamics, the law of equivalence and the law of transformation, are based on Thomson's conclusions. He also proposed a metric temperature scale based on absolute zero. In the scale, absolute zero is zero degrees, ice melts at about 273 degrees, and water boils at about 373 degrees. In recognition of his contributions to science, Thompson was awarded the title of Lord Kelvin in 1892. The temperature scale that he proposed is known as the *Kelvin scale.* One thing that Kelvin did not possess, however, was a knack for predictions. He once said, "I have not the smallest molecule of faith in aerial navigation other than ballooning." And at an address to the British Association for the Advancement of Science in 1900, he said, "There is nothing new to be discovered in physics now. All that remains is more and more precise measurement."

Tiffany, Charles

Charles Tiffany was born February 15, 1812, in Killingly, Connecticut. He began his career in the country store operated by his father. In 1837, Tiffany's father lent him $500, and with another $500 contributed by a partner, John Young, he opened a stationery and fancy goods store on Broadway. Tiffany & Young's first two days sales amounted to only $4.95, and their first week's profits were a meager 33 cents. Of course, it got better. Within 12 years, Tiffany's inventory had grown to include watches, clocks, silverware, and bronzeware. In 1845, Tiffany and Young published "The Catalogue of Useful and Fancy Articles," its first mail-order catalog. The company continued to grow and thrive, in part because of Charles Tiffany's showmanship. He sold bits of the transatlantic cable, laid in 1850. He designed a tiny silver horse and carriage for the wedding of P. T. Barnum's famous midgets, Tom Thumb and Lavinia. Most notably, he bought and sold Marie Antoinette's Girdle of Diamonds and several other French crown jewels. In 1853, Tiffany bought out his partner, and moved the business, which he renamed *Tiffany & Company,* uptown. In 1867, Tiffany became the first American silvermaker to earn first prize at the Paris Exposition Universelle, enhancing his reputation even further. Ten years later, Tiffany purchased a large diamond that had been extracted from the new Kimberly Mines in South Africa. The *Tiffany Diamond* is the largest flawless and perfectly colored canary diamond ever mined. By then, Tiffany was selling about $6 million in diamonds each year. In 1885, Tiffany redesigned the Great Seal of the United States, which is still on the American dollar. When he died in 1902, Charles Tiffany was worth $35 million. The Tiffany Company continued to prosper. In 1940, Tiffany's opened a new Fifth Avenue store, the first fully air-conditioned building in New York. In 1961, the movie *Breakfast at Tiffany's*, based on the book by Truman Capote and starring Audrey Hepburn, was released, making the name Tiffany familiar to those who had never been to New York. In the 1990s, the pop band Deep Blue Something had a hit with a song also called "Breakfast at Tiffany's," which alludes to the film.

Tiffany, Louis Comfort

Charles Tiffany was disappointed that his son Louis wanted to study art instead of joining the Tiffany Company. After studying painting with artists George Inness and Samuel Colman in New York City, Louis went to study in Paris. He continued to travel. He went all the way to the Middle East and was intrigued by the iridescence of ancient glass he found there. When he returned to New York in 1879, his father helped Louis found the Associated Artists interior design studio, a decorator service. In 1885, Louis established a glass-making factory and experimented with stained glass for decorative art objects, inventing a process for making an opalescent glass known as *Tiffany favrile glass*. "Favrile" is an Old English word meaning "handmade." Louis was also known for his lamps, which used colored glass to make a lampshade that glows in daylight as well as at night. *Tiffany lamp* has become a generic term for such a fixture, whether it was actually made by Tiffany or not. The name tiffany has made its way into Webster's dictionary, which defines it as an adjective meaning "being glass or an article of glass made by or in the manner of Louis C. Tiffany." After his father's death, Tiffany finally took charge of the company.

Townshend, Thomas

Thomas Townshend's blood was blue. He was born in 1733, the grandson of Charles Townshend, the Second Viscount Townshend, eldest son of Sir Horatio, First Viscount Townshend of Raynham, in Norfolk. Following family tradition, Thomas Townshend graduated from Clare College, Cambridge, and then entered Parliament in 1754. He was made Lord of the Treasury in 1765, Joint Paymaster of the Forces in 1767, and Secretary of War in 1782. In 1783, his title was elevated from Baron to First Viscount Sydney. By 1788, Townshend had become the British Home Secretary. That year Captain Arthur Phillip established the first European settlement in Australia. He named it *Sydney Cove*, after the viscount.

Toyoda, Sakichi

Sakichi Toyoda created Japan's first power loom, which became the cornerstone of the Japanese textile machinery industry. To sell the looms, Toyoda built a company called Toyoda Shoten in the seaside city of Nagoya. In 1935, his son, Kiichiro, expanded the family business to include automobiles. The first vehicle to be marketed by the fledgling automaker was the Model G1 truck in 1935. But the road to automobile success was to be long. Auto manufacturing stopped at the plant during World War II. After the war, while United States automakers were experiencing booming sales, Japanese industry was slowly rebuilding. The automakers of Tokyo laughed at the idea of cars being built at Toyoda's loom works, located in the Japanese equivalent of the boondocks, but the Toyoda family was not deterred. They worked with nearby supplier plants to produce the cars as efficiently as possible. When the company began exporting its cars, they changed the spelling of the name to *Toyota*. They're not laughing any more. Today Toyota is Japan's biggest manufacturer and the world's third largest automaker, behind General Motors and Ford.

Tupper, Earl Silas

Earl Silas Tupper was born in 1907 on a farm in New Hampshire. While working as a *DuPont* chemist in the 1930s, he became convinced that plastic was the material of the future. So in 1938 he left DuPont to form his own company, Tupper Plastics. He began experimenting with plastic shoe heels, and eventually moved on to bathroom cups. By 1945, he had created a plastic cup out of pastel polyethylene, or, as he called it, Poly-T. Next he crafted plastic bowls with tops that sealed in air. These he called "Poly-T Wonder Bowls." For the most part, the public simply wondered what the bowls were, and they weren't curious enough to buy them to find out. It was a fortuitous accident that changed all that. A Detroit woman named Brownie Wise had been given a set of the new plastic bowls. "It took me three days to figure out how the seal worked," she said. Once she had the bowl sealed, she dropped it one day as she was putting it into the refrigerator. Instead of breaking open, it bounced and remained sealed. Wise was sold, and she decided to start selling. She was already selling Stanley Home Products at demonstration parties, and she added *Tupperware* to her line. She was so successful with the parties that Tupper decided to sell the products exclusively at home parties. By the late 1970s, more than $900 million worth of Tupperware was being sold at parties each year.

U/V/W

Upjohn, William Erastus

Dr. William Erastus Upjohn graduated from the University of Michigan in 1875 and opened a medical practice in Hastings, Michigan. At the time, most pills had hard coatings that often did not dissolve in the stomach. They simply passed through. Upjohn set to work to develop a better pill, and in 1885, at age 32, he patented his first "friable" pill. "Friable" does not mean that it could be fried, but that it could be crushed. A year later, Upjohn and his brother Henry opened the Upjohn Pill and Granule Company in Kalamazoo, Michigan. Henry died a year later, but two other Upjohn brothers soon joined the company. The company introduced more pills, tablets, and a highly successful laxative called Phenolax. After some family squabbles, W. E. Upjohn bought out his brothers. He hired a researcher named Frederick W. Heyl to develop new products. In 1920, Upjohn turned over the daily operations of his company to others and spent the majority of his time gardening until his death in 1932. Today, the combined Pharmacia and Upjohn company has more than 30,000 employees worldwide and annual sales of more than $7 billion.

Valentine

There were two (some sources say three) Christian martyrs by the name of Valentine who were sainted and share a feast day of February 14. One of the Valentines lived in Terni in Umbria and performed miracles around the year 220. A philosopher named Crato who heard of the bishop's powers to heal asked him to come to Rome and cure his terminally ill son. Valentine agreed to do so if Crato would agree to convert to Christianity. He did. Many of Crato's students were also convinced and became Christians. This angered the prefect, Abundius. To stop all this conversion, he had Valentine beheaded. His body was taken back to Terni, and he became the patron saint of that city. The second Valentine was also a Christian bishop who lived in Rome around the year 270 under the reign of Emperor Claudius II. Claudius believed that married men made poor soldiers, so to ensure that Rome would have a strong military, he outlawed marriage. Valentine disagreed with the edict, and continued to marry young lovers in secret. He was brought before Claudius, who told Valentine that he could live if he would convert and follow the Roman gods. Valentine refused, and was beheaded on February 24. Before Christianity took hold in Rome, there had been an annual celebration in honor of the god Lupercus. The fertility festival took place in mid-February. One of the most popular parts of the festival was a game in which the names of young unmarried women were placed in a box, and drawn out at random by the young men. The young man and woman would then spend the next year in each other's company. When Christianity became the religion of the land, the popular old festival was no longer encouraged, but church officials knew that simply outlawing the festivities would meet with opposition. In 496, Pope Gelasius outlawed the Lupercus celebration, but replaced it with a similar festival with a Christian theme. Now the young people drew the names of saints from the box and were expected to emulate the life of the saint for the next year. The patron of the new festival was *St. Valentine*. Still, the original, more romantic intentions could not be suppressed, and *Valentine's Day* came to be known as a lover's holiday once again.

Van Allen, James

James Van Allen was a rocket scientist. Born in Mount Pleasant, Iowa, in 1914, he graduated from Mt. Pleasant High School as valedictorian in 1931. As the chairman of the physics department at the State University of Iowa, he focused on high altitude research and rocket development. He studied cosmic rays and supervised work on the first U.S. satellite. The satellite carried a package of instruments that measured micrometeorites and the temperature within the satellite. The instruments were called the *Van Allen package*. As he continued his work with cosmic rays and radiation, Van Allen discovered radiation belts around the Earth. They were named the *Van Allen Belts* in his honor.

Vandiver, Pendelton

Pendelton Vandiver lived in the hills of Kentucky. He was loved in his community for his musical skill and entertaining personality. When his family got together, the old man would play his fiddle and everyone would dance and sing. One of the relatives at those get-togethers was Vandiver's nephew, a youngster named Bill Monroe. Monroe was so taken with the man's playing that he decided to take up the fiddle, too. After his uncle died, Monroe continued to play his music. Bill Monroe and His Blue Grass Boys went on to become regulars on the Grand Ole Opry. The musician was always inspired by his uncle's memory, and finally he wrote a song called "*Uncle Pen.*" In the early 1980s, country star Ricky Scaggs decided to record the bluegrass number as a tribute to *his* musical inspiration, Bill Monroe. In October 1984, "Uncle Pen" finally reached the top of the country charts.

Van Rensselaer, Stephen

After Stephen Van Rensselaer of Albany, New York, graduated from *Harvard*, he returned to the Albany area, where he became lieutenant-governor of New York and later congressman. He was also a wealthy landowner, with real estate in three counties, one of which is now called *Rensselaer*. Despite, or perhaps because of, his classical education, Rensselaer believed in practical training. So he established a school to teach the "business of living" to the children of farmers and mechanics. In 1832, the name of the school was changed from Rensselaer School to Rensselaer Institute. Then in 1861 it was changed again to *Rensselaer Polytechnic Institute*.

Vernon, Edward

Edward Vernon was a Vice Admiral of the Royal Navy. He fought in the battle of Jenkin's Ear and was a friend of George Washington's brother. Because of this relationship, *Mount Vernon* was named in his honor. Vernon, however, was not terribly popular with his men. The soldier's gave him the nickname "Old Grog" because of his heavily textured grogram cloak. Vernon became very unpopular when he ordered that Navy rum be watered down to make it harder for sailors to become inebriated. The men gave the nickname "grog" to this unpalatable drink.

Vespucci, Amerigo

Amerigo Vespucci was born in Florence, Italy, and grew up to be an explorer. As a young man, Vespucci worked as a merchant while studying navigation. One of his first major voyages was in 1499, when he traveled to South America on a Spanish expedition. He later took part in a Portuguese expedition in 1501. In a letter written in 1504, Vespucci claimed that he had also made an earlier voyage in 1497, and that he was the first European to set foot in the New World. Many modern scholars do not believe Vespucci's claim. But he was convincing enough at the time. In 1507, a German mapmaker, Martin Waldseemuller, suggested that the new continent be named with the Greek or Latin version of Vespucci's name: Americus or America. National Public Radio's commentator Leslie Blunetta has pointed out that Amerigo is the Italian equivalent of "Henry," making this country, in essence, the United States of Henry. "How much patriotism could we instill by requiring our schoolchildren to chant, 'I pledge allegiance to the flag of the United States of Henry'?" she asks. "And how much worse would our trade deficit be if General Motors tried to attack the Japanese with, 'It's the heartbeat of Henry, it's today's Chevrolet.'"

Vick, Joshua

Joshua Vick was a medical doctor and pharmacist in North Carolina in the early 1900s. Vick gave a job to his brother-in-law, H. S. Richardson, who was studying for his own pharmacist's licence. Richardson went on to a variety of odd jobs. He worked as a streetcar conductor and as a blanket salesman before his father, Lunsford Richardson, asked him to take over his "home remedy" business. The elder Richardson had also run a drugstore in the little town of Slema, North Carolina. Most of his customers complained of the common ailments, cold and flu. In those days, people treated congestion by placing plasters on the chest to increase the flow of blood to that area. Many of the ingredients in the plasters were simply ineffective, and sometimes they caused the skin to blister and swell. Richardson started working on a more effective salve that would use a new ingredient, menthol. The result was a chest rub called "Richardson's Croup and Pneumonia Cure Salve." The menthol scent opened the air passages, while the salve stimulated the flow of blood in the chest. Richardson went on to develop several other "home cures" and to launch his own company, "Richardson's Home Remedies." By the time he handed the business over to his son in 1907, the company had 19 products. Most of them, however, were ineffective. H. S. decided that his first task was to drop all of the products but one—the menthol salve. He also changed the name of his father's formula. First, he called the product Vick's Salve, after his brother-in-law. Later the name was changed again to *Vick's Vaporub*.

Vitus

Born in Southern Italy, Vitus was instructed in Christianity by his tutor, Modestus, and his nurse, Crescentia. Vitus' father was a senator and a proud follower of old-time religion, which is what we'd now call pagan. Outraged that his son had been converted, he had all three heretics arrested. It is said that while they were in prison, angels came to dance with them. The Christians were sent to the lions, but the lions refused to eat them. So they were boiled in oil instead. Vitus became a sainted martyr, the patron of actors, comedians, dancers, and the island of Sicily. In Germany, it was said that anyone who danced in front of St. Vitus' statue on his feast day, June 15, would have good health for a year. The enthusiastic dancing of believers reminded people of involuntary spasms that accompany some nervous disorders. Chorea, the technical name for the affliction, became popularly known as *St. Vitus dance.* "Chorea," incidentally, comes from Greek, and also means "dance."

Volta, Alessandro Giuseppe Antonio Anastasio

Alessandro Volta was born in Como, Italy, and educated in public schools there. In 1774, he became professor of physics at the Royal School, and the following year he devised the electrophorus, an instrument that produced charges of static electricity. Next, he applied himself to chemistry, studying atmospheric electricity and devising experiments such as the ignition of gases by an electric spark in a closed vessel. In 1779, he became professor of physics at the University of Pavia, a chair he occupied for 25 years. By 1800, he had developed the so-called *voltaic pile,* a forerunner of the electric battery, which produced a steady stream of electricity. In honor of his work in the field of electricity, Napoleon made him a count. The *volt,* an electrical unit, is named for him.

Walker, John

Not to be confused with the English druggist who invented the friction match, this John Walker was born in 1805, and by the time he was 15 he owned a distillery. The concoction of choice? Scotch whisky. It was Walker's two sons, George and Alexander, who made *Johnnie Walker* a worldwide brand. The striding man on the bottle of Johnnie Walker is the company's founder. In 1933, the Walkers were granted a royal warrant of appointment to supply whisky to King George V, and in case you wondered what the royals drink, Johnnie Walker is still an official source of spirits for the British monarchy. Scotch whisky is Scottish. British law states that it can only be produced in Scotland—but don't call the people who make it Scotch, unless you want to be laughed at. They're Scots. About 85 percent of the whisky made in Scotland is exported. The United Kingdom is, in fact, the world's largest exporter of spirits. About 7.5 million cases of that is Johnnie Walker Red Label, which outsells its nearest rival by almost a million cases a year.

Walton, Sam

Sam Walton was born in Kingfisher, Oklahoma, in 1918. His family was poor, and Walton learned the value of a dollar early on in life. After high school, he worked his way through the University of Missouri by expanding the newspaper route he had started as a high school student. His first job after college was at *J. C. Penney* in Des Moines, Iowa. Walton later said that he was thrilled when "*James Cash Penney* himself visited the store one day." During the war, a heart irregularity prevented Walton from serving overseas. Instead, he was stationed in California. In 1950, now out of the military, Walton opened Walton's Five and Dime. A chain of drugstores followed. By 1960, Walton's 15 stores were taking in $1.4 million a year. But Walton soon saw a challenging new competitor arise— the discount store. He believed that discount stores might put drugstores out of business. Instead of trying to beat them, he decided to join them. Inspired by a store called Fed-Mart, Walton decided to call his new business *Wal-Mart.*

Wanamaker, John

In 1860, when 22-year-old John Wanamaker married Mary Brown, he gained not only a wife but also a business partner, her brother Nathan. Wanamaker and Nathan Brown opened a clothing store called Oak Hall. It didn't prosper until the Civil War broke out, and they received a large order for uniforms. Wanamaker used the windfall to create an advertising budget. Wanamaker's brother-in-law died in 1868, and Wanamaker continued on his own. His plan was to open a huge store with one of the most varied selections of merchandise available at the time. He bought an abandoned Pennsylvania Railroad shed and converted it into a store, which opened in 1877. That *Wanamaker's* is generally considered to be the first department store.

Ward, Aaron Montgomery

In 1844, a boy was born in Chatham, New Jersey, to a family whose ancestors had fought in the French and Indian War and the American Revolution. The boy's patriotic parents named him Aaron Montgomery Ward after Gen. G. Aaron Montgomery Ward, who served in George Washington's army. When he was nine, the family moved to Niles, Michigan. Ward dropped out of school at 14 and worked as a laborer to support himself. He traveled to Chicago, the center of the wholesale dry goods trade, and got a job with a store called Field Palmer and Leiter. A hard worker, Ward quickly earned a raise from $5 a week to $12 a week, but the restless youth moved on after only two years. He worked at a series of Chicago stores before trying his luck as a traveling salesman. He soon tired of life on the road and decided to settle down. With $1,600, he and two partners filled a warehouse with goods and sent farmers a catalog of items they could purchase by mail. The first mailing was only one page and contained 163 items, but soon business had grown enough to warrant an entire bound catalog. "Ward's Wish Book," as it came to be known, predated that of *Richard Sears* and *Alvah Roebuck* by 14 years.

Warner, Harry, Albert, Samuel, and Jack

Harry Warner was born in Poland, as were his two younger brothers, Albert and Samuel. In the late 1800s, however, the family moved to Canada where another brother, Jack, was born in 1892. In 1903, Harry Warner launched a career as a film distributor. Two years later, his brothers joined him in the purchase of a nickelodeon in New Castle, Pennsylvania. The nickelodeon spawned a chain of shops, but by 1912 the brothers had set their sights on another side of the business—making movies. Their first successful production was the 1917 film *My Four Years in Germany*. They took the money they earned from the picture and opened their own studio, which they called *Warner Brothers*.

Watt, James

James Watt was born in Scotland in 1736 and trained as an instrument maker. He got a job at the University of Glasgow, and there he met a physicist named Joseph Black. Black inspired Watt to study thermodynamics. Steam engines were new at the time, and Watt began to look for ways to improve them. He discovered various ways to make the engines more efficient, including a newly designed condensation chamber. Watt left the academic world to join forces with a manufacturer and businessman named Matthew Boulton. Watt designed the engines, gears, and governors, and Boulton sold them. Watt's designs revolutionized manufacturing and helped fuel the Industrial Revolution. Soon most factories were powered with engines that followed Watt's design. Watt measured the power output of the engines in "horsepower," a term he invented. The unit of measurement was later officially changed to the *watt.*

Webster, Noah

Noah Webster was a researcher and editor of *The American Magazine.* He published many books over the course of his career, including such page-turners as *A Brief History of Epidemic and Pestilential Diseases, Sketches of American Policy,* and *Dissertations on the English Language.* Far and away his most successful book, however, was *An American Dictionary of the English Language.* It was the first truly American dictionary. It included 12,000 new American words and simplified spellings of many British words. It is thanks to Webster that we do not put a "u" in "color." Today Webster's is practically synonymous with "dictionary."

Welch, Thomas

Dr. Thomas Welch was a minister with a degree in dentistry from Syracuse Medical College. He was also a prohibitionist, and deeply troubled by the use of wine in religious ceremonies. So in early 1870s, he decided to do something about it. He developed a non-alcoholic grape beverage that he called Dr. Welch's Unfermented Wine. He discovered, much to his dismay, that ministers were not interested in his alternative to wine. After only four years, he gave up on the project and returned to a career in dentistry. Dr. Welch's son Charles followed in his father's footsteps. He became a dentist in Washington D. C., but his father's idea for grape juice preoccupied him. He returned to the family home in New Jersey, and suggested a father and son grape juice business. Thomas Welch thought it was a ridiculous idea, and they opened a dental supply business instead. But

Charles worked at selling the grape juice on the side. Over time, Charles' business shifted from mostly dental to mostly grape. By 1909, *Welch's Grape Juice* was selling one million gallons a year.

Wellesley, Arthur

Arthur Wellesley was born in Ireland in 1769. As a young man, he was not particularly ambitious, but it didn't matter because he was very well connected. His father was first Viscount Wellesley of Dangan and first Earl of Mornington, descended from a family that settled in Ireland in the 16th century. Arthur was educated at Eton and the military academy of Angers in France. Then, as expected, he entered the army in 1787. His money and family ties helped him rise quickly to the rank of lieutenant colonel. He saw no action until 1794, when he served in the Duke of York's unsuccessful campaign in the Netherlands. Wellesley's brother, the governor general of India, offered him a post, and Wellesley served in India until 1805. This time, he was successful. Many military successes followed, earning Wellesley the official title of the Duke of Wellington, and the unofficial title of "the Iron Duke." His greatest military victory came in 1815 when he defeated Napoleon at the Battle of Waterloo. Interestingly, if you visit Waterloo today (it is located in Belgium), you will find a great deal of information on Napoleon, but little mention of the winner. Back in England, however, Wellington was a national hero. Soon people copied his habits and style of dress. He was fond of a dish made of prime beef wrapped in bacon and paté and cooked in a puff pastry shell. That dish was soon known as *Beef Wellington*. The *Wellington overcoat*, and a style of boots simply known as *Wellingtons* are also named after him.

Wells, Henry

Born in Thetford, Vermont, in 1805, Henry Wells was the son of a Congregationalist clergyman who moved to New York when Henry was eight. In 1836, to take advantage of the rush for westward expansion, Henry went to work as a freight agent on the Erie Canal. By the 1840s, he had his own express company. He met William Fargo, a freight agent from Auburn, New York.

The two men formed the American Express Company in 1850. By then, gold had been discovered in California. There was an insatiable need for express and banking services in the West. Wells and Fargo formed *Wells, Fargo & Company* to meet that need. Besides being the man behind the *Wells Fargo wagon,* Wells built the first commercial telegraph lines in the United States and established *Wells College* for women.

Welty, Eudora

Eudora Alice Welty was born in 1909 in Jackson, Mississippi. She attended Mississippi Women's College, and graduated from the University of Wisconsin in 1929. In 1936, she published the story "Death of a Traveling Salesman." This was the beginning of her writing career. Welty became known for stories and novels set in rural Mississippi. In 1941, she won the first of six O. Henry Memorial Contest awards and published her first collection, *A Curtain of Green.* One of the stories in the collection; "Why I Live at the P.O.," captured the imagination of a team working to produce a new electronic mail system. In the author's honor, they called their new program *Eudora.*

Wenceslas

There was a King Wenceslas, but whether he was "good" or not is up for debate. Wenceslas was 13 years old when his father, Wratislaus, died. Until Wenceslas reached maturity, his mother, Drahomira, was in command. The boy was put in the custody of his grandmother, Ludmilla. Ludmilla urged Wenceslas to take the throne by force and make Christianity the religion of the land. Hearing of the plan, Drahomira had Ludmilla killed. One of Wenceslas' first acts as king was to banish his mother from Bohemia. He went on to enforce Christianity by beating those who refused to follow. He aligned his country politically with those nations that had also accepted Christianity as the state religion. On the "good king" side, Wenceslas also built churches and worked tirelessly for charity. In the end, the king was executed by his brother Boleslaus. Wenceslas became the patron saint of Czechoslovakia, and a symbol of Czech nationalism. Many years later, an English man, perhaps holding a Czech coin bearing Wenceslas' face, found he liked the sound of the good king's name, and he fit it into a traditional melody. The song became a favorite timeless Christmas carol. When *Good King Wenceslas* looked out in the famous carol, it was on the *Feast of Stephen.* Who was Stephen? He was one of Jesus' original 12 disciples. After Jesus' death, Stephen was accused of preaching blasphemy and was executed by stoning, becoming the first Christian martyr. Later he was sainted. The Feast of St. Stephen is December 26, the day after Christmas. So "Good King Wenceslas" is, technically, a Boxing Day carol.

Westinghouse, George

George Westinghouse was a precocious and prolific inventor. Born in Central Bridge, New York, on October 6, 1846, he was the eighth of 10 children. When he was 10, the family moved to Schenectady, where his father established a shop for agricultural machinery and small steam engines. It was here that Westinghouse discovered his love of machines. At the age of 19, he received his first patent for a rotary steam engine and set to work to create a more reliable railroad braking system. He founded a company called the Westinghouse Air Brake Company. For the next 10 years, Westinghouse created one railroad improvement after another, receiving an average of a patent every 20 days during that period, a total of 134 in all. In 1885, he turned his attention to electric power, and founded the Westinghouse Electric Company. He bought the patent for *Nikola Tesla's* polyphase system of alternating current and the induction motor, which allowed electricity to travel farther than Thomas Edison's direct current. On March 20, 1886, in Great Barrington, Massachusetts, Westinghouse demonstrated how the new transformer could work for lighting for the first time. For several years the two methods of delivering current battled it out like VHS and Beta. It seemed at first that Westinghouse would win out. By 1890, the company's annual sales totaled $4 million, and Westinghouse had installed more than 300 central power stations. In 1893, he won the bid to provide electricity for the Columbian Exposition. In a short time, alternating current represented 95 percent of all electric power generated around the globe. Then Edison, aided by a wealthy friend, J. P. Morgan, set up his own AC system. Westinghouse sued, but he couldn't compete with Morgan's money. Westinghouse and Edison finally settled on co-patents.

Wilson, Sam

Troy, New York, resident Sam Wilson worked as a meat packager. His reputation for friendliness earned him the nickname "Uncle Sam." During the War of 1812, Wilson acted as inspector for a government contractor. The meat that passed Wilson's inspection was stamped "U.S.," for "United States." The nation was quite new then, and "U.S." was not yet a common abbreviation, so when soldiers asked what the "U.S." stood for, some people supposed it must stand for *Uncle Sam*. This is how "Uncle Sam" came to symbolize the U.S. government. The first caricature of an Uncle Sam figure, attired in stars and stripes, appeared in political cartoons in 1832.

Winchester, Oliver Fisher

Oliver Fisher Winchester was born in Boston in 1810. His father died when he was just a boy. His widowed mother could barely support the family, so Winchester went to work at an early age. Along the way he learned carpentry. Then he opened a men's clothing shop. This led to an interest in the manufacturing end of the business, and in 1848 Winchester patented a shirt-making process and opened a factory in New Haven, Connecticut. The business made him a wealthy man. He thought firearms might be a good investment, so he bought himself some firearms companies. He became president of the Volcanic Arms Company, which he renamed the New Haven Arms Company. In 1860, his company introduced the Henry repeating rifle, named for Benjamin Tyler Henry, its designer. Then in 1867, he reorganized his company again under name Winchester Repeating Arms Company. It was not long before he was introducing his company's most famous product, an improvement on the Henry repeating rifle called the *73 Winchester*, so named for the year of its release. The 73 was the first of the famous *Winchester rifles*, which would become standard equipment for Western pioneers.

Wistar, Caspar

Caspar Wistar was a Philadelphia Quaker who taught anatomy, midwifery, and surgery at the College of Pennsylvania. He wrote the nation's first anatomy textbook and succeeded Thomas Jefferson as the head of the American Philosophical Society. The popular and noted scholar died in 1818. Thomas Nuttall, the curator of Harvard's Botanical Garden, named a newly discovered flower in his honor. Unfortunately, Nuttall made a mistake when he wrote the name in his ledger. Instead of writing "Wistaria," he wrote *wisteria*, and the spelling was never corrected.

Woolworth, Frank Winfield

Frank Winfield Woolworth was born in 1852 on his grandfather's farm, 40 miles from the Canadian border in New York State. When he turned 19, Woolworth was so anxious to jumpstart his sales career that he offered to work for free at Augsbury-Moore, a dry goods firm. After two and a half years, Woolworth had increased his salary from zero to $6 a week. He left the company for a dry goods firm that offered an incredible $10 a week, but his employers were not impressed with his performance and cut his salary to $8 a week. In 1877, his old employer at Augsbury-Moore, who had been impressed with Woolworth's work, offered to match the $10 a week, and he returned. After two more years with the company, Woolworth convinced his boss to lend him the money to open his own "Great 5-Cent Store" in Utica. It flopped. Woolworth tried again, in Lancaster, Pennsylvania. This time, it was a success. He later added 10-cent items, creating the first "Five and Dime." Many imitators were to follow. A generation grew up buying sodas from lunch counters in "dime stores," a term that is rapidly disappearing as 10-cent items become more and more scarce. In its heyday, Woolworth had more than 2,100 variety stores throughout the world, but as the 20th century drew to a close, large discount stores such as *Wal-Mart* replaced the Five and Dime. Woolworth announced it would close its American dime stores.

Wrigley, William

William Wrigley, Jr., grew up in Philadelphia. His father, William Wrigley, Sr., was a soap manufacturer. The younger Wrigley began his career selling his father's product, Wrigley's Scouring Soap. In 1891, when he was 26, he went to Chicago with $35 and a plan to sell soap. When sales didn't go as well as he had hoped, Wrigley began offering free baking powder as a bonus to his customers. It turned out that they wanted the baking powder more than the soap, and so he changed products. But selling baking powder on its own was not easy without a gimmick. Giving away freebies had worked for him before, so he tried again. This time, Wrigley tried offering chewing gum to potential customers. He found, to his surprise, that the gum was even more popular than the baking powder. So in 1893 he started a company to sell *Wrigley's gum*.

Wurlitzer, Rudolph

Rudolph Wurlitzer, the man who gave his name to the most famous jukebox of the 1940s and 1950s, died in 1914, long before the big band and rock eras. In 1853, the German immigrant arrived on U.S. shores, determined to make his fortune. He got a job with a Cincinnati dry goods store, and slept in a box in the back room to save rent money. In three years, he managed to save $700. He started his own business importing and selling musical instruments wholesale to dealers. By 1861, he decided he could lower costs by manufacturing the instruments in the United States. The Civil War proved to be a boon to the instrument maker, who got a contract with the U.S. Army to make bugles. Near the turn of the century, as electrical power became more commonplace, Wurlitzer began manufacturing coin-operated player pianos and mandolins. Wurlitzer died in 1914, but his son Farny shared his interest in electrical instruments. He developed a huge pipe organ known as the *Mighty Wurlitzer* and in 1934 introduced the *Wurlitzer Simplex*, the company's first jukebox.

X/Y/Z

Yale, Elihu

Elihu Yale was born in Boston in 1648. When he was four, his family moved to England, and he never returned to the United States. For 20 years, Yale was part of the East India Company, and he became governor of a settlement at Madras. He was suspended from the post, however, in 1692 after disagreements with his council and his superiors. Yale amassed a fortune in his lifetime, and he was generous with the proceeds. In 1718, a man named Cotton Mather contacted Yale and asked for his help. He represented a small institution of learning. It was founded as the Collegiate School of Connecticut in 1701, and it needed money for a new building in New Haven. Yale sent Mather a carton of goods that the school sold, earning them 560 pounds, which was a substantial sum in the early 1700s. In gratitude, officials named the new building for Yale, and eventually the entire institution became Yale College. The first benefactor of *Yale University* is buried in the churchyard of Wrexham, North Wales. His tomb is inscribed with these lines:

> Born in America, in Europe bred,
> In Africa traveled, in Asia wed,
> Where long he lived and thrived, in London dead;
> Much good, some ill he did, so hope all's even,
> And that his soul through mercy's gone to heaven.

Zamboni, Frank

Today the name *Zamboni* is widely recognized by hockey fans and skaters. "If our name had been Smith or Brown, I don't think any of this would have happened," Richard Zamboni, president of Frank Zamboni, Inc., once said. "It's kind of a screwball name. There's such a uniqueness to it, the machine kind of took on a character of its own. My father was always surprised at that." Richard's father was Frank Zamboni, the son of Italian immigrants. He was raised in Utah, and at age 21 moved to California to seek his fortune in the ice business. There was a time, of course, when people did not have refrigerators. Instead, they had ice boxes, which kept food cold with a block of ice. Frank Zamboni supplied the ice blocks. By the late 1930s, however, ice boxes were slowly being replaced by home refrigerators. With his life savings tied up in refrigeration equipment, Zamboni decided to build an ice rink. His least favorite task as ice rink manager was resurfacing the ice. This was accomplished with a planer pulled by a tractor. The planer would level the ice, and the shavings were then swept off manually. Next, the ice was washed by a large hose, and smoothed with a squeegee. The task would take an hour and a half. So Zamboni went to work on a machine to make the task easier. After ten years of less successful models, Zamboni rolled out his first workable resurfacer in 1949. The machine was spotted by skating champ Sonja Henie, who ordered one for her ice show. Her use of the machine popularized it in the United States and helped make the unlikely moniker *Zamboni* a household word.

Zeppelin, Ferdinand

Count Ferdinand von Zeppelin was born in Baden, Germany, on July 8, 1838. He began a military career in 1857. In 1863, he traveled to America as a military observer in the Civil War. He then joined an expedition along the Mississippi River. His first voyage into the sky occurred in St. Paul, Minnesota, where he floated in a balloon. He returned to Germany, where he became a brigadier general, but his lighter-than-air experience remained on his mind. After he retired in 1891, he began experimenting with dirigible balloons. He was able to secure sufficient financial support to build a working model. His first 18-minute flight took place on July 2, 1900. Although most of Zeppelin's airships were less than stellar–13 of them crashed between 1900 and 1914–the Germany military was impressed with their potential and ordered several of the crafts, which were then known as *Zeppelins*. Zeppelin died on March 8, 1917, before dirigibles came into vogue as a method of travel for the wealthy in the 1920s and 1930s. The age of the Zeppelin came to a dramatic end when the *Hindenburg* burst into a ball of flame while landing in New Jersey on May 6, 1937, as reporters looked on.

Zildjian, Avedis

In the 1600s in Turkey, people were still called by their profession. A man named Avedis adopted the last name "Zildjian," which meant "cymbal smith." He developed a great reputation for his trade within his country, but the cymbals were not widely known outside Turkey. Over the years, the cymbal-making trade was passed on from generation to generation. Avedis Zildjian III, the cymbal-making heir apparent, had other plans. He moved to the United States in 1908 and worked as a candymaker near Boston. Eventually, he bought his own candy factory, married a native-born Boston girl, and built a home in Quincy, Massachusetts. He had no thoughts of going into the cymbal-making business, until his uncle Aram sent him a letter. Having never married, Aram had no sons to carry on the family tradition, so he contacted his brother's son and asked him to learn the trade. Avedis did not want to return to Turkey. Instead, he convinced his uncle to join him in America. Avedis learned the family cymbal secrets, and they began making cymbals in a small plant near Avedis' Massachusetts home. Today, Zildjian is the world's leading cymbal and drumstick maker. It is still a family-run business headed by Armand Zildjian and his daughters Craigie and Debbie.

Shorts

To quote William Shakespeare: "To expostulate/ what majesty should be, what duty is, why day is day, night is night, and time is time/ were nothing but to waste day, night and time. Therefore, since brevity is the soul of wit . . .," I will briefly recount the stories of the following souls:

Addison, Thomas

Thomas Addison was a physician at Guy's Hospital in London. In 1849, he described a disorder resulting from insufficiency of the adrenal glands. So Addison earned the distinction every doctor dreams of, having a disease named after him. *Addison's disease,* also known as *Addison's anemia,* was at one time almost always fatal. It is treatable today, however, with daily doses of cortisone.

Aesop

Aesop was a slave owned by Iadmon the Thracian. He lived in the 6th century B.C. Not much is known about Aesop, except that he was a man of words. Most notable were *Aesop's Fables,* a collection of morality tales. Less famous were his off-color stories, which apparently displeased the priests of the time and led to his death. He was thrown over a cliff at Delphi.

Akademos

The ancient Greek Akademos was a hero of the Trojan War. Because of his heroic stature, a man named Cimon named his park for him. The garden near Athens featured walks and fountains. Among those who found the park a perfect place to study and think were Socrates and Plato. Plato instructed his students in the park. The group of students came to be called "*academics.*"

Allen, Roy

One day a hotelier named Roy Allen met a soda fountain operator. It was the era of Prohibition, and the soda fountain operator told him there was a fortune to be made in root beer. Allen was convinced, so he opened a western-style saloon in Lodi, California, that sold the legal, non-alcoholic beverage. The saloon did so well that he and a partner, Frank Wright (not the architect), opened a second saloon in 1922. This time they named the saloon *A&W*, which stood for Allen and Wright.

Ayoub, Diana

Diana Ayoub attended Paul Anka's church and babysat for his younger brother and sister. Fifteen-year-old Paul was in love. Twenty-year-old Diana was not interested. The lovesick youth wrote a poem about it, and then set it to music. His recording of "*Diana*" later sold a million copies.

Barocci, Federigo

Federigo Barocci lived from 1528 to 1612 in Italy, where he was a painter. He was regarded as a master of tender sentiment, and his flamboyant art was thought to evoke the mood of a movement known as Counter-Reformation. In the 17th and 18th centuries, such elaborate, ornamented art was given popularity by artist Francesco Borromini, and became the standard of the time. The style is known today as *baroque*, in honor of Barocci.

Batty, Fitzherbert

According to at least one English scholar, Fitzherbert Batty was a Jamaican lawyer who became well known when he was declared insane in 1839. His notoriety gives us the term *batty*, meaning crazy.

Bernard of Montjoux

Until the 11th century, pilgrims on the path to Rome from France and Germany would cross the Alps on foot, even in the coldest of winters. Bernard was an Augustinian missionary who built rest houses for the pilgrims who crossed the Alps. St. Bernard did not breed dogs, however. It was his followers who bred them long after his death and named them in his honor.

Beukel, William

William Beukel—or perhaps he spelled it Beukelz—was a 14th century Dutch fisherman. He was the first to preserve fish by a method that was named after him. Over time, Beukel was transformed into pekel, and from pekel came *pickle*.

Booze, E. G.

According to etymologists, E. G. Booze was a distiller in Philadelphia in the 18th century. He sold his own *Booze whiskey*, which proved so popular that the name "booze" is interchangeable with alcoholic drinks today.

Bowler, Thomas and William

The Bowlers were an English hat-making family in the 1850s. A customer named William Cole asked the Bowlers to design a hat for him to wear on hunting trips. Today, the round, stiff, felt hat with the curled brim is called a *bowler*. In America, such a hat is also known as a *derby*, so named for the *Earl of Derby*, who once wore a bowler to the races at Epsom Downs.

Brown, Leroy

Leroy Brown was in the army, stationed at Fort Dix, New Jersey. One night, Brown got fed up with army life and walked out. After a month of being AWOL, he returned to the barracks to collect his paycheck. His brashness made an impact on another young recruit named Jim Croce. The song Croce wrote, "*Bad, Bad Leroy Brown*," topped the charts in 1973.

Brownell, Frank

Kodak founder George Eastman popularized photography with the first easy-to-use camera, known as the *Brownie*. The Brownie was the first camera to use roll film that could be sent back to Kodak for development. "You press the button, and we do the rest" was the company's slogan. Eastman named the Brownie after his manufacturing collaborator, Frank Brownell.

Burnside, Ambrose

Ambrose Burnside was a Union general in the Civil War. He was easy to spot because of his distinctive side whiskers and mustache. Eventually, side whiskers came to be known as burnsides. Since they are on the side of the face, the syllables became transposed, and burnsides became *sideburns.*

Casey, Dennis P.

With the help of Dennis P. Casey, the Baltimore Orioles made it into the first division in the American Association. It was the mighty Casey's hitting and pitching that helped the team to accomplish what no Baltimore team had done before. In 1888, Casey inspired a poem by Ernest L. Thayer called "*Casey at the Bat.*"

Charley

Charley only had one name because Charley was a horse. Charley was, in fact, a horse with a limp who pulled a roller in the Chicago White Sox ball park. When baseball players pulled a muscle and began to limp like the animal, it was said that they had a *charley horse.*

Dahl, Anders

Anders Dahl was a Swedish botanist who worked at Madrid's Royal Botanical Garden. One day a German explorer, Friedrich von Humboldt, discovered a plant in Mexico that was prized by the Aztecs. He sent the new species of flower to the botanic garden. When it arrived, Father Cavanilles, keeper of the garden, named it *dahlia* after his friend Dahl, who had died earlier that year. Rumor is that the plant's bloom reminded him of Dahl's ever-untidy hair.

Dassler, Adolph

Adolph Dassler and his brother, Rudi, formed Dassler Brothers Shoes in Germany in 1925. After World War II, the brothers decided to go their separate ways. Rudi formed his own shoe company called Puma, and Adolph kept the old company, which he renamed. Adolph's nickname was Adi, and he called the company *Adidas*, the first six letters of Adi Dassler.

Day, Mathias

In 1870, Mathias Day purchased a tract of land in northern Florida. In 1876, the city was incorporated as Daytona.

De Silhouette, Etienne

Etienne de Silhouette was a French author and politician who served briefly as minister of finance. He was so unpopular that his name became associated with anything plain and cheap. He was a fan of shadow art and decorated his chateau at Bry-sur-Marne with many such portraits. The portraits came to be called *silhouettes* as well.

De Tourette, Georges Gilles

In 1885, French neurologist Georges de Tourette identified for the first time a rare medical disorder. The disorder, known today as *Tourette's Syndrome*, is characterized by involuntary body movements, attention deficit, and vocal, sometimes obscene, outbursts. The syndrome appears more often in males than females and the cause is unknown. No cure yet exists, but symptoms are often treatable with tranquilizers.

Deringer, Henry

Henry Deringer was a gun manufacturer who supplied military rifles and pistols to the U.S. government. In 1852, he invented a short-barreled, large-bore percussion pocket pistol. The pistol spawned many imitators. They could copy Deringer's technology, but apparently they could not master the spelling of his name. That is why today we know that style of pistol as the *derringer*.

Di Lellio, Alfredo

Alfredo di Lellio was a Roman restaurateur in the 1920s. Mary Pickford and Douglas Fairbanks made his restaurant famous when they ate there every day during their honeymoon. They were especially fond of his signature dish, fettuccine with butter cream and Parmesan cheese. Today the dish is known alternately as "a heart attack on a plate" or "*fettuccine Alfredo*."

Doberman, Ludwig

Ludwig Doberman was a watchman in Apolda, Germany. In 1890, he started experimenting with dogs to help him in his guard duties. He combined a German shepherd, a Rottweiler, a black and tan terrier, and the German pinscher. The resulting breed, the *doberman pinscher*, was employed first as a watchdog and later trained for police and military work.

Downing, George

Sir George Downing was scoutmaster general to Oliver Cromwell's army in Scotland in 1650 and secretary of the British treasury in 1667. The famous *Downing Street*, home of the British prime minister, was named after him. Another Sir George Downing, his grandson, willed his estate to found *Downing College* in Cambridge, England.

Doyley

Etymologists believe that the lace *doily* takes its name from a prosperous 18th century textile merchant. Doyley, recorded by some authors as Doily or Doiley, was the owner of a linen shop in central London and prospered by selling lightweight cloth and "Doyley napkins," which we now call placemats.

Du Lhut, Daniel Greysolon

In 1679, French explorer Daniel Greysolon Du Lhut made a treaty with the Sioux and Chippewa Indians. After the treaty, he was able to build a trading post on the shore of Lake Superior in what is now Minnesota. The English settlers in the area had some trouble with the Frenchman's name, and the town he founded became known as *Duluth*.

Duesenburg, Frederick

Frederick Duesenburg was a champion bicyclist. In his quest for greater speed, he began experimenting with motors. He built the Manson motor in 1903. Ten years later, he designed an engine he was proud to call the Duesenburg. In 1917, he headed up his own business, the Duesenburg Motor Company, as chief engineer. By 1930, the *Duesenburg* was known as a truly outstanding car. Anything else that was highly regarded was called by the car's nickname: *a real duesey.*

Dula, Tom

Tom Dula was a Civil War veteran who apparently had a temper. In a jealous rage over a rival suitor, Dula murdered his girlfriend, and was sentenced to death. We remember him today because he wrote a song about his plight. "*Tom Dooley*" became a hit for the Kingston Trio in 1958.

Eastman, Linda

Jack Lawrence was visiting his attorney, Lee Eastman, in 1947. He was quite taken with Eastman's four-year-old daughter, Linda. Lawrence wrote a song for the girl. "*Linda*," by Jan and Dean, rose to number 28 on the charts in 1963. Little Linda grew up to inspire many other songs composed by her husband, Paul McCartney.

Ellis, Sam

Sam Ellis ran a tavern on a small New York island. Other accounts say that Ellis was a butcher. In any case, the Ellis family sold their island to the United States government in the late 1700s. It is still called *Ellis Island.*

Finn, Mickey

Mickey Finn was a 19th century saloon keeper. His San Francisco bar was especially popular with sailors. His clientele had a penchant for rowdiness, so to keep the peace, Finn would slip drugs into the drinks of certain troublemakers. Today, a knockout drink is known as a *Mickey Finn.*

Folger, James

Along with his brothers Edward and Harry, James Folger headed for San Francisco in 1849 to prospect for gold. Part of the way across the country they ran low on money, so Edward and Harry decided to leave their younger brother behind. James needed a source of income, so he started roasting coffee beans and selling them. Since most merchants at the time were selling coffee unroasted, *Folger's Coffee* was a great success. There is no word on whether the older Folgers struck gold.

Forsyth, William

William Forsyth was a Scottish horticulturist who became super-intendent of the royal gardens at Saint James and Kensington in London. In this role, Forsyth introduced many plants to England. One of them was a yellow flowering shrub that Forsyth had imported from China. The plant had a characteristic necessary for success in British gardens—it grew well in the shade. It was named the *forsythia* in the horticulturist's honor.

Freymann, Robert

Dr. Robert Freymann was a German-born physician who prac-ticed in New York. Freymann's clients included many jazz and rock musicians. He was known for liberally prescribing amphetamines. Among his patients were jazz greats Theolonious Monk and Charlie Parker. (It was Dr. Freymann who signed Parker's death certificate.) One of his patients, John Lennon, immortalized the good doctor in the Beatles song "*Dr. Robert.*"

Captain Fudge

Captain Fudge's first name has been lost to history. What is known about him was that he was a British Navy captain in the 1600s. When he would return to port, he liked to impress people with highly embellished and outright fictional tales of his adventures. His fellow seamen began to call him "Lying Fudge," and when they would embellish a story, they were said to be *fudging it.*

Garden, Alexander

With a name like "Garden" it was probably predestined that Alexander would become a botanist. He gained such prominence as a botanist, in fact, that the Royal Society of Botany in London named a newly discovered tropical plant in his honor: the *gardenia.*

Giocondo, Mona Lisa

Mona Lisa, the wife of the wealthy Giocondo, posed for an artist named Leonardo da Vinci. Her portrait was completed in 1504 and purchased by Francis I. English speakers call the famous painting by the subject's given names, *Mona Lisa.* In Europe, the portrait is referred to by the subject's married name. In Italian it is known as *La Giocondo* and in French as *La Joconde.*

Gobelin, Jehan

Jehan and Giles Gobelin invented a unique dye in 1435. The dye was a brighter red than had ever been imagined possible. People began to say that the Gobelins had sold their souls to the devil to get the secret of that brilliant red. In the early 1400s, tales of bewitching were not taken lightly. So the bright dye earned the Gobelins a place in the dictionary. Over time, the name Gobelin became synonymous with evil creatures, and the spelling evolved to *goblin.*

Goose, Elizabeth Foster

When 27-year-old Elizabeth Foster married Isaac Goose, she gained not just a husband but 10 children, too. As a new stepmother, she had no trouble winning the kids over. She entertained them with old rhymes. Later, one of her step-daughters married a printer, and he also loved the tales. In 1719, he decided to publish a collection of the verses. He called his volume *Songs for the Nursery, or Mother Goose's Melodies.* *Mother Goose* died in 1757 at the age of 92.

Gordon, Alexander

Alexander Gordon was a London distiller. In 1769, he began producing what is now known as *Gordon's Gin.* Gordon's is today the world's most popular brand of gin, with annual sales of over 5.4 million cases.

Gucci, Guccio

Guccio Gucci was born in Florence, Italy, in 1881. Around 1900, he left for London, where he found employment as a waiter at the ritzy Savoy Hotel. There he studied the behavior of the well to do. He returned to Florence, and after a brief stint with a leather goods manufacturer named Franzi, Gucci opened his own handbag business. He named it *Gucci*.

Gunter, Edmund

Although the expression is no longer heard, "*according to Gunter*" was as popular an expression at one time as "*according to Hoyle*" is today. Gunter was an English mathematician and astronomer and the inventor of the modern slide rule. He introduced the terms "cosine" and "cotangent" to the English language. Mathematicians are familiar with *Gunter's quadrant* and *Gunter's scale*, which were named for the scientist.

Hall, Sir Benjamin

Sir Benjamin Hall was chief commissioner of works in London from 1855 to 1888. One of his responsibilities was to oversee the casting and mounting of a great bell in the clock tower of the House of Parliament. The bell was to be called "St. Stephen." The press, however, dubbed the bell *Big Ben* after Benjamin Hall, and the name has endured.

Hanson, Timothy

Timothy Hanson carried grass seed from New England to plant in Maryland. This particular strain of grass, with seeds at the end of the long stem, had come from Great Britain originally. Scientifically, it is called *phleum pretense*. Most people, however, now refer to it as *timothy grass*.

Harvey

According to *The Dictionary of American Food and Drink* by John Mariani, Harvey was a surfer who did not perform to expectations at the Manhattan Beach tournament. Following his disappointment, Harvey began swallowing drinks made up of orange juice, vodka, and Galliano. Several drinks later,

Harvey was banging into the walls. Thus, allegedly, the *Harvey Wallbanger* was born.

Hasbrouck, Jonathan

Jonathan Hasbrouck was an American judge who died in 1846. The *Jonathan apple* was named in his honor.

Hazyan, Geber ibn

Gaber ibn Hazyan was an Arab alchemist. To avoid being executed for sorcery, Hazyan wrote his formulas in a completely unintelligible form of writing. It is believed that we get the word *gibberish* from his name.

Heath, Lawrence

At age 45, Lawrence Heath tired of working as a school principal and decided to open a candy store in Robinson, Illinois. On January 7, 1914, he went into business with his sons, selling fountain drinks, ice cream, and a popular homemade English toffee. In 1932, *Heath* went national, marketing individually wrapped toffee bars bearing his name.

Heisman, John

John Heisman played and coached football in the late 1800s and early 1900s. He brought many innovations to the game, including the center snap, the forward pass, and, reportedly, the scoreboard. He also coined the word "hike" to begin a play. In 1916, Heisman's team ran up the highest score in football history, 220-0, against Cumberland College. Oh, yes, and they named a trophy after him.

Henri, viscount of Turenne

Henri was viscount of Turenne and marshal of France. During the Thirty Years War, he was commander of the French army. Legend has it that during one battle the viscount, having no dishes, used his helmet as a soup bowl. The soldiers began calling any large serving dish a *tureen*. Many scholars dispute this claim, however, speculating that the word comes from the French word for an earthen container, *terrine*.

Henry

The Williamson Candy Company in Chicago hired many young women to make its candy. Every day around the same time a local lad named Henry would stop by for a visit and flirt with the girls. The candymakers would also flirt with the engaging young man, saying such things as "Oh Henry, will you do this for me?" or "Oh Henry, will you do that for me?" The company joke became the name of a candy bar in 1920.

Hines, Duncan

Duncan Hines was a renowned food critic and the author of *Adventures in Good Eating*. This guide to restaurants along major highways was so popular that Hines' name became a household word. In the early 1940s, a businessman named Roy Park was trying to promote a new line of baked goods. He asked Hines, whose name was now synonymous with good food, to be his partner. They formed Hines–Park Foods in 1948. In less than three weeks Duncan Hines cake mixes had captured 48 percent of the American cake mix market.

Hirschfield, Clara

Austrian immigrant Leo Hirschfield's daughter Clara had a nickname: "Tootsie." She also had a sweet tooth. So Hirschfield rolled homemade candies—*Tootsie Rolls*—for her.

Hunter, Jan

Singer Marvin Gaye wrote the song "*Jan*" for a California high school student named Jan Hunter. Hunter later became Gaye's second wife.

Johnson, Samuel

Wisconsin native Samuel Johnson made his living selling parquet flooring. He traveled to Europe to study the floors of castles. While he was there, he learned that wax was used to make the floors shine. When he returned home, Johnson introduced carnauba wax to his line of products. He was soon floored to find his floor-care products were selling better than his flooring. So Johnson stopped making floors and concentrated on floor wax.

Jones, Davy

This Davy Jones was not the lovable moptop of the Monkees, but he of the locker. It is theorized that *Davy Jones' locker* belonged to the Jones of the 16th century ballad "Jones Ale is Newe." This Jones was a barman, and it is believed that his locker was where he stored his spirits.

Kaposi, Moritz

Moritz Kaposi was an Austro-Hungarian dermatologist in the mid-1800s. In 1872, he identified a rare tumor found primarily in elderly men of Italian or Eastern European Jewish ancestry. The appearance of the red, purple, and brown patches was quite rare, but they were found more often in individuals with suppressed immune symptoms. HIV and AIDS unfortunately have made *Kaposi's sarcoma* much more common today than when the scientist first identified it.

Kent, Herbert A.

Herbert A. Kent was an executive at the Lorillard Tobacco Company. He was so well liked at the office that in 1952 the company named a cigarette after him.

Ketch, Jack

Jack Ketch is a catchall term for an executioner. Many experts believe the term dates back to a real Jack Ketch, who was a real executioner. Perhaps he was the English hangman in the 17th century who barbarously executed William Lord Russell, Duke of Monmouth. Others believe that the name evolved over time from Richard Jaquette, Lord of the Manor of Tyburn, where executions were performed until 1783. There are still others who believe there was no Jack at all, and that it was simply a play on words for "jack-catch."

Knickerbocker, Diedrich

Diedrich Knickerbocker was the pseudonym of Washington Irving. The supposedly Dutch author wrote *A History of New York From the Beginning of the World to the End of the Dutch Dynasty* in 1809. The book was illustrated by George Cruikshank, who drew the author in a style of knee pants that came to be known as *knickerbockers*.

Krupp, Bertha

Frau Krupp was the matriarch of the Krupp family who manufactured weapons of war. Most notably, they manufactured a huge cannon that in World War I was nicknamed *Big Bertha*. Although Bertha is an Old German name meaning "shining," surveys show that because of "Big Bertha," most people picture Berthas as being overweight.

La Forge, George

George La Forge was a loyal fan of the "Star Trek" television series who did not let muscular dystrophy keep him from attending numerous "Star Trek" conventions. La Forge died in 1975, but he made an impression on the series creators. When they began work on a new "Star Trek" series, they decided to include a character with a physical disability. They named the character Geordi La Forge in his honor.

Latan, Dr. A. M.

Dr. Latan peddled a variety of health tonics and potions in Paris in the 1840s. He was instantly recognizable as he traveled because of his opulent coach. His coach, "le char de Latan," became strongly associated with his style of selling. The term later came into the English language as *charlatan*.

Lawrence, Sarah Bates

Throughout her life, Sarah Bates Lawrence of New York gave freely of her time to further the cause of women in her state. When she died, her husband, a wealthy man named William Van Duzer Lawrence, thought a fitting memorial would be the creation of a college in Bronxville. William Lawrence died in 1927, one year before *Sarah Lawrence College* opened. At the time of his death, he had given a total of $1,250,000 to the institution.

Lee, Maria

In the early 1800s, a formidable black woman named Maria Lee ran a Boston lodging house for sailors. She would allow no trouble from her boarders. If any of the sailors in residence became unruly, Lee wasted no time calling the police. Boston natives called the woman *Black Maria*, and the term came to be applied to the police vans that carried the prisoners away.

Lee, Mr.

Mr. Lee was a teacher at P.S. 109. A couple of girls from his class formed a singing group with some friends. They called their group the Bobbettes. Mr. Lee was apparently not a beloved teacher. When the Bobbettes went to record the song "*Mr. Lee*,"Atlantic Records asked them to alter the lyrics from "He's the ugliest teacher I ever did see" to "He's the handsomest sweetie I ever did see."

Lennon, Julian

Born John Charles Julian Lennon, the son of Beatle John Lennon was also known, at least indirectly, as Jude. When John Lennon moved in with Yoko Ono, the Japanese artist who was to be his second wife, he began proceedings to divorce his first wife, Cynthia. One day Paul McCartney was thinking about John and Cynthia's son and began to compose a song for him. The song, "Hey Jules," eventually became "*Hey Jude,*" which sold over five million records. John Charles Julian Jules Jude Lennon grew up to become a musician in his own right.

Lufkin, E. P.

The moral of this story is, don't mess with a railroad surveyor. E. P. Lufkin was such a surveyor. As he was laying out the railroad route across Texas, some of his workers got themselves arrested for drunkenness in a town called Homer. Lufkin decided to take his revenge on the town by routing the railway lines to avoid it completely. Instead of locating the station in Homer, he placed it in an uninhabited spot that he named after himself—*Lufkin*. The new town of Lufkin, Texas, prospered. Homer disappeared.

Lynch, Charles

Charles Lynch was a planter and Virginia justice of the peace. During the American Revolution, justice and peace were often hard to come by. Lynch was in favor of swift justice, and he often dispensed with the formality of an actual trial and went straight to the punishment, usually a flogging. The practice of inflicting punishment without a proper trial came to be known as *lynching*.

MacIntosh, Charles

Charles MacIntosh was born in 1766 and raised in his father's dye-making plant. In 1823, MacIntosh patented a waterproof fabric made of two or more layers of cloth cemented together with rubber. He advertised them as "life preservers" for anyone who had to go out in rainy weather. The process was patented in 1823. With a slight change in spelling, his *mackintosh* came to be synonymous with a rain jacket.

McIntosh, John

John McIntosh was a farmer in Ontario, Canada. One day in 1796 he was clearing some annoying trees from his land when he discovered a red apple tree. He sampled the fruit, and decided that not only would he not clear the tree, but he would plant an entire orchard. Today *McIntosh apples* account for about 10 percent of the U.S. apple harvest.

Macbeth

Macbeth was a commander under his cousin King Duncan I. In 1040, Macbeth murdered Duncan and claimed the kingdom, which he ruled for 17 prosperous years. In 1057, Macbeth was killed in battle by Malcolm Canmore, a son of Duncan I, who later became Malcolm III, king of Scotland. Lady Macbeth was known as a patron of the church. That image would be significantly altered by a later biographer named William Shakespeare.

McKay, G.

In the 1870s, a distiller in Edinburgh, Scotland, named G. McKay began advertising its whisky as "the real McKay." The phrase somehow was changed to Macoy, and finally to McCoy. "*The Real McCoy*" was commonly used for decades, especially during the Prohibition era when it was once again applied to liquor. Real alcohol was "the real McCoy."

Menasche, Lillian

In 1952, Lillian Menasche borrowed the name Vernon from George Washington's Mount Vernon and put an ad in *Seventeen* magazine to sell monogrammed belts and bags. She ran her mail-order business from her kitchen table. Her catalog slowly grew, incorporating housewares, garden tools, and numerous inexpensive knick-knacks, most of which could be monogrammed. When asked about the secret of her success, Vernon said, "I know my customer because I am my customer." By 1988, the *Lillian Vernon Catalog* had sold enough merchandise to take the company public.

Montagu, James

James Montagu, the Earl of Sandwich, would spend hours at the gambling table. To avoid having to stop gambling to eat, he would have servants bring him sliced cold meat between two pieces of bread. His blue-blooded guests began to refer to this type of meal as a *sandwich*. Captain James Cook also named the *Sandwich Islands* after the earl. Unlike the food, the islands were later renamed. We now know them as Hawaii.

Monteveccio, Romeo

Authors and playwrights are often inspired by stories they read in the news. On March 11, 1302, Romeo Monteveccio and Juliet Cappelleto were married in Citadela, Italy. The event led a writer named Arthur Brooke to compose a poem in 1562 entitled the "Tragicall Historye of Romeus and Juliet, containing a rare example of loves constancie." A playwright named William Shakespeare was inspired by the poem to write a play.

Morton, Joy

In the early 1900s, salt was sold in barrels. When the weather was damp the salt would clump. To keep the salt dry and make it easy to pour, Joy Morton developed a paper canister with an aluminum spout. *Morton Salt*'s packaging and memorable advertising made it a popular staple on America's tables. Interestingly, "When it rains, it pours" was not Morton's first slogan. Morton's original idea for a slogan was the somewhat more cumbersome "Even in rainy weather it flows freely."

Nehru, Jawaharlal

Nehru was the first prime minister of independent India, serving from 1947 until 1964. This was not enough to make Nehru a household name, however. Luckily, he liked to wear a jacket with a stand-up collar and no lapel. The Nehru jacket caught on with the Beatles and hippies who favored Indian culture. Briefly in the late 1960s, the Nehru jacket was a trendy fashion item. By 1969, it was appearing in the Sears catalog. Its trendiness gone, the fashion soon ran its course.

Nicholas, Nick

"Big Nick Nicholas" was a world-renowned tenor saxophonist who played with everyone from Earl "Fatha" Hines to Dizzy Gillespie. He is best remembered by jazz fans for a 16-bar solo on Gillespie's African-Cuban jazz piece, "Manteca," in 1947. Nicolas was also a great influence on John Coltrane, whose song "*Big Nick*" was named in Nicholas' honor.

Nielsen, Arthur Charles

Arthur Charles Nielsen founded a market research company in 1923. His company studied consumer shopping habits and appreciation of various products. In 1952, Neilsen decided to survey viewers about their favorite television programs. The *Nielsen ratings* became the standard by which networks and sponsors could gauge a program's success.

Noble, Charley

Since the mid-19th century, the galley stack on a ship has been known as a *Charley Noble*. Many people have theories as to who Mr. Noble was. The honor has been attributed both to a merchant sea captain who insisted that the copper galley funnel be kept brightly polished, and to a ship's cook whose galley funnel became a symbol of his excellent meals.

O'Donnell, Lucy

At age four, little Lucy O'Donnell sat beside a boy named Julian in nursery school. Julian was quite fond of his classmate. One day he drew a picture of her and brought it home to show his dad. His father commented, "That's a nice drawing, Julian. What is it?" Julian Lennon told his father that it was "*Lucy in the sky with diamonds.*" Thus, a new Beatles song was born. These days, grownup Lucy is still in the classroom, teaching children with special needs.

Orbison, Claudette

Roy Orbison began his musical career as a staff songwriter for Acuff-Rose Music. One of his first songs was "*Claudette,*" written about his wife. The Everly Brothers recorded the song and made it a hit. In the late 1960s, as Orbison reached the height of his success, Claudette was tragically killed in a motorcycle crash.

Paulmier, Madeleine

Madeleine Paulmier was a pastry cook in 19th century Comercy, France. She concocted a small shell-shaped cake that we know today as *madeleines.*

Phillips, Charles Henry

Charles Henry Phillips moved from England to New Jersey, where he opened a drugstore. There he concocted such cures as Phillips Palatable Cod Liver Oil Emulsion and Phillips Phospo-Muriate Quinine Compound. You won't find Phillips Phospho-Nutritive on the shelves today, but one of his inventions has stood the test of time. It is magnesium hydroxide suspended in water, also known as *milk of magnesia.*

Purdue, John

When John Purdue died in 1876, he had no family to carry on his name. He was buried in an unmarked grave on a university campus. Were it not for the $150,000 he donated to found a college in Lafayette, Indiana, John Purdue's name might be completely forgotten today. Instead, it graces *Purdue University.*

Pye, Joe

Joe Pye was an Indian medicine man who lived near Salem, Massachusetts, in colonial times. Pye used a common tall weed from the area to cure the colonists' illnesses. It cured the patients by causing "copious perspiration." The purple flowering weed, still common to New England, is known today as the *joe-pye weed.*

Pygmalion

Pygmalion was an ancient king of Cyprus. According to legend, the king hated women. He fell in love with something else—an ivory statue he had carved of the ideal woman. He asked the goddesses to breathe life into the statue, which they did, and he married the woman. The myth of the creation of the perfect woman intrigued George Bernard Shaw, who used *Pygmalion* as the title of a famous play.

Raffel, Forest and Leroy

Brothers Forest and Leroy Raffel wanted to call their Akron, Ohio, fast food restaurant Big Tex. That name was already taken, however. So the brothers named it after themselves. Raffel Brothers, or R.B.'s, became *Arby's.*

Reese, Harry

Pennsylvania native Harry Reese's first big job was managing a dairy farm for Milton Hershey of the Hershey Chocolate Company during World War I. In 1923, Reese decided to open his own company. He moved to Hummelstown, Pennsylvania, and set up a candy-making kitchen. He created the "Johnny Bar" and the "Lizzie Bar," but his most famous sweets were the *peanut butter cups.*

Robinson, Jack

As the story goes, Jack Robinson was a gentleman who was fond of dropping in on friends unannounced. He would then take his leave as unexpectedly as he had arrived. Soon people were using the expression "*before you can say Jack Robinson*" to refer to anything that happens quickly.

Rogers, Mary

A young New York City woman named Mary Rogers was murdered in 1841. The news story inspired Edgar Allen Poe to write *The Mystery of Marie Roget.*

Ryder, James

James A. Ryder was a Florida truck driver. In 1937, he won a contract to distribute beer and moved into the truck-leasing business. He retired in 1978, having little further contact with the company that bears his name, *Ryder Truck Rentals.* Ryder passed away in March 1997 at the age of 83.

Shaw, Henry Wheeler

Henry Wheeler Shaw was born in Lanesboro, Massachusetts, in 1818. He roamed around for two decades before settling into a career in real estate in Poughkeepsie, New York. When he was about 50 years old, he began to write rural tales, using intentional misspellings. He wrote the stories under the pen name Josh Billings and became one of the country's best-known humorists. After his death, people began to use the word *josh* as a synonym for joking.

Skinner, Leonard

Mr. Skinner was a high school teacher. He once suspended some students for having long hair. Those students went on to form a rock band and name it after him—*Lynard Shynard.* Of course, they probably would have spelled his name better if they hadn't been tossed out of school. Years later, Skinner and the band settled their differences. When the former teacher was working in real estate, he introduced the band at one of their hometown concerts.

Smith, James

James Smith was a Poughkeepsie, New York, candymaker. One day in 1870, Smith got a recipe for "cough candy" from a customer. Smith's first batch of the candy sold out quickly, and demand was steady. Soon, cough drops were the main business of the Smith family. When other companies began selling their own cough candy, Smith's sons, William and Andrew, put their likenesses on the boxes so that customers could be sure they got authentic *Smith Brothers Cough Drops.* The Smiths' pictures are still on the boxes today.

Spalding, Albert Goodwill

Baseball's first 200-game winner was a pitcher named Albert Goodwill Spalding. Spalding played for the Boston Red Stockings and the Chicago White Sox, winning 241 of 301 games pitched. He was a unique pitcher in that he used only balls that he made himself. When he retired from baseball, Spalding went into business selling his baseballs to the public. A year after his retirement, the National Baseball League was formed and made Spalding's product the official league ball.

Spooner, W. A.

W. A. Spooner was a minister and educator and was often called upon to speak to groups. He had an amusing habit of reversing sounds in his words and sentences. Some of the *spoonerisms* that have been attributed to him include "half-warmed fish" for "half-formed wish" and "you are occupewing my pie" instead of "you are occupying my pew." Before Spooner gave his name to the cause, people had to use a much more cumbersome word for the transposition of syllables: theametsis . . . I mean, *metathesis.*

Stroganoff, Paul

Count Paul Stroganoff was a 19th century Russian diplomat. He was fond of thinly sliced beef fillets, sauteed and served with mushrooms and sour cream. Soon others were as taken with the count's dish, and they referred to it by his name, *beef stroganoff.* In his book *Namesakes,* author Tad Tuleja wrote, "As far as Mother Russia is concerned, it is his only memorial. *The Great Soviet Encyclopedia* gives the czarist functionary not a nod."

Tate, Sir Henry

Henry Tate was a successful and rich sugar broker in Liverpool, England. His hobbies included art collecting. In 1897, he donated 80,000 pounds to construct an art gallery. The *Tate Gallery* was built on the site of an old prison and opened with a collection of 65 pictures from Tate's private collection.

Thomas, Samuel Bath

Samuel Bath Thomas was born in Plymouth, England, and moved to America in 1875. Upon his arrival in New York City, Thomas found a job in a bakery. In only five years, he had saved enough money to open a bakery of his own. He lived above his shop, and did all the baking in the basement. At the time, most of his competitors were selling wheat and rye breads. Thomas decided that he needed to have something the others didn't. He came up with bread dough rolled and cut into rounds, baked on a griddle, and split and toasted just before eating—in other words, English muffins.

Thompson, John Taliaferro

John Taliaferro Thompson was born in Newport, Kentucky, in 1860. In 1882, he entered the army and later became a private consultant on armaments. In 1920, Thompson and a partner named John N. Blish developed a .45 caliber submachine gun with a stick magazine, a pistol grip, and a detachable stock. It wasn't until World War II that it got much attention as a military weapon. But the *Thompson submachine gun*, known as the *tommy gun* for short, became very popular with Capone-era gangsters in Chicago.

Tibbets, Enola Gay

Col. Paul Tibbets was selected to pilot a historic bombing mission over Japan during World War II. He was to drop the first atomic weapon to be used in war. His plane was one of 15 specially modified B-29 bombers designed to carry atomic weapons. Tibbets named his plane the *Enola Gay* in honor of his mother, and had the name painted on the side just before takeoff. Her name will be forever associated with the bombing of Hiroshima. The bomb also had a name. It was called Little Boy.

Tull, Jethro

One has to wonder how the 18th century inventor of the seed drill would feel about lending his name to a famous rock band.

Uncle Remus

There was a real Uncle Remus. He was a gardener in Forsyth, Georgia. In the late 1800s, Joel Chandler Harris began collecting traditional African tales by talking to former slaves. A man called Uncle Remus was especially helpful to him. So Harris framed his collection of tales by using an old narrator named Uncle Remus.

Vassar, Matthew

Matthew Vassar was born in 1792 in England. He made a fortune in whaling and brewing. One thing he didn't have, however, was a child. As he got older, Vassar began to wonder if his name would die with him. He was inspired, however, by a relative who had founded Guy's Hospital in London. So Vassar decided to give $440,000 and 200 acres of land in 1861 to establish *Vassar Female College*. In his will, he left another $388,000. The plan worked. Vassar's name lives on.

Wedgewood, Josiah

Josiah Wedgewood was born at Burslem, Staffordshire, on July 12, 1730. When his father died, he was taken from school to work for his brother in a pottery shop. After his apprenticeship, he moved to Stoke-on-Trent, where he began making ornamental pottery and stoneware. He returned to his hometown in 1759 and opened a new factory to manufacture pottery and china. His skill and design made Wedgewood pottery famous, especially the white and *Wedgewood blue*. He died in 1795, but his name, and progeny, lived on. His daughter Susannah had a son named Charles Darwin.

Weiss, Chuck E.

In the early 1970s, a young Rickie Lee Jones moved to Los Angeles and started hanging out at the Troubadour, the center of the West Coast folk music scene. There she met Chuck E. Weiss, a musician who was earning his pay in the kitchen. A great friendship developed among Jones, Weiss, and another musician, Tom Waits. One evening, Jones got a call from Denver. It was her friends calling. Tom Waits shouted into the telephone, "Chuck E.'s in love!" Jones recognized a song title when she heard it. The love story itself she made up later.

Wenburg, Charles

Charles Wenburg was a shipping mogul in the 19th century. He brought a recipe for lobster that he had discovered in his travels to restaurateur Lorenzo Delmonico. Delmonico named the popular dish *lobster Wenburg*. Later, Wenburg was thrown out of the restaurant for fighting and asked not to come back. To further express his displeasure, Delmonico changed the name of the lobster dish by rearranging Wenburg's name. We know the dish today as *lobster newburg*.

Whistler, Anna Mathilda

On July 10, 1834, Anna Mathilda gave birth to a healthy boy she named James Abbott McNeil Whistler. James would become a noted artist. His most famous painting would be the one that he painted of his mother. *Whistler's Mother*, by the way, is not the title of the painting. It is officially called "Arrangement in Grey and Black no. 1, A Portrait of the Artist's Mother."

William of Occam

William, who hailed from Occam, England, was a Franciscan scholar under the tutelage of *Duns Scotus*. William spent most of his life reading, reflecting, and writing. Sometimes his writing got him in trouble, as it did in the 1320s when he was investigated for heresy by the papal court. In 1328, he went to France, where he wrote for the French court. A recurring theme in his writings was that one should not look for complicated explanations. In philosophy, this is known as *Occam's razor*, which states that "entities should not be multiplied except where necessary."

Williams, Mabel

Mabel Williams' brother ran a mail-order catalog business. One day he asked Mabel about some eye makeup she had made for herself out of petroleum jelly and black pigment. He decided to sell it in his catalog, calling it Lash-Brow-Line. It became one of his best sellers. As a gesture to his sister, he changed the name to *Maybelline*.